OUR

SACRAMENTAL

LIFE

OUR SACRAMENTAL LIFE

Living and Worshiping in Christ

Patricia Morrison Driedger

ave maria press   Notre Dame, Indiana

The Ad Hoc Committee to Oversee the Use of the Catechism, National Conference of Catholic Bishops, has found this catechetical text, copyright 2002, to be in conformity with the *Catechism of the Catholic Church*.

Nihil Obstat: Bishop Noël Delaquis
Titular Bishop of Bravelbourg
Censor Ad Hoc

Imprimatur: Archbishop Emilius Goulet, P.S.S.
Archbishop of Saint Boniface, Manitoba, Canada
Given on 17 December 2001.

The *Nihil Obstat* and *Imprimatur* are official declarations that a book or pamphlet is free of doctrinal or moral error. No implication is contained therein that those who have granted the *Nihil Obstat* or *Imprimatur* agree with its contents, opinions, or statements expressed.

Scripture texts in this work are taken from the *New American Bible with Revised New Testament and Revised Psalms* © 1991, 1986, 1970 Confraternity of Christian Doctrine, Washington, D.C. and are used by permission of the copyright owner. All Rights Reserved. No part of the *New American Bible* may be reproduced without permission in writing from the copyright owner.

English translation of the *Catechism of the Catholic Church* for the United States of America copyright © 1994, United States Catholic Conference, Inc.—Libreria Editrice Vaticana. Used with permission.

Other references cited as Endnotes with each chapter.

www.avemariapress.com

International Standard Book Number: 0-87793-719-2

Project Editor: Michael Amodei

Cover and text design by Brian Conley

Printed and bound in the United States of America.

To my mom, Patricia A. Morrison

In memory of my dad, Richard C. Morrison (1938-1999)

Thank you for your love and support and for giving me the gift of the

Church and the sacraments.

Contents

Introduction

"For as often as you eat this bread and drink this cup, you proclaim the death of the Lord until he comes."

In an oft-told story, St. Augustine, the famous theologian and Church Father, was walking along the seashore trying to figure out the mystery of the Blessed Trinity.

"How could there be one God and yet three distinct persons?" he was said to ponder.

Augustine was so engrossed in meditation and thought that he nearly trampled a little boy who was sitting near the shore in the wet sand, pouring a pail of water into a hole he had dug into the sand.

Augustine stopped to chat with the boy. "What are you doing?" he asked.

"I'm going to empty the ocean into this hole," the boy replied.

Augustine laughed. "You'll never get the whole ocean into that little hole!" he said.

The little boy stood up and looked directly at Augustine.

"And you, sir," he said, "will never put the whole mystery of the Trinity into your little mind."

Then the boy disappeared.

God and his plan for our lives are much too awesome to fit into human-size brains, but God does not want us to remain in ignorance of him or his plan for our salvation.

Our own desire for God—and the accompanying mystery of God's plan for our salvation—is written in our hearts. God has created us with faculties capable of coming to a knowledge and existence of him. But in order for us to enter into real intimacy with God, he must reveal himself to us and give us the grace to be able to welcome and understand that revelation in faith.

God's revelation to mankind has been established in several stages. The works of God in the Old Testament set the stage for Christ who completed the work of salvation and gave perfect glory to God. Jesus accomplished this work principally through his passion, death, resurrection from the dead, and his ascension into heaven. These events of our salvation are known as the *Paschal mystery*. The Paschal mystery has two key aspects, as the *Catechism of the Catholic Church* teaches:

- First, by his death, Christ liberates us from sin.
- Second, by his Resurrection, Christ opens for us the way to a new life. This new life is justification that reinstates in us God's grace. It is the source of our own future resurrection (654).

Our new life is here now. At Pentecost, a new era of God's revelation has begun—the age of the Church. In this age, Christ now lives and acts in and with the Church. In the sacramental liturgy, the Church proclaims and celebrates the Paschal mystery through which the Lord saves us.

Liturgy, itself, is a word that traditionally meant "public work" or "people's work." Today, it refers to the people's participation through prayer and worship in "the work of God." The entire liturgical life of the Church revolves around the Eucharistic sacrifice and the other sacraments.

What Are Sacraments?

You can likely recite all seven sacraments. You may have received the sacraments of initiation and the sacrament of Penance or Reconciliation. But how much of your understanding of the sacraments is relegated to only the immediate preparation you received as a young child?

What *are* the sacraments? The *Catechism of the Catholic Church* offers a definition that will serve us as we work through an exposition of each of the individual sacraments. The sacraments are:

- "powers that come forth" from the Body of Christ, which is ever-living and life-giving;
- actions of the Holy Spirit at work in his Body, the Church;
- "the masterworks of God" in the new and everlasting covenant.

The seven sacraments are all instituted by Jesus Christ. The mysteries of Christ's life are the foundation for what he would later dispense in the sacraments, through the ministers of the Church. What was visible in the life of Christ on earth has now passed on through the Holy Spirit to his Church.

The sacraments make visible the mystery of God's love for us. It is easy to see how Jesus did that. Jesus is God-made-flesh. The Incarnation is the primary sacrament of our salvation. The Father has spoken his Word in the visible form of Jesus.

The Church, too, is a sacrament because it continues Jesus' work of salvation. Jesus acts through the sacraments in what is called the "sacramental economy," the sharing of the fruits of Christ's Paschal mystery in the celebration of the sacraments. This, too, is how you participate in the sacramental life. You have a sacramental vocation to be an authentic sign of God's love. The Church's faith precedes and nourishes your faith. Through the grace of the sacraments you are called by the Lord to witness to him and to live his message, and to live a grace-filled life that attracts others to the gospel.

As Catholics, this is our call until the Lord comes again.

1 The Sacraments Continue the Work of Christ

"If I but Touch His Clothes..."

Though Mark's gospel is the shortest of the four New Testament gospels, it offers a vivid description of Jesus' ministry. Mark takes the reader from one incident to another in Jesus' life at a breakneck pace, beginning with the very opening of his ministry—his baptism—and ending with the discovery of his resurrection by some of the women who were his followers.

Mark uses several interesting writing techniques to make important points. In one of these techniques, Mark sandwiches one story within another, a type of framing device that suggests that the reader look closely at the middle story in order to discover a very important lesson.

The story of the raising to life of Jairus's daughter (Mk 5:21-43) is one example of the use of this technique. The story is told in two parts. In the middle of its telling is the account of the cure of a woman who has suffered from hemorrhages. As with any framing model, Mark intends for his readers to focus on what is in the middle as a way of going deeper into what he is teaching in the story used as a frame.

Let's look at the lessons the story of the woman with the hemorrhage offers in comparison with the story of Jairus that surrounds it:

The woman in the story had been afflicted for twelve years.

She had heard about Jesus.

She was milling around in the crowd of people who were following Jesus.

She said, "If I but touch his clothes, I shall be healed."

The cure was instantaneous and complete.

Jesus had not laid hands or spoken to the woman. But he was aware at once that the healing power had gone out from him.

Why is this short story so important in relationship to its frame? What are the important lessons it teaches?

For one, Jesus was in full control of each situation. He knew of the divine powers he possessed.

Secondly, the incident shows that faith accompanied by physical contact with Jesus could bring about a cure. (Likewise, in the story of the raising of Jairus's daughter, the father, too, has faith that Jesus' presence will bring his daughter back to life. But some of the people around him are not so sure. They tell him that his daughter has died; to not bother Jesus anymore. Jesus responds, "Do not be afraid; just have faith.")

Throughout his ministry Jesus called his followers to a deeper faith. He claimed the authority not only to teach and to heal, but to reconcile and forgive sins. Perhaps the greatest challenge to faith that he issued to his disciples came in the prediction of his passion, death, and resurrection. He did this on three separate occasions:

> *He began to teach them that the Son of Man must suffer greatly and be rejected by the elders, the chief priests, and the scribes, and be killed, and rise after three days. He spoke this openly (Mk 8:31-32).*

Jesus' words were powerful. They instilled faith in those who came to believe in him, and they challenged believers to ever deeper faith. These two healings—of Jairus's daughter and the woman with the hemorrhage—illustrate the power of Jesus' words. Jesus' very presence was also powerful. It was simply by touching his cloak that the woman was healed.

Jesus continues to touch us as he did the women in Mark's gospel. Through his word and his presence in the sacraments we too are called to grow in faith. And like his disciples, we too are called to accompany him in his dying and rising.

All of Jesus' words and actions bring about our salvation for they anticipated the power of his Paschal mystery. Christ continues to act in the Church, which is his Body, through the seven sacraments.

Read the text of the framing stories in Mark 5:21-43. Which character are you most like in either story? Why?

The Church Is the Body of Christ

To understand how the sacraments are the work of Christ and continue Christ's work on earth even now, we must understand more about his Church.

The Church is a multidimensional reality. We will look briefly at two aspects of the Church as a foundation for our study of the sacraments: the Church as the Body of Christ and the Church as the Sacrament of Christ. While this is not a complete study of the Church, it will help us understand the sacraments as both actions *of* the Church and actions *for* the Church.

Our understanding of the Church as the Body of Christ is rooted in our faith in Jesus Christ, the eternal Son of God, who became man. As John's gospel says, "The Word became flesh, and made his dwelling among us" (1:14). Jesus, who was true God and true man, had a human body just like ours. He was like us in everything but sin. He died and rose again, and appeared in his risen body to his disciples. At his ascension into heaven, the presence of his risen body with his followers ceased. But he continued to be present to them, as he is to us, through the gift of the Holy Spirit—given at Pentecost—in the Church.

The foundation for our understanding of the Church as the Body of Christ comes from St. Paul's writings. In the First Letter to the Corinthians Paul wrote: "As a body is one, though it has many parts, and all the parts of the body, though many, are one body, so also Christ. For in one Spirit we were all baptized into one body" (12:12-13a).

The Second Vatican Council expressed this teaching very succinctly:

> *Rising from the dead [Christ] sent his life-giving Spirit upon his disciples and through this Spirit has established his body, the Church, as the universal sacrament of salvation. Sitting at the right hand of the Father, he is continually active in the world, leading men to the Church, and through her joining them more closely to himself and making them partakers of his glorious life by nourishing them with his own body and blood (Lumen Gentium, 48).*

There are many implications to this image of the Church, but these three are especially important for our understanding of the sacraments:

How does the Church's description as the Body of Christ help you to understand how Christ continues his work in the Church even to today?

- *The Church is one body.* As members of the Body of Christ we are all united to Christ and therefore to one another. Members of the Church become more intimately united with Christ and one another through the sacraments. This unity is founded in Baptism, which unites us to the death and resurrection of Christ, and finds its ultimate expression in the Eucharist. As we share in the Body and Blood of the Lord we are joined in communion with him and with other believers.

- *Christ is the Head of the Body.* Our understanding of Christ as the head of the Body is also rooted in the New Testament, in the Letter to the Colossians:

> He is in the image of the invisible God,
> the firstborn of all creation.
> For in him were created all things in heaven and on earth,
> the visible and the invisible,
> whether thrones or dominions or principalities or powers;
> all things were created through him and for him.
> He is before all things,
> and in him all things hold together.
> He is the head of the body, the church.
> He is the beginning, the firstborn from the dead,
> that in all things he himself might be preeminent (Col 1:15-19).

All members of the Church strive to be like Christ. Though there are many different gifts that we have been given, and various vocations and roles in the Church, we all seek to follow the one Lord and to share in his dying and rising. The sacraments form us and help us to understand our own joys and sufferings in light of the Paschal mystery.

- *The Church is the Bride of Christ.* Christ and the Church are not the same. Though unified, the head and members of one body have a distinct relationship. The image often used to describe this relationship is that of a bride and a bridegroom. Jesus referred to himself as the "bridegroom." In describing the relationship between a husband and wife, Jesus said that "the two will become one flesh." In the same way, Jesus and the Church, though two distinct parts, form one body (cf. Eph 5:32). Christ has joined himself with the Church in an everlasting covenant and will never stop caring for the Church as he would his own body.

Christ instituted the Church to accomplish the salvation of men and women throughout the earth to the end of time. The Church was born from Christ's total self-gift on the cross. When the soldier pierced the side of Christ with a lance, John's gospel tells us that "blood and water flowed out" (Jn 19:34). The Fathers of the Church saw in this a sign of the sacraments, specifically of the water of Baptism and the Body and Blood of Christ in the Eucharist. Christ's self-gift on the cross was anticipated when Jesus celebrated the first Eucharist at the Last Supper. There he said, "This is my body, which will be given for you; do this in memory of me," and "This cup is the new covenant in my blood, which will be shed for you" (Lk 22:19-20). These words were fulfilled with his death on the cross. They are the source of the Eucharist, and of our understanding of the Church as the Body of Christ.

The Church is the pledge of Christ's fidelity to his people. Through nearly two thousand years of history, the Church continues to survive, proof of the Lord's promise that he will be with us until the end of the world. The Church's first purpose is to be the sign and source of the spiritual union of all people with God. This awareness of the Church's mission leads us to consider how the Church is also a sacrament.

The Church Is the Universal Sacrament of Salvation

The Church exists not for herself, but to point others to Jesus Christ, the Savior of the world and the source of God's grace and love for us. The Church shares Christ with others when it proclaims the gospel and serves others. In doing so, the Church is both Christ's instrument and the visible sign of God's plan of love for all humanity.

The *Catechism* expresses this reality in these words:

> As sacrament, the Church is Christ's instrument. "She is taken up by him also as the instrument for the salvation of all," "the universal sacrament of salvation," by which Christ is "at once manifesting and actualizing the mystery of God's love for men." (LG 9 #2, 48 #2; GS 45 #1.) The Church "is the visible plan of God's love for humanity," because God desires "that the whole human race may become one People of God, form one Body of Christ, and be built up into one temple of the Holy Spirit." [Paul VI, June 22, 1973; AG 7 #2; cf. LG 17.] (CCC, 776)

As a sacrament, the Church has both a visible and invisible or spiritual dimension. It is both human and divine. Because it is human, it is sometimes weak and sinful, and its clarity as a sign of Christ's presence can be obscured. But because it is divine, Christ's presence in the Church is assured, and we know that despite human weaknesses, Christ is always at work.

The Church in Time

As a visible community founded by Christ, the Church is an entity in history. The Church's authority and mission, its orientation and goal all come from Christ and his ministry of salvation. All members of the Church—lay and ordained—are called to carry on Christ's work. Christ is the source of all ministry in the

Tell about someone you know or know of whose life is primarily concerned with pointing others to Christ.

Name your current bishop. Look up and report on some biographical information on him from your diocese's web site or diocesan handbook.

Church. Each member, in accordance with their call and place in the People of God, contributes to the Church's sacramental presence in the world. In this way, the Church shares in the work of Christ to serve as a "light to all nations."

Early Christians were fond of saying, "The world was created for the sake of the Church." Through the eyes of faith we can see how the Old Testament foreshadows the coming of the Christ and the establishment of the Church. The people of Israel were its foundation. The remote preparation for the Church began when God called Abraham and promised that he would be the father of a great people. Its immediate preparation began with Israel's election as the People of God. When Israel was accused by its prophets of infidelity to the covenant, a new and eternal covenant was announced. In Christ, the New Covenant was established.

Christ has established the Church and he sustains it as a visible organization set up with a hierarchical structure through which he communicates truth and

grace. This hierarchy, instituted with Peter and the apostles, continues in the same way today: the bishop of Rome, the Pope, is Peter's successor, and the bishops are the successors of the apostles. The Pope, and the bishops, with their priests and deacons as co-workers, carry on the work of Christ by their preaching, their pastoral leadership, and their liturgical work of celebrating the sacraments.

Their first task is to preach the gospel to all of the world. This only makes sense. For no one can preach the Good News of salvation to himself. No one can grant the authority to preach on his own either. Using the Good Shepherd as a model, the bishops, with priests as their delegates, also govern the Church, exercising their authority in communion with the whole Church under the Pope's guidance.

The *sanctifying office* of the bishop helps bishops and priests "channel the fullness of Christ's holiness in many ways and abundantly" (*Lumen Gentium*, 26). By virtue of their ordination, bishops and priests receive the sacred power to represent Christ in their sacramental ministry; in other words, to act in the person of Christ.

The bishops sanctify the Church with their example, calling to mind the Good Shepherd who does not domineer those whom he is in charge of, but rather is an example himself of holiness for them. As Pope John Paul II taught, "The Church's structure is totally ordered to the holiness of Christ's members" (*Mulieris dignitatem*, 27).

The Church Transcends History

At the same time, the Church is a spiritual reality, a mystery that transcends history and is only visible through the eyes of faith. As a mystery, the Church "both contains and communicates the invisible grace she signifies" (*CCC*, 774). God the Father planned for the Church from the beginning of time. Jesus accomplished the work of the Church through his life, death, resurrection, and ascension. When this was complete, the Holy Spirit was sent on Pentecost to continue the work of making the Church holy for all time to come. The Church on earth is the beginning of God's kingdom.

Only in heaven at the time of Christ's second coming will the Church be perfected, and not before the Church and the world go through great trials. Until then the pilgrim Church journeys along, receiving God's graces and consolations, and led by Christ himself, present in many ways, including in the seven sacraments.

Thus it is that the Church is called a "sacrament." As the Council taught: "By her relationship with Christ, the Church is a kind of sacrament or sign of intimate union with God, and of the unity of all mankind" (*Lumen Gentium*, 1). Since the Church's role as sacrament is rooted in Christ, we will also examine how Christ himself is a sacrament.

Read Peter's speech at Pentecost from Acts 2:14-36. Explain how Peter recounts how the Church was planned for from the beginning of time.

Christ, the Sacrament of Salvation

Jesus has been called the prime, or primordial sacrament. The New Testament term for sacrament is the Greek word *mysterion*, translated as "mystery." It was used to refer to the secret thoughts of God, thoughts which transcend human reason and consequently can only be known if God reveals them. St. Paul uses the word *mysterion* to refer to Christ.

The term sacrament applies appropriately to Christ himself:

- Jesus is the great mystery of God's love for humanity. In him, the Father's plan of salvation for the world has taken place.
- Jesus is also the pledge of our salvation. He lived his life for the salvation of all.
- Jesus is the sign of God's grace. The Father's love for us is visible in Jesus.
- Jesus is an *efficacious* sign—one that causes what it points to. His very life, passion, death, resurrection, and ascension have conquered sin and death and won eternal life for us with the Blessed Trinity.

Read Chapter 1 of Lumen Gentium. Write five quotations that describe for you how Christ lives in the Church.

What Are the Sacraments?

Having looked at the Church as the Body of Christ and as a Sacrament of Christ, and having seen how Christ himself is a sacrament, we turn now to the sacraments themselves. The *Catechism of the Catholic Church* offers us this definition.

> *The sacraments are efficacious signs of grace, instituted by Christ and entrusted to the Church, by which divine life is dispensed to us. The visible rites by which the sacraments are celebrated signify and make present the graces proper to each sacrament. They bear fruit in those who receive them with the required dispositions (1131).*

Before we cover the Church's understanding of the sacraments as "efficacious signs of grace," we will explore other important aspects of this definition.

Divine life is dispensed to us in the sacraments. This is a natural connection, for Christ himself is the prime sacrament, and the Church is his Body. This was so from the time of Jesus' ministry. He told his disciples:

> *Remain in me, as I remain in you. Just as a branch cannot bear fruit on its own unless it remains on the vine, so neither can you unless you remain in me. I am the vine, you are the branches. Whoever remains in me and I in him will bear much fruit, because without me you can do nothing (Jn 15:4-5).*

When someone uses the language of the sacraments (e.g., "preparing for the sacraments" or "receiving the sacraments") it is generally understood they are referring to the Catholic Church. The sacraments are a distinguishing element of being Catholic.

The sacraments were "instituted by Christ." In the chapters ahead we will look at how each sacrament is rooted in the specific actions of his ministry. But first and foremost, we must affirm that the sacraments are "of Christ." His words, teachings, miracles, his whole life, and especially the events surrounding his passion, death, and resurrection reveal God the Father. The same Jesus who healed the woman with the hemorrhage, whose words forgave sinners, who fed the multitudes with bread and his own words, is present today in the Church and the seven sacraments. Christ is present to us in the visible signs of water and oil, bread and wine, words and touch. As St. Leo the Great put it, "What was visible in our Savior has passed over into his mysteries."

The sacraments put us in touch with the mystery of Christ. The sacraments are actions of the Holy Spirit at work in Christ's Body, the Church. Like Jairus and the woman healed of the hemorrhage, having faith in their power helps us to meet Christ face to face.

Because we are part of the Church, we are intimately united with Jesus. This is especially true through our participation in the sacraments. In Baptism, we were formed in the likeness of Christ. Through the sharing of the body and blood of the Lord at Eucharist, we are taken up into communion with Christ and with one

✔ Memorize this definition of sacraments: "The sacraments are efficacious signs of grace, instituted by Christ and entrusted to the Church, by which divine life is dispensed to us." Recite it to a classmate.

another. Three sacraments—Baptism, Confirmation, and Holy Orders—confer a sacramental *character* or seal that relates the person to a share in Christ's priesthood according to a different state or function. These sacraments cannot be repeated.

The sacraments have been "entrusted to the Church." The Church's saving mission was given by the Father to his Son and then passed on by Jesus to his apostles and finally to their successors, the bishops. Through the sacrament of Holy Orders priests and deacons share in the work of the bishop. Thus Christ is guaranteed to act in the sacraments through the Holy Spirit for the Church. It is the ordained minister who ties the words and actions of the sacraments to the words and actions of Christ, their foundation.

The sacramental bond of the ordained to Christ helps us to understand how the sacraments are "by the Church." The sacraments also "make the Church," as St. Augustine described, and are "for the Church" since they communicate to all people, especially in the Eucharist, the mystery of communion with the God of love, Father, Son, and Holy Spirit.

Efficacious Signs of Grace

Recall that the definition of a sacrament says that they are "efficacious signs of grace" and that each one confers the particular grace that is proper to it. In order to understand what happens in the sacraments when we receive grace, we need to understand what grace is. The *Catechism of the Catholic Church* defines grace as "a participation in the life of God." Grace is "the free and undeserved help that God gives us" so that we can respond to his call (1997, 1996). The *Catechism* goes on to say that grace is first and foremost the gift of the Holy Spirit himself, but that grace also includes the ability which God gives us to participate in and collaborate with his work (2003).

Each sacrament enables us to participate in the life of God in a particular way. This distinct gift is called the *sacramental grace* of the sacrament. This grace makes us holy and pleasing to God, adopted children of God, temples of the Holy Spirit, and heirs of eternal life. The sacrament of Baptism, for example, brings us into God's family, and the sacrament of Penance restores God's life in those who have sinned and separated themselves from it.

The life of grace begins in us at our Baptism when we are given the gift of *sanctifying grace.* Sanctifying grace is the ongoing or habitual gift of God's life in us (*CCC*, 2000). It disposes us to God and opens us to receive even more of his life, the way a flower opens to the sun. Sacraments can also confer actual graces upon us. *Actual grace* is God's particular way of helping us to overcome our sins or grow further in our Christian vocation. For example, when we receive the Eucharist we

Write definitions clarifying the differences between sacramental grace and sanctifying grace.

may have a sense of God calling us in a particular way, or when we confess our sins the priest may give us some helpful counsel.

In the sacraments we are given the grace to take part in and benefit from all that Jesus has done and is doing for the people of the world. Sacraments strengthen and deepen our relationship with Jesus and with his people. They draw us into the wonder and completeness of divine life.

There are seven sacraments in the Church: Baptism, Confirmation, Eucharist, Penance, Anointing of the Sick, Holy Orders, and Matrimony. The Church teaches that the seven sacraments have several things in common. Most prominently is that they immerse us in the Paschal mystery.

Faith and the Sacraments

Our faith is witnessed in the sacraments. On the other hand, the sacraments do not only express our existing belief, they instruct us in faith. They also nourish and strengthen our faith.

The mission to share our faith with others was given to the Church by Christ. From the very beginning, this task was a sacramental mission. Jesus' mandate to them was twofold: to preach the gospel and to baptize. He said, "Go therefore and make disciples of all nations, baptizing them in the names of the Father and of the Son and of the Holy Spirit" (Mt 28:19). Before one can be baptized one must first hear the word of God and assent to it. The *assent* (saying "yes") is the meaning of faith.

The faith of the Church comes before the faith of the new believer. That is why, for example, we baptize infants. That is also why the Church stresses that the celebrations of the sacraments are communal celebrations. They are rooted not in the faith of the individuals who participate in them, whether it be the ministers of the sacraments or the recipients, but in the faith of the whole Church. In celebrating the sacraments, the Church confesses the faith it received from the apostles.

The particular words that the Church prays in the sacramental rites expresses our faith. An ancient Latin theological axiom *lex orandi, lex credendi* explains this: "the law of praying is the law of believing." The axiom can also be expressed in the opposite direction *lex credendi, lex orandi.* In this formulation it expresses the role that liturgy and prayer have in forming, shaping, and nurturing our faith. The words of the liturgy, similar to the words of the creeds, are a foundational element of the Church's Tradition.

Recall that the "liturgy of the Church" is its official public worship of God. Christian liturgy is primarily addressed to God the Father in union with Christ and the Holy Spirit. The liturgy, as expressed through the sacraments, makes us holy, builds up the Body of Christ, and gives worship to God.

For this reason, the words and actions that are central to the sacramental rites may not be adapted or manipulated according to the desires of the local community, the pastor, or the bishop. Even the Pope may not change the liturgy arbitrarily, "but only in the obedience of faith and with religious respect for the mystery of the liturgy" (*CCC*, 1125). These central rites are called the matter and form of the sacraments, and we will look at them in detail as we study each of

In your own words, explain the meaning of the saying, lex orandi, lex credendi, that is, "the law of praying becomes the law of believing."

the sacraments. The matter is the symbolic element and/or the ritual action that is essential to the celebration of the sacrament. In Baptism, for example, the matter is water. The accompanying action is either the threefold pouring of the water or the immersion of the recipient in the water. The form is the verbal formula that the Church has determined to be essential. In Baptism the form is, "I baptize you in the name of the Father, and of the Son, and of the Holy Spirit."

In 1439 the Council of Florence named three things that are necessary for each sacrament:

1) proper matter;
2) correct words or form;
3) the person of the designated ministrant who has the intention of doing what the Church does in the sacraments. (In other words, even a priest cannot perform a sacrament while acting in a play because he is just acting and not intending to do what the Church does.)

Through the centuries since the time of Christ and the apostles, the matter and form of the prayers and rites of the liturgy have remained the same. If either the necessary matter or form of the sacrament is not present, the sacrament is not celebrated and is said to be invalid. Also, matter and form cannot be modified indiscriminately by the Church. The elements chosen by Christ must be respected.

How Do the Sacraments Work?

Recall again that the sacraments are *efficacious*, that is, "capable of producing a desired effect." This means that the sacraments actually confer the grace that they signify (e.g., forgiveness, healing, communion). How does this happen?

The sacraments are effective because Christ is acting in them. In union with the Father and by the power of the Holy Spirit, Christ is really present in the Church and acts in a real and effective way in the sacraments. He is the "great high priest" as the letter to the Hebrews says (4:14). "The Church celebrates the sacraments as a priestly community structured by the baptismal priesthood and the priesthood of ordained ministers" (*CCC*, 1132). Christ is present in a particular way in the ordained minister of the sacrament who acts "*in persona Christi*," in the person of Christ.

The power of the sacraments does not come from the personal holiness or demeanor of the minister, but rather from Christ himself. God the Father hears the prayer of his Son who acts through the Church and by the power of the Holy Spirit. This guarantee of God's action in the sacraments is described as an action *ex opere operato* (by the very fact that the action has been done). It is by virtue of Christ and his sacrifice made once for all that the sacraments continue to be effective.

The effectiveness of the sacraments is not dependent on the faith or holiness of the minister or the recipient. As long as the priest intends to do what the Church intends in the sacrament, it is effective. The degree to which we benefit from the sacraments is dependent upon our own disposition. The sacraments will

List some actions and customs associated with a family ritual. How are these important to the life of your family?

Pretend you were asked to explain the meaning of sacraments to an eight-year-old. How would you do it?

bear richer fruit in our lives if we take the time to understand them, prepare for them, and reflect upon them. This aspect of the sacraments is called their fruitfulness. The fruitfulness of the sacraments can be enhanced by the reverence and beauty with which they are celebrated and the ways in which they express the faith and experience of the local community that celebrates them. That is why the rituals themselves allow for certain options in the readings and prayers to be used in different celebrations.

Finally, the sacraments are effective by virtue of their symbolic power. The material used—bread, wine, water, words, touch—also have an effect. Jesus chose these materials because they speak so strongly to us. The water of baptism cleanses because it is water, and the bread of the Eucharist nourishes because it is bread.

A Proper Disposition

The fruit which the sacraments bear is dependent upon the disposition of those who receive them. In other words, the sacraments can change us if we are prepared to be changed, but if we are unprepared or resistant the sacraments will have little to no effect upon us. God does not force us to receive what we do not want. Even Jesus could not perform miracles where the people had no faith (Mk 6:5). People who receive the Eucharist without faith or love will have received the body of Christ, but that fact will make no significant difference in their lives. On the other hand, people who receive the Eucharist *with* faith and love will experience a more intimate union with Jesus. They will be able to believe more strongly, love more deeply, and serve more generously.

It is difficult to receive the sacraments with faith and love if one is unaware of their meaning and what Jesus is offering us through them. Too often we do not take the time to prepare to receive the sacraments or to reflect upon what we have received. Our experience of the sacraments is like the experience of two Sudanese refugees participating in their first cross-country skiing trip.

James and Thomas grew up in war-torn Sudan. When they were fourteen they were dragged from their homes and told, at gunpoint, that they were now members of the army. They joined hundreds of other teenagers from other villages on a long forced march through the dense forest. After a few days they had no idea where they were or where their home was. Once the soldiers were sure that none of the boys could find their way home, they relaxed their guard somewhat. James and Thomas along with several others were able to escape during the middle of the night. They spent days forcing

Name an experience you had that was enhanced because you took the time to prepare for it and later reflect on it.

Name a second experience that could have been better had you taken more time for preparation and reflection.

(A Proper Disposition cont.)

their way through dense undergrowth heading in the direction of the Kenyan border. Some of the boys died along the way, but eventually James and Thomas found their way to a refugee camp. After a long wait, they were finally given permission to immigrate to Canada. They arrived at their new home in the middle of a very cold and very snowy winter.

One Saturday morning, two days after their arrival, they were having breakfast with Dave, one of the people from the refugee committee of the parish that had sponsored them. This is Thomas's account of what happened:

> *After breakfast Dave said he had a surprise for us. He told us to put on our warm clothes and go out to the car. He handed us a pile of sticks which we were supposed to strap to the roof. I wondered what the sticks were for, but Dave seemed to be in a hurry, so I didn't ask. We all got into the car. Dave drove us to the edge of a forest and told us to get out. He gave each of us two of the long sticks and told us to strap them to our feet. Then he gave us two more sticks with sharp points and told us to start walking. I took two steps and fell. The snow hurt my face and the sticks were holding my legs in a strange position so I couldn't get up. I was terrified, I thought I had escaped from the forests of the Sudan to die in the forests of Canada![1]*

Because James and Thomas had never seen skis or heard of skiing, they were unable to appreciate the gift of skis or the surprise and beauty of a cross country ski trip. When they looked at the skis, they did not see sporting equipment or a mode of transportation. Instead they saw sticks and possibly implements of pain.

How often do we look at the Eucharist and fail to see the food which will save us from starvation and instead see a tasteless wafer or a long ritual?

How often do we look at baptism and fail to see the water which can wash away death and decay and instead see a way to make babies cry and Mass longer?

If James and Thomas had been prepared for their first skiing trip, it would have been a very different experience. If we are prepared to celebrate the sacraments (or if we take time to reflect upon the unrepeatable sacraments which we have already celebrated), they will be very different experiences for us.

Liturgy: The Work of the Holy Trinity

The celebration of the sacraments is called the Church's liturgy. The liturgy is central to the life of the Church and so is central to our lives as Catholics. The liturgy celebrates the Paschal mystery which brought about our salvation. In the liturgy, the Lord continues his work of redemption. "The liturgy is the summit toward which the activity of the Church is directed; at the same time it is the fountain from which all her powers flow" (*Sacrosanctum Concilium*).

Recall that the word liturgy comes from the Greek for "public work" or "people's work." This root meaning of liturgy also reminds us that the liturgy is the "public" prayer of the Church. It is public in the sense that it is communal rather than private prayer. Every liturgical celebration, whether it be an outdoor Mass in a huge stadium or an emergency Baptism in a hospital, is part of the public prayer of the Church. Every liturgical action is an action of the whole Body of Christ. Liturgy especially refers to the Eucharist. It also refers to the other sacraments and the *liturgy of the hours*, or divine office, the official prayer of the Church.

The liturgy allows us to experience and celebrate our salvation. During the liturgy Christ is always present and shares with us the fruits of the Paschal mystery until he comes again. This is known as the *sacramental economy*, that is the way Christ uses to disperse the graces of his saving actions to the world. The word "economy" may seem strange to us in this context because we associate it with monetary issues. But it actually comes from two Greek words meaning "management of the household." Thus the sacramental economy refers to the way in which Christ cares for his household, the Church.

From a historical perspective, the events of our salvation occurred only once. But by the power of the Holy Spirit, the liturgy makes these events present and real for us today. The liturgy brings us in communion with God and with one another. The liturgy also allows us to participate in Christ's prayer to the Father, made in the Holy Spirit.

One of the best ways to understand the liturgy is to examine it more closely as the work of the Blessed Trinity and to explore the distinct roles of the three divine Persons in it.

✔️ Why is it necessary for people to come to the liturgy? See the <u>Constitution on the Sacred Liturgy</u> (nos. 9 and 11).

God the Father: Source and Goal of Liturgy

Through the liturgy, the Church blesses, praises, adores, and thanks God the Father as the source of all blessings in creation and salvation history. There is a second dimension as well. The Church gives back to the Father his own gifts (for example, in the Eucharist we offer the gifts of bread and wine) and begs him to send the Holy Spirit on that offering, as well as on the whole Church and world. We offer these gifts so that through communion with the Paschal mystery and by the power of the Spirit, these gifts will bring about the fruits of God's grace.

From the beginning of time through the duration of salvation history, all of God's work is *blessing.* A blessing is a "divine and life-giving action" (*CCC*, 1078). God's blessings were witnessed in the dramatic, saving events of the Old Testament. At the time of Abraham, the divine blessing entered into human history, which was consumed by sin and moving towards death, in order to redirect it to life. With Abraham, this history of salvation began. The birth of Isaac, the Passover and Exodus, the election of David as king, God's presence brought to the Temple in the Ark of the Covenant, the exile to Babylon, the return of the small remnant, and the written word of the Law, Prophets, and Psalms included in the liturgy of the Chosen People—all these events remind us of God's blessings. At the same time they call us to respond to them with our own blessings of praise and thanksgiving.

Now, in the Church's liturgy, the Father's blessing is fully revealed and communicated. The Father is acknowledged as the source and end of all blessings, and of creation and salvation. The incarnate Son died, rose from the dead, and ascended to the Father to fill us with his blessings. Through him, the Father pours into our hearts the gift of all gifts, the Holy Spirit. Thus the priest, lifting the consecrated bread and wine, prays on behalf of the Church at the conclusion of the Eucharistic prayer:

> *Through him,*
> *with him,*
> *in him,*
> *in the unity of the Holy Spirit,*
> *all glory and honor is yours,*
> *almighty Father,*
> *for ever and ever.*
> *Amen.*

Christ Is Present and Acts in the Liturgy

Jesus Christ instituted the sacraments through the words and actions of his life. Now, sitting at the right hand of God the Father, he acts through the sacraments

What does it mean to say that God the Father is "the source and end of all blessings, and of creation and salvation"?

What would it mean for you to share in some way in Christ's glory?

in order to share his grace. As perceptible signs to our human nature, the sacraments make present the grace they signify.

In the liturgy, Christ's suffering, death, and resurrection are made present. The Paschal mystery is a real, historical event: Jesus actually died, was buried, rose from the dead, and ascended to the right hand of the Father. These events are not repeated in the liturgy, for they occurred once for all. But through the liturgy they are made present to us and their effects are real and accessible to us (*CCC*, 1364). This is the uniqueness of the Paschal mystery—that it is not relegated only to the past. The saving works of Christ continue to be carried out through all time. The Paschal mystery then, transcends history while being present in it in every age.

All of the structures of the liturgy and liturgical life were set in motion by Christ. Just as he was sent by the Father, so Jesus sent his apostles, filled with the Holy Spirit, to preach the Good News. Christ also willed that this work of preaching salvation should be conducted through the sacrifice of Eucharist and the sacraments.

Christ remains ever present in the Church, particularly in the liturgy. He is present in the following ways:

- especially in the Eucharistic species, the bread and wine which become his Body and Blood;
- in the person of his minister, the priest;
- in the word, since it is Christ who speaks when the scriptures are read at Mass;
- when the Church prays and sings, for he promised, "where two or three are gathered together in my name, there am I in the midst of them" (Mt 18:20).

The *Documents of Vatican II* remind us that,
> *Christ indeed always associates the Church with himself in the truly great work of giving perfect praise to God and making men holy. The Church is his dearly beloved Bride who calls to her Lord, and through him offers worship to the Eternal Father* (Sacrosanctum Concilium, 7).

Besides his presence in the earthly liturgy, Christ is also present at the heavenly liturgy that is celebrated with angels and saints. We live in hope that someday we will take part in this heavenly liturgy and that we too will share in some way in Christ's glory.

The Holy Spirit and Our Role in Liturgy

*First, the Holy Spirit prepares **our hearts** to encounter the Lord*. The Holy Spirit is a "teacher of faith" and the "artisan" of the sacraments (*CCC*, 1091). It is the Spirit who gives us the gift of faith and enables us to respond to Christ. When the Holy Spirit hears our response of faith, he cooperates with us. Because of this cooperation, the liturgy is truly the common work of the Holy Spirit and the Church.

Christ is the center of the liturgy and every dimension of it points to him. When we hear the word of God proclaimed from the Old Testament, when we pray the Psalms, or when we recall the saving events and significant realties which have been fulfilled by Christ, the Holy Spirit inspires us to see how the Old Testament prefigured Christ and was fulfilled in him. Re-reading the Old Testament with the inspiration of the Holy Spirit and using Jesus as the starting point reveals the newness of Christ. The meaning of previously veiled events from the past are unveiled. For example, the great flood and Noah's ark prefigures Baptism, and the manna in the desert prefigured the Eucharist, "the true bread from heaven" (Jn 6:32).

In every liturgical action of the Church today, especially the Eucharist and the sacraments, an encounter is forged between Christ and the Church. This unity comes from the working of the Holy Spirit, who gathers all of God's people—all races, cultures, and social backgrounds—into the one Body of Christ.

Second, the Holy Spirit makes the mystery of Christ present in the here and now. The Holy Spirit is the Church's living memory. The Spirit and the Church cooperate to make Christ and his work of salvation present in the liturgy. Besides recalling God's work in the Old Testament, the Holy Spirit also "gives a spiritual understanding to the Word of God to those who read or hear it, according to the dispositions of their heart" (*CCC*, 1101). The Spirit gives to the Church the grace of faith, strengthens it, and makes it grow in the community.

The "remembering of faith" (e.g., the events of salvation history) is known as *anamnesis*. The liturgy always refers to God's saving actions in history. These words of remembering are contained in the Liturgy of the Word when the Holy Spirit recalls all that Christ has done for us. Anamnesis is central to all our sacramental celebrations, and especially to the Liturgy of the Eucharist. In fulfillment of Christ's command to the apostles, the Church keeps his memorial by recalling his Paschal mystery in the eucharistic prayer.

However, the liturgy not only remembers the events of our salvation, it also makes them present to us today. By the power of the Holy Spirit, we can participate in Christ's Paschal mystery. This most dramatically takes place at Eucharist during the *epiclesis* ("invocation upon"), an intercessory prayer in which the priest begs the Father to send the Holy Spirit so that the gift offerings of bread and wine may become the body and blood of Christ. In every sacramental celebration there is an *epiclesis*. The Spirit is called upon to come and sanctify the elements to be used in the liturgy, e.g. water or chrism, and to come and sanctify the Church that has gathered to celebrate the sacrament.

The greatest gift of the Holy Spirit is love (see 1 Cor 13:1-13). Read the passage and list five qualities of love that St. Paul writes about and examples of how you can live each of these qualities.

In your own words, share the "joyful hope" you have for Christ's coming.

The Holy Spirit is the agent that joins us to Christ and to each other. The Spirit empowers us—especially through the reception of the body and blood of Christ—to become a living offering to God. We are to bring the love of Christ into the world.

Eternal Life and the Sacraments

One of the earliest prayers of the Church was *Marana tha*, an Aramaic expression that means "O Lord, come!" This prayer expresses the ultimate goal of Christians and of the liturgy—eternal life.

The sacraments help us share in eternal life even now while we await Christ's coming. In the sacraments, we have received the guarantee of everlasting life while at the same time we "continue to wait in joyful hope for the coming of the Lord."

As the *Catechism of the Catholic Church* teaches: "The Church celebrates the mystery of her Lord 'until he comes,' when God will be 'everything to everyone'" (1130).

Chapter 1

Review Questions

1. Why is it important to understand more about the Church in order to understand how the sacraments are the work of Christ?

2. Are Christ and the Church the same?

3. How is the Church herself a sacrament?

4. How does the Church contribute to Christ's sacramental presence in the world?

5. When will the Church be perfected?

6. How is Christ himself a sacrament?

7. What are the sacraments?

8. Which three sacraments confer a sacramental character or seal?

9. Define *grace*.

10. According to the Council of Florence, what are three things necessary for each sacrament?

11. What does it meant to say that sacraments are "efficacious"?

12. What is meant by the "sacramental economy"?

13. What is God the Father's role in liturgy?

14. Name the ways that Christ remains present in the Church, particularly in the liturgy.

15. How is our role in liturgy helped by the Holy Spirit?

16. Define *anamnesis*.

17. Define *epiclesis*.

Endnotes

1. This story was told to the author.

Celebrating the Church's Liturgy

A Life of Signs and Symbols

Fr. Mychael Judge's life was in many ways marked by signs and symbols.

As a Franciscan priest, Fr. Mychael wore the usual brown friar's habit and sandals of St. Francis when he helped serve food to the homeless or chat with the maids who cleaned at the hotels near his parish in lower Manhattan.

But when the fire alarm for FDNY Engine 1/Ladder 24 sounded, Fr. Mychael changed into his fireman's uniform and helmet and headed out to the scene with his unit.

The situation was no different on Tuesday, September 11, 2001. In the same way he had for nearly thirty years as a fire department chaplain, Fr. Mychael raced out to be with the others in his company after the first plane struck the World Trade Center.

Fire engulfed the top floors of Tower 2 of the World Trade Center building. Trapped people were leaping from windows nearly one hundred stories up to escape the flames that would kill them. A falling woman struck one of the firefighters from Engine 1/Ladder 24.

Fr. Mychael knelt down by the dying man. He removed his helmet, began to locate his pyx (containing the Blessed Sacrament) and the sacred oils, and prepared to administer the Anointing of the Sick or last rites to the firefighter. Only seconds later a piece of debris crashed into Fr. Mychael, killing him as well.

Five firemen broke from their duties, picked up Fr. Mychael's body, carried him to a nearby church, and laid him before the altar. They covered him with a white cloth and his stole, and put his helmet and fireman's badge on his chest.

Later in the day, they came back and took Fr. Mychael's body to their firehouse. There, they laid him in the bed of the fire truck. Engine 1/Ladder 24 lost ten other firefighters that day. Those who survived came to mourn and pay their respects near where Fr. Mychael was laid. So did his Franciscan brothers. At his funeral, the coffin was covered with a simple white alb with Fr. Mychael's helmet marked "Chaplain" placed upon it.

His Franciscan habit and fireman's helmet, the pyx and the sacred oils, his stole and the altar before which his comrades laid him—all of these are signs and symbols of Fr. Mychael's life and dedication, his very identity as a priest and fire department chaplain.

He went to Ground Zero with the expectation that he would administer the sacrament of the last rites to the victims. Fr. Michael Duffy explained in his homily at Fr. Mychael's funeral that "Two to three hundred firemen are still buried there. It would have been physically impossible to administer the sacraments to all of them in this life. In the next life, Fr. Mychael will greet them with 'Welcome. Let me take you to our Father.'"

Fr. Mychael Judge's death certificate administered by the City of New York has the number 1 on it. His body was the first released from Ground Zero.

"His role was to bring firemen to their death and meet their maker," Fr. Duffy added.

Mychael's Prayer

The following prayer was written by Fr. Mychael Judge:

Lord, take me where You want me to go;
Let me meet who You want me to meet;
Tell me what You want me to say, and
Keep me out of Your way.

Our lives too are filled with signs and symbols. Signs can be anything that point to something else, words, objects, and actions can all be signs. A school bell tells you when the period is over. A red light means "stop." There are natural signs too that are not created by people: smoke is the sign that fire may be near; a wagging tail on a dog and a smile on a person help us to conclude that each is happy.

Symbols are special signs that go beyond just "pointing" to something. Symbols are part of what they point to, but not all of it. Fire, for example, is a symbol of warmth. Fire is a source of warmth and is necessary for it, but there is more to warmth than fire. Symbols evoke deeper meanings than signs do, they elicit both conscious and unconscious feelings within us. For example, the nation's flag may evoke feelings of pride and patriotism. An old photo may stir up special thoughts and feelings for the person and time depicted. The flag and the photo also convey another dimension of a symbol: something that both reveals and conceals the fullness of the reality it communicates. The flag may inspire pride in a country's virtues, but may also conceal the nation's failings; the photograph may capture a dimension of a person, but can only reveal certain aspects of one's essence. Some symbols, like fire or water, are so rooted in our  human existence that we grasp their meaning without any need for instruction. Others, like a ring or a stole, become symbols as we grow in our understanding of their meaning.

People can be signs and symbols too. Fr. Mychael Judge was certainly a sign of courage, goodness, and his faith for people who heard about his life and how it ended on September 11. The religious habit and firefighter's uniform he wore were visible signs of who he was.

Symbols are more powerful than signs. They have a depth of meaning that signs do not and they can capture our attention and emotions in a way signs can't. Yet despite their ability to communicate a greater reality, they are not identical to it. This, as we have begun to discover already, is how they differ from sacraments.

Sacraments are celebrations that are "woven from signs and symbols" (*CCC*, 1145). Signs and symbols play a central role in their celebration, as we will discover in this chapter. Having explored how the fruits of Christ's Paschal mystery are dispensed in the sacraments in Chapter 1, this chapter treats what is common to the celebration of the seven sacraments by answering the following questions:

- Who celebrates the liturgy?
- How is the liturgy celebrated?
- When is the liturgy celebrated?
- Where is the liturgy celebrated?

Who Celebrates the Liturgy?

Recall our discussion of the meaning of liturgy from Chapter 1. The *Catechism* defines liturgy as: "The participation of the People of God in 'the work of God.' Through the liturgy Christ, our redeemer and high priest, continues the work of our redemption in, with, and through his Church." (1069).

The liturgy is first of all celebrated by Christ. He is the celebrant of the Eucharist and all the sacraments. In them, he is active in the Church, both in the People of God as a whole, and in the distinctive ways that the ordained and laity participate in the liturgy.

Just as Christ acts "in, with, and through his Church," so the Church acts in, with, and through Christ. The Church also celebrates the liturgy. "It is the whole community, the Body of Christ united with its Head, that celebrates" (*CCC*, 1140).

The Church on earth is united with the Church in heaven in its praise of the God. Those already in heaven—angels, ancestors from the Old Testament, martyrs, Mary, the Mother of God, and the entire communion of saints—celebrate the heavenly liturgy completely in communion with the Blessed Trinity and with one another.

We, the Pilgrim Church, participate in this eternal liturgy whenever we participate in the sacramental liturgy on earth. And, our participation is absolutely needed because liturgy is an action of *Christus totus*, the "whole Christ." When we are absent from liturgy one piece of the body of Christ is missing.

Prior to the Second Vatican Council, liturgy was often celebrated in private or quasi-private. In many Catholic churches designed prior to Vatican II, you can witness evidence of this today as the nave often included one main sanctuary and altar and two side altars where Mass may have been offered privately. Also, in those times, the assembly's participation was understood in less active terms. Hence, some people prayed the rosary or other devotions while remaining on the outskirts of the liturgy.

Nowadays, the Church reminds us that it is the whole community, united with Christ, that celebrates liturgy. According to the fathers of the Second Vatican Council:

> *Liturgical services are not private functions but are celebrations of the Church which is the "sacrament of unity," namely, the holy people united and organized under the authority of the bishops* (Sacrosanctum Concilium, 26).

☑

Why do you go to Mass when you do go?

Why do you not go to Mass when you don't go?

Celebrated in community, liturgy involves all members of the Body of Christ, each according to their calling. The distinct roles within the liturgy flow from the distinct ways that the "common priesthood" of all the baptized and the "ministerial priesthood" of the ordained participate in the one priesthood of Christ.

Two Ways to Participate in the One Priesthood of Christ

St. Thomas Aquinas correctly taught that "Only Christ is the true priest, the others being only his ministers." The letter to the Hebrews describes Christ as a high priest who is "holy, innocent, undefiled, separated from sinners, higher than the heavens" (7:26). Christ is different from the priests of the Old Testament who offered sacrifice day after day. Christ offered one sacrifice—the sacrifice of the cross—that is made present in the Eucharistic sacrifice of the Church. In the same way, Christ's one priesthood is made present through the ministerial priesthood without diminishing Christ's unique priesthood.

In fact, the entire Church is priestly. Through the sacraments of Baptism and Confirmation, we each share in Christ's mission as priest, prophet, and king. This is what is known as the *common priesthood.* As Catholics, we share this priestly ministry of Christ whenever we use our talents to continue his work to bring God's love to others. Some of the ways we do this include:

- *Witness.* We must share the Good News with our words and actions. By being honest and sincere with our love for others and by not shrinking when asked about Christ and our values, we witness him to the world.
- *Live in Community.* We live in community with people through the whole world. When we build up this community through the reconciling of differences, acting for peace, and working for justice, we bring Christ to the world.
- *Serve.* Jesus modeled service when he washed the feet of his disciples at the Last Supper. We, too, in humility must serve the physical, emotional, and spiritual needs of all, especially our least brothers and sisters.
- *Worship.* It is through the sacraments—especially the Eucharist—that a vital function of the common priesthood takes place. When we gather together and pray, we permit the Holy Spirit to pray in and through us. We adore and

Name several ways you use your talents to bring God's love to others.

thank God, ask for forgiveness, and petition for our needs. Joined to Christ, the High Priest, our prayers become his prayer.

The *ministerial* or *hierarchical priesthood* is different than the common priesthood, yet nevertheless related. The ministerial priesthood is at the service of the common priesthood. The ministerial priesthood is the means by which Christ builds up and leads his Church. That is why it is transmitted by its own sacrament, the sacrament of Holy Orders (*CCC*, 1547). By the sacred power he has been given in the sacrament, the ministerial priest molds and rules the priestly people.

The priest also acts in the name of the whole Church when presenting to God the Father the prayer of the Church, and above all when offering the Eucharistic sacrifice to the Father in the name of the people. The priest represents Christ when presiding at Eucharist.

The assembly joins in the offering of the Eucharist and the other sacraments by virtue of their priesthood given in Baptism and Confirmation. The *Constitution on the Sacred Liturgy* of Vatican II taught that the "full, conscious, and active participation" of the faithful in the liturgy is a right and duty that comes from our Baptism. We participate in liturgy through acclamations, responses, singing, actions, gestures, and other body positions. Silence, too, is a proper response at certain times in the liturgy.

At liturgy generally and the Eucharist specifically, other people with particular ministries not consecrated in the sacrament of Holy Orders serve in roles such as servers, readers, commentators, extraordinary ministers of holy communion, and members of the choir.

How Is the Liturgy Celebrated?

Sacraments are celebrated with signs and symbols, words and actions, singing and music, and holy images called *icons*.

The signs and symbols used in liturgy come from God's creation. For example, light and darkness, wind and fire, water and earth, the tree and its fruit, tell of God and symbolize his greatness and nearness.

Signs and symbols used in liturgy also come from our human life. These include washing and anointing, breaking bread and sharing the cup—things that are part of our everyday lives.

There are also signs and symbols taken from the Old Testament. Some of these were once cosmic signs that may have been incorporated from other social traditions of the time. Yet, in making his covenant with them, Yahweh transformed actions and events like circumcision, the anointing and consecration of kings and priests, laying on of hands, sacrifices, and the harvest festivals into actions and events with religious meaning. These signs also are understood to prefigure the sacraments of the New Covenant.

Jesus, too, used signs to help make known the mysteries of God's kingdom. He performed healings and used symbolic gestures to accompany his preaching. His life itself gives meaning to the signs of the Old Testament—especially the Exodus and Passover—because in him the hidden meaning of those signs is revealed.

Since Pentecost, the Church has incorporated even more signs, symbols, gestures, actions, and words into its liturgy. These include Scripture reading, processions, holy water, kneeling, blessings, anointing with oil, candles, incense, standing and sitting, musical instruments, singing, and more.

Many of the signs and symbols of liturgy have been taken from everyday life. Things like washing, anointing with oil, and the sharing of food and drink are incorporated into our religious life where they help us express our relationship with God. The fact that water is used in Baptism helps us to see and feel the cleansing that is happening. The food of the Eucharist helps us to see, feel, and taste the nourishment and strength that Christ is giving us. The fact that our worship was formed in the created world and uses everyday actions makes it accessible to all people and not just the well educated. If a person can understand that food gives us energy, or that water makes us clean, or that certain ointments protect us and heal us, he or she can understand the gifts of the sacraments.

List five natural signs and their meaning. For example, lightning is a sign of thunder.

Tracing the Meaning of the Term "Sacrament"

The New Testament term for sacraments is the Greek word *mysterion* which translates to "mystery." St. Paul used the word *mysterion* to refer to Christ, apostolic preaching, those things that are spoken in the Spirit, and the relationship between Christ and the Church and a husband and wife.

The word sacrament itself comes from the Latin word, *sacramentum*, which is translated from *mysterion*.

For Romans, sacrament originally referred to a bond, seal, or sign that took the form of a pledge of property or money. Roman soldiers applied the term to the oath they took to their commanders and gods.

Church Father Tertullian applied the term *sacramentum* to the Christian rites of Baptism, Confirmation, and Eucharist. He did so in an attempt to inform Roman citizens about the formal pledge Christians made to be loyal to Jesus and to serve God faithfully.

Explain the difference between a sacrament and an ordinary symbol.

(Tracing the Meaning of the Term "Sacrament" cont.)

St. Augustine, in the fifth century, developed the meaning of sacrament as a special sign or symbol. Augustine's definition of sacraments as a "visible sign of invisible grace" refers to sacraments being holy signs through which we can both perceive and receive invisible grace. Grace, in this understanding, refers to what was later defined as sanctifying grace. At the time, Augustine used the term "sacrament" to describe many things including the giving of salt at Baptism, the giving of ashes, the creed, and the Lord's Prayer.

St. Thomas Aquinas referred to sacraments as efficacious symbols. Recall that ordinary symbols communicate a greater reality while remaining distinct from it. A sacrament, as an efficacious symbol "effects what it symbolizes and symbolizes what it effects." As the *Catechism* explains: "As a fire transforms into itself everything it touches, so the Holy Spirit transforms into the divine life whatever is subjected to his power" (1127). In a sacrament, there is a *pointing to* and *effecting of* the reality symbolized. A sacrament not only signifies a sacred reality but actually puts us in touch with it.

Words, Actions, Songs, Images

The words spoken and the actions performed by the assembly (the people) at liturgy are the means by which the assembly ministers to one another in liturgy. The fact that the people say and do the same thing at the same time is a sign of unity which liturgy establishes and strengthens.

In particular, liturgy includes the use of the Word of God which has been given to us in the scriptures. "The liturgy of the Word is an integral part of sacramental celebrations" (*CCC*, 1154). The Second Vatican Council also taught the importance of the Scriptures in liturgy for,

> *it is from Scripture that lessons are read and explained in the homily, and psalms are sung; the prayers, collects, and liturgical songs are scriptural in their inspiration, and it is from Scripture that actions and signs derive their meaning (*Sacrosanctum Concillium, 24).*

Prior to the Council only a select few of Old Testament and New Testament passages were read at Mass. Now the Church has a three-year cycle of Sunday readings and a two-year cycle of weekday readings so that Catholics at Mass are able to hear a good selection of the Old Testament and samples from virtually all of the books of the New Testament over that period. All of the readings are now done in the vernacular, the common language of the people.

At liturgy, several visible signs which accompany the Word of God are emphasized. For example:

- The Word of God is contained in a special book—a lectionary or a book of the gospels.
- The Word of God is venerated with a procession, incense, and candles.
- The Word of God is proclaimed in an audible and intelligible way.
- The Word of God is extended through the homily, which derives its teaching from the Scriptures.
- The Word of God is responded to by the assembly through acclamations, psalms, litanies, and professions of faith.

The other words which are used in the liturgy are also words of God. The Church has chosen the words of our prayers, responses, and creeds because they express the faith the Holy Spirit stirs within us. Our faith is the faith of the Church. Through the Church God gives us the ability to speak and respond to him as a people who are truly united. Each of the prayers and the responses of the liturgy help shape our relationship with God. When we say them week in and week out, they work their way into our lives and very souls and shape us as a people of faith. For example, the *Kyrie* ("Lord Have Mercy") helps us to see ourselves as people who are dependent upon God. Over time it helps us to develop the desire and the ability to ask for and receive forgiveness.

The Church also celebrates liturgy with music. The Second Vatican Council called music "a necessary or integral part of solemn liturgy" (*Sacrosanctum Concilium*, 112). Music allows us to express what is in our hearts. It also moves us in ways that words alone cannot. When music accompanies liturgical actions or gives expression to liturgical words, those actions and words have greater impact on us. Music with liturgy expresses prayerfulness, builds community, and increases the solemnity of the liturgical rites.

 Locate and read the scripture readings from the coming Sunday's liturgy. What theme do the first reading and the gospel have in common? How does this message speak to your life?

The setting for liturgy is also important. *Icons* are holy images that help us to focus our attention on Jesus, the Son of God. Statues, paintings, stained glass, and other sacred art present images of Jesus as well as the images of Mary and the saints who have been transfigured into his likeness. When we contemplate on the sacred icons together with meditation on the Word of God and the singing of liturgical hymns, we enter more deeply into the signs of the liturgy so that their meaning becomes part of our lives and we are able to share it with others.

A Treasure of Immeasurable Value

Share the lyrics of a particular liturgical song that has special meaning to you and tell why that is so.

St. Augustine said, "He who sings prays twice." The Second Vatican Council described the musical tradition of the Church as "a treasure of immeasurable value." Among some of the other teachings of the Council regarding music are:

- Liturgical action is given a more noble form when sacred rites are solemnized in song, with the assistance of sacred ministers and the active participation of the people.
- Choirs are to be promoted and trained, but whenever the liturgy is to be celebrated with song, the entire assembly should actively participate.
- The teaching and practice of music must be promoted in seminaries, in novitiates, schools, and other Catholic institutions. Composers and singers should be given liturgical training.
- Gregorian chant is proper to liturgy in the Roman Catholic Church. It should be given a place of pride in liturgical services.

- Religious singing by the people is to be skillfully taught so that their voices may ring out.
- When possible, the native music of people of mission lands and other parts of the world should be adapted to worship.
- The pipe organ is a traditional musical instrument that should be held in high esteem.
- Composers, filled with the Christian spirit, should feel called to cultivate sacred music.
- The musical texts should be drawn chiefly from the scriptures and from liturgical sources; they should be in conformity with Catholic doctrine.

When Is the Liturgy Celebrated?

Even though God is outside of human history, he enters our time and our space so that we might know him. This is one of the fundamental principles of the Judeo-Christian tradition. We do not need to escape time in order to relate to God. God communicates with us in time. For this reason our worship does not release us from the routine of our lives. Instead it plunges us more deeply into the rhythms of time and invites us to rework each aspect of our lives in light of what God has done and is doing for us.

The worship of the Church is structured around yearly, weekly, and daily schedules. Yearly events help us to understand God's constancy in the midst of change. They also help us to see the faithfulness of God and to find direction in our lives. Weekly events help us structure our work and our family life around our relationship with God. And daily events help us to shape our self-identity around that same relationship.

As our worship plunges us into the rhythms of time, it makes all time part of the *present*. "Today" is the word that marks the prayer of the Church. As we celebrate the Paschal mystery in all of its dimensions on a daily, weekly, and yearly basis, all of the events of salvation history become part of our own lives. They become events of today.

The celebration of Christ's birth, life, death, and resurrection unfolding over the course of the year is called the liturgical year. It is the basic rhythm of our Christian life through which we experience the natural cycle of the year as "a year of the Lord's grace."

Examine the statements: 1) God enters our time and space, and 2) All time is part of the present. How do these statements help you to understand how Jesus is present in the sacraments?

Jewish Roots

The liturgical year has its roots in Judaism. Jesus, as a faithful Jew, observed the various festivals of the Jewish year, most notably the Passover. It was during the Passover in Jerusalem that the Last Supper and his passion and death took place. The defining moment in Jewish history is the Exodus. The Book of Exodus records not only God's liberation of the Jews from slavery in Egypt, but gives explicit instructions for a yearly commemoration of these saving events. The Passover and the Exodus are annual events which allow all Jews to continue to experience God's saving work. By celebrating this festival each year in memory of God's action, the Jewish people continue to consciously participate in this saving work.

They grow in their awareness of all of the ways in which God is continually acting to bring them freedom, life, and salvation. The yearly celebration of Passover helps Jews of each generation to make God's gift of freedom their own.

Along with Passover there were two other major festivals which shaped the Jewish year at the time of Jesus: Pentecost (also called *Shavuot*) which celebrated the giving of the commandments and was also a time of thanksgiving for the wheat harvest; and *Succoth* (Feast of Booths) which was a time of thanksgiving for the grape harvest and which culminated with a celebration that recalls the giving of the Torah.

In Jesus' time all Jewish men over age twelve were expected to travel to Jerusalem for at least one of these three festivals each year. Passover, Pentecost, and Succoth were the principal feasts of the Jewish year in Jesus' time. Today Passover remains at the center of the Jewish year, along with *Rosh Hashanah*, the new year feast, *Yom Kippur*, the feast of atonement, and *Hanukkah*, the feast of the dedication of the Temple. Besides these four, *Shavuot* and *Succoth* are still celebrated along with *Purim*, the Jewish carnival.

Historically, these feasts helped the Jewish people find their identity and their place within creation. One thing that we should note about the Jewish calendar is that all of the significant events of the natural world—things like planting harvests and the major seasonal changes—are linked to and understood in light of God's saving actions. As Christians began to develop their own annual calendar they continued this same pattern, interpreting and celebrating all significant events in light of God's saving action.

The Lord's Day

Sunday is the original feast day for Christians. The first day of the week according to the Jewish calendar, it is the day on which Christ rose from the dead. From the Church's very beginning, Christians have gathered on this day to celebrate the Eucharist and to proclaim their faith in the resurrection.

St. Jerome (ca. 380-420), one of the Fathers of the Church, wrote:

> *The Lord's day, the day of the Resurrection, the day of Christians, is our day. It is called the Lord's day because on it the Lord rose victorious to the Father. If pagans call it the "day of the sun" we willingly agree, for today the light of the world is raised, today is revealed the sun of justice with healing in his wings (quoted from CCC, 1166).*

Sunday is the first day of the week, the day on which God began the work of creation. It is also called the "eighth day" because on it we look forward to Christ's return in glory when the work of creation and salvation is finished.

"On the evening of the first day of the week" Jesus appeared to his disciples and said to them, "Peace be with you" (Jn 20:19). Throughout the New Testament we find the Church gathered for Eucharist on "the first day." In the middle of the

☑

Research some of the liturgical practices for one of the Jewish feasts described above.

second century, Justin Martyr tells us that the Church in Rome would gather on Sunday. The "apostles or prophets were read," the priest gave instruction, prayers were offered, and the bread and wine were blessed with thanksgiving and distributed (*First Apology*, 67).

The New Testament also refers to a special meal shared by Christians known as an *agape*, or a "love meal." This was a meal of sharing, usually held in a "house church," a Christian's home. The Eucharist was shared in many places in conjunction with an agape. Read about two examples of *agape* in Acts 2:46 and 20:7 and some abuses of this practice in 1 Corinthians 11:17 ff. which caused the Eucharist to be separated from it.

The earliest Jewish Christians continued to celebrate the Sabbath along with the commemoration of the Resurrection on the first day of the week.

The word Sabbath comes from the Hebrew word, *Shabbat*, which literally translates "cease or desist." It is the seventh day when God rested after completing the work of creation. "So God blessed the seventh day and made it holy, because on it he rested from the work he had done in creation" (Gn 2:3).

For the first three centuries of Christianity there was no mention of abstaining from work on Sundays. Jews and Jewish Christians continued to keep Saturday as a day of rest however. In 321 the Emperor Constantine declared Sunday to be a day of rest for all judges, city dwellers, and business people. Farmers were allowed to work so as not to miss the good weather.

Even as Sunday began to take on the connotations of the Jewish Sabbath and become a day of rest, the primary focus for the day remained on gathering as a community to listen to the word of God and to share the Eucharist. In the early years of Christianity, when Sunday was still a work day, Christians gathered in the morning for a liturgy of the Word and sometimes a baptism, and in the evening to share the primary meal of the day and celebrate the Eucharist. After a short while the practice of sharing a meal before the Eucharist disappeared, but the separate services remained. In fact, by the fifth century, Sunday worship in the major Christian centers such as Jerusalem, Antioch, Alexandria, Rome, and Constantinople consisted of a series of services which took up most of the day and were parceled throughout the entire city. Very few people actually attended every piece of the Sunday worship, but the series of services shaped the day and even the Christian sense of time itself.

Sunday Eucharist remains the foundation and heart of Catholic life. When we participate in the communal celebration of Sunday Mass, we give a public testimony of belonging and being faithful to Christ and to his Church.

Church law requires Catholics to go to Mass on Sundays and all holy days, or on the evening preceding either. This obligation is a serious one. Those who deliberately miss Mass commit a grave sin. Only valid excuses like being ill or having to care for an infant or being excused by a pastor free a person from this obligation.

The Second Vatican Council said that Sunday is "the original feast day." It should be a day of joy and freedom from work (*Sacrosanctum Concilium*, 106). The *Catechism of the Catholic Church* teaches that

> *On Sundays and other holy days of obligation, the faithful are to refrain from engaging in work or activities that hinder the worship owed to God, the joy proper to the Lord's Day, the performance of the works of mercy, and the appropriate relaxation of mind and body (2185).*

To accomplish this, we must spend Sunday relaxing, spending time with our families, visiting older relatives or neighbors, and doing charitable works for those in need: the elderly, poor, and sick. Also appropriate as activities are things that refresh our mind like meditating, reading, and taking a walk in nature. Some Catholics, because of their jobs (e.g., medical, retail, and the like) have to work on Sundays. However, they, too, should set aside time for prayer, reflection, and rest. Christians especially should take care to not make unnecessary demands on others that would keep them from resting on the Lord's Day.

Describe what you consider to be three inappropriate actions for Sunday as well as three appropriate actions for commemorating the Lord's Day.

The Sabbath

Name a concrete plan you can suggest to your family for rest on the next Sunday.

A weekly commemoration of God's work in creation has always been one of the defining elements of Judaism and Christianity. For Jews, the Sabbath is Saturday. Jews are called to make every seventh day holy, to set it aside as a day to rest from ordinary activity and focus their energy on God. As they structure their week around the Sabbath they begin to understand that all time belongs to God and that God's agenda and not our own is what matters not only in the long term but also in the day to day.

The Sabbath exists because God rested on the seventh day of creation. Because its roots are in the creation story, the Sabbath draws our attention to that story. The Sabbath is a reminder that God created us out of love. It is also a reminder that God invites us to join him in the work of creation and to return love to God by loving one another and by caring for his world. The Sabbath is to be a day of rest for all people, rich and poor alike. It provides a means for caring for those who are weaker than we are, and it reminds us that God has cared for us in our weakness.

Easter

Easter was the first annual feast celebrated by the early Church. Because the first Christians maintained aspects of Jewish practice, and because they expected the imminent return of Christ, at first there was no need for a separate calendar which would carry them from year to year. There is evidence in the New Testament, however, that the earliest Christians did observe an annual remembrance of the Resurrection. For example, in his first letter to the Corinthians (5:7-8) Paul seems to indicate that Christians had reinterpreted the festival of Passover. It seems likely that, during the days when the Jewish community celebrated Passover, the Christians also celebrated, but with a focus on Christ as the Paschal lamb. In fact the Greek word for Easter was *pascha*, a translation of the Hebrew word for Passover.

There is much evidence over the second and third centuries that Christians celebrated Easter each year. Around the middle of the second century, a homily preached by a Church Father named Melito of Sardis (in present day Turkey) described the structure of the Pascha. It lasted from sunset to midnight and consisted of fasting, Scripture reading, chanting, and the Eucharist.

A controversy developed in the second century about when Easter should be celebrated. Some parts of the Church observed it according to the Jewish calendar at the same time as Passover. This was the fourteenth day of the Jewish month called Nisan. In other parts of the Church Easter was celebrated on the Sunday following Passover.

The matter was resolved by the Council of Nicea in 325 at which it was agreed that Easter should be celebrated on the Sunday following the first full moon after the Spring equinox (the first day of spring). That is how we calculate the date for Easter today.

By the end of the fourth century the annual Easter celebration was divided into several days to better reflect the historical events of Christ's suffering, death, and resurrection. The Church's practice in Jerusalem was very influential and spread throughout the Roman Empire. Holy Thursday marked the Last Supper and the arrest of Jesus. Good Friday commemorated his crucifixion and death. The Easter Vigil service began in a dark Church, the sign of the chaos that existed before creation and of the darkness of despair when Christ was in the tomb.

The first week of the Easter season was of particular importance in the early Church. St. Augustine (d. 430) described it as a time when the faithful did not work, but instead celebrated the liturgy daily and helped introduce the newly baptized into the mysteries of the faith, particularly the sacraments.

The annual celebration of the Easter Triduum, which reaches its climax at the Easter Vigil, is the focal point of the Church's calendar. Easter is the feast of feasts. The liturgical year truly becomes a "year of the Lord's favor" as the light of the resurrection pours out from the celebration of Easter and fills the year with its brilliance. As the words of the *Exultet*—the Easter proclamation sung at the vigil—proclaim:

> This *is our Passover feast, when Christ, the true Lamb, is slain* . . .
> This is the night *when first you saved our fathers: you freed the people of Israel from their slavery and led them dry-shod through the sea.*
> This is the night *when the pillar of fire destroyed the darkness of sin!*
> This is the night *when Christians everywhere . . . are restored to grace and grow together in holiness.*
> This is the night *when Jesus Christ broke the chains of death and rose triumphant from the grave.* . . .
> Of this *night scripture says: "the night will be as clear as day: it will become my light, my joy."*
> The power of this holy night *dispels all evil, washes guilt away, restores lost innocence, brings mourners joy; it casts out hatred, brings us peace, and humbles earthly pride (from the Easter vigil liturgy, emphasis added).*

☑ A traditional Catholic Easter custom is to eat lamb on Easter Sunday to celebrate the rising of the Lamb of God. What Easter customs do you celebrate with your family?

The fifty day period after Easter is called the Easter Season and it is one of the holiest seasons of the liturgical year. We celebrate the Eucharist with the joy of the first disciples who recognized Jesus in the breaking of the bread. During the Easter season we fulfill what has traditionally been called our "Easter duty." "Prepared by the sacrament of Reconciliation, [we] receive the Eucharist at least once a year, if possible during the Easter season" (*CCC*, 1389).

The Easter season is crowned with the celebration of the Ascension of Christ into heaven, forty days after Easter on Ascension Thursday, and Pentecost, fifty days after Easter, the day on which the Holy Spirit descended upon the Apostles. Pentecost is called the "birthday" of the Church. The Easter season invites us to immerse ourselves and our lives into the Paschal mystery, to make our whole lives a celebration of God's grace.

Lent

We cannot celebrate Easter fully if we have not taken the time to prepare for the celebration. We cannot be restored if we have not taken the time to identify the ways in which we are broken. By the second century Christians were preparing for the Easter celebration with a two-day (forty-hour) fast. No one within the community was to take food or water during the hours that Christ was in the tomb. Also, during the same time, Lent developed as a forty-day period of preparation for those who were to be baptized at Easter. Catechumens were to fast with just one meal per day for forty days in imitation of the forty days that Jesus spent in the wilderness.

This fast was seen as having several purposes. First, people believed that fasting gave fervor to prayers, strengthened them to fight against evil and helped prepare them for the reception of the Holy Spirit. Second, fasting allowed one to give money to the poor that would otherwise be used for food. For many fasting was a response of love. The rest of the Church participated in the fast as a way of supporting the catechumens and as a way doing penance for their sins and recommitting themselves to their own baptism.

In some parts of the early Church, Lent—the word means "springtime"—was the appropriate time for those guilty of serious sin to complete their process of reconciliation. At the beginning of Lent those who were called penitents would put on special garments. They would be sprinkled with ashes and then be solemnly expelled from the Church. They would not be able to participate in the prayers of the faithful or the Eucharist until they were solemnly reconciled with the Church on Holy Thursday.

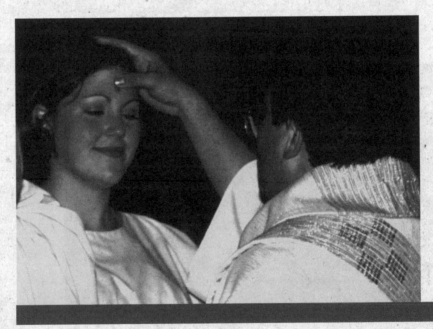

The Lenten season originally began on the sixth Sunday before Easter and ended with the celebration of the Lord's Supper on Holy Thursday. Because there was no fasting on Sundays, the Church of the fifth century decided that six more days should be added to Lent in order to have forty fast days. To accomplish this, Good Friday and Holy Saturday were separated from the Easter Triduum and added to Lent and the four days preceding the sixth Sunday before Easter were also added. Thus Ash Wednesday was born as the first day of the season of penance. When the practice of expelling serious sinners at the beginning of Lent and restoring them to the Church at the end of Lent faded out of existence at the end of the first millennium, the practice of sprinkling ashes was retained for all the faithful.

A common modern practice during Lent is for Catholics to substitute a meal of soup and bread or other simple items on Ash Wednesday and the Fridays of Lent. Then, the difference in cost between what is usually spent on meals for these days is donated to the poor. Describe other communal or individual penitential acts you are aware of for Lent.

Today, Lent is seen as a time of conversion with a threefold emphasis on prayer, fasting, and almsgiving. We seek a greater openness to the word of God, a more complete participation in the liturgy, and a stronger commitment to works of charity (almsgiving). Our practice of fasting (not eating) and abstinence (giving up certain foods or behaviors) is designed to turn our hearts to God and remind us of the plight of those who are hungry. During Lent we abstain from meat on Ash Wednesday, and on every Friday including Good Friday. On Ash Wednesday and Good Friday we also fast between meals. Today's Lenten season extends from Ash Wednesday to the Mass of the Lord's Supper on Holy Thursday. It is forty-four days long if Sundays are included and thirty-eight days if they are not.

Christmas

In the first two centuries, the entire Christian story was viewed by the Church as a part of the Easter celebration. Gradually, however, people began to celebrate different aspects of Christ's saving work on independent feast days. The Eastern Church (centered in Constantinople) began to celebrate Epiphany as the feast of Christ's birth, the visit of the magi, his baptism, and his first miracle all in one

while marking the fact that God had revealed himself to the world. The word epiphany means "revelation" or "showing forth." The dating of Epiphany to January 6 seems to have had its roots in the popular belief that Jesus was conceived on the date of his death. His death was widely held to be April 6, and January 6 is exactly nine months later.

In the Western Church, there is evidence that by 336 Christmas day was being celebrated on December 25. There are two theories about this date for Christmas. One is that this was the date for the pagan festival of the Unconquered Sun. According to many scholars the Church introduced the celebration of the Incarnation on this day to help Christians understand that Christ is the true light that has come into the world, the "sun of justice" mentioned in Malachi 3:20. By celebrating Christ's birth on the day of the pagan festival Christians could proclaim that their feast celebrated the only true unconquered Son who alone can give light and bring salvation to the world.

The second theory relates to early Christian theologians being inclined to pay particular attention to equinoxes and solstices. For example some believed that John the Baptist was conceived at the autumn equinox and born at the summer solstice. Since Luke 1:26 reports that Jesus was conceived six months after John, he would have been conceived at the spring equinox (March 25) and therefore born on December 25.

For Christians of the third and fourth century it made perfect sense for God to choose the winter solstice as the day of Christ's birth; on the darkest day of the year God sent the Light to the world. Christians came to understand the winter solstice in light of the Incarnation. The solstice became a reminder of the true light which came into the world in Christ and which gave us hope even in the midst of darkness. The Christian observance of Christmas put the solstice at the service of God.

Near the end of the fourth century the Eastern Church and Western Church began to celebrate the events surrounding Jesus' birth on both December 25 and January 6. December 25 became the day for the whole Church to celebrate Jesus' birth and January 6 became the day to celebrate his baptism and his first miracle at Cana. The coming of the Magi was celebrated in the East on December 25 and on January 6 in the West.

Christmas has been celebrated in the Church since at least 354. Read the story of the Incarnation and subsequent events from Luke 2:1-38. Use accompanying biblical notes to cite a date when scholars believe Jesus Christ was born.

Advent

Advent as a season of preparation for Christmas seems to have developed in the East during the fifth century. It may have begun as a forty-day fast for those who were preparing for their own baptism to be celebrated on the day of Christ's baptism. At the end of the sixth century the Advent Masses for the city of Rome focused on the Incarnation of Christ and preparation for the celebration of Christmas.

In other regions, particularly in Gaul, Advent became a time of preparation for Christ's second coming. The Irish missionaries in Gaul tended to emphasize the fact that Christ would come again to judge the people, pointing out the importance of preparing through penance. By the twelfth century some of the penitential characteristics of the Gaelic Advent liturgies had made their way into Rome, resulting in the elimination of the Gloria from the liturgy and the wearing of purple vestments.

Today Advent is viewed in two ways. The first two weeks of Advent direct our minds to the second coming of Christ and the time when God "will wipe every

Advent is Latin for "to come." There are many Advent traditions in the church. Research and report on at least one of the following: Advent calendar, Advent wreath, Jesse tree, crèche, "O" antiphons, or posadas.

tear from our eyes" (Rv 21:4). It is thus a season of joyful and spiritual expectation. The Gloria is still omitted during the Advent liturgies, but this is not because we are mourning our sin, but rather in order that the song of the angels might ring out in all its newness on Christmas.

The elimination of the Gloria during Advent draws our attention to a second important characteristic of the season: Advent is a time to *prepare* to celebrate Christmas. It is not a time to *begin* celebrating Christmas. During the Sundays of Advent we focus on the fact that without Christ we would be in darkness. We also reflect upon the promises that God made which were fulfilled when Jesus entered the world. During the season of Advent we live in spirit with those who were relying on God's promise to send a Savior. When we celebrate the coming of that Savior at Christmas we find new confidence in God's faithfulness.

Ordinary Time

The Easter cycle, which goes from Ash Wednesday to Pentecost, and the Christmas cycle, which goes from the first Sunday of Advent until the feast of Christ's baptism on the Sunday after Epiphany, are the supporting pillars of the liturgical year. During the other weeks of the year "the mystery of Christ in all its fullness is celebrated." (*General Norms for the Liturgical Year and the Calendar,* #43). These weeks are referred to as "ordinary time." During this time of the liturgical years the Sundays are counted (e.g., The Third Sunday of Ordinary Time). The word "ordinary" refers to the numbers, as in ordinal numbers.

Ordinary time has thirty-three or thirty-four Sundays, depending upon the total number of Sundays in a given year. In years with only thirty-three Sundays in ordinary time, a week is omitted between the Sunday of ordinary time immediately before Ash Wednesday and the Sunday immediately after Pentecost. The last Sunday of the year—whether it be the thirty-third or thirty-fourth Sunday—is never eliminated because the readings for that day focus on the second coming and are necessary to finish the liturgical year and lead the Church into Advent. This last Sunday is the celebration of the feast of Christ the King.

Ordinary time is punctuated by numerous feast days. Over time the Christian calendar came to include feasts to remember events in the life of Mary and memorials of martyrs and saints. Several of the Marian feasts have very ancient roots. The earliest Marian feast began some time before the council of Ephesus which was held in 431. It was the "commemoration of the holy, ever-virgin mother of God" which was celebrated on December 26 in the East. The Assumption of Mary was a feast commemorating Mary's death or her "falling asleep." It was extended to the entire Byzantine Empire in the sixth century. The Feast of the Annunciation on March 25 was also being celebrated by the middle of the sixth century in the East and the seventh century in the West. The Feast of the Immaculate Conception (the conception of Mary) was first celebrated around 700 in the East. The mystery of the Immaculate Conception was officially named a dogma of the Church on December 8, 1854, by Pope Pius IX.

Each of these feasts celebrates the incredible love of God for his people and the grace which God offers to those who will receive it. In his encyclical *Marialis Cultus*, Pope Paul VI stressed the fact that celebrations and devotions which honor Mary should draw our minds and hearts to Christ and to the Trinity. "The ultimate purpose of devotion to the Blessed Virgin is to glorify God and lead Christians to commit themselves to a life which conforms absolutely to his will" (#39).

As for the saints, according to the *Constitution on the Liturgy*, "the feasts of the saints proclaim the wonderful works of Christ in his servants and offer to the faithful fitting examples for their imitation" (*Sacrosanctum Concilium*, 111). The Solemnity of All Saints on November 1 has its origins in the East where a memorial of all the martyrs was celebrated as early as the fourth century.

The other feast days which punctuate ordinary time draw our attention to particular truths of the faith. These feasts began to appear in the Middle Ages as a way of helping people to grasp particular teachings. Many are still celebrated today, like the Solemnity of the Trinity, Corpus Christi, the feast of the Sacred Heart, Christ the King, and the feast of the Holy Family.

The liturgical year helps us to relive the key points in salvation history and make them our own. There is no end to the things that God will reveal to us throughout the year. For this reason the liturgical year is a constant source of grace for the Church. The liturgical year calls us to look beyond ourselves and the things that we do and to focus our attention on the things that God has done and is doing. The Christian calendar offers balance to the calendars of our daily lives and all the things we "have to do." It reminds us that we are able to do what we do only because of what God has done for us. As we live through the great events of salvation history we are challenged to examine our priorities in light of God's plans and not just our own.

Research and report on a saint's feast or memorial that occurs on or near your birthday.

The Liturgy of the Hours

Pray all or part of the liturgy of the hours for a day. Use a printed resource or look up today's readings on the web (for example: www.liturgyhours.org). Report on your experience.

Both the Sunday celebration of the Mass and the annual unfolding of the Paschal mystery through the course of the liturgical year focus on the wonderful things that God has done for us. They help us open our hearts and prepare our lives so that we can receive the gift which God is offering us. Once we have received that gift we cannot help responding with prayers of praise. The liturgy of the hours—the daily public prayer of the Church—is the praise of the community offered to God in the midst of our daily lives. It is the prayer of a people whose lives are being shaped by what God has done and is doing.

The liturgy of the hours is modeled at least in part on the daily prayers of Judaism. When Jesus lived, faithful Jews set aside specific times of the day for prayer in the morning and evening, and also during the third, sixth, and ninth hours of the day (9:00, 12:00, 3:00). The early Christians continued the practice of praying at these times of day. The morning and evening prayer, however, ceased to be private. Christians in the early Church would gather publicly for prayer and praise each day before and after work. This practice was described by Hippolytus around the year 217 and continued to grow and spread for the next century or so.

By the sixth century, however, morning and evening prayer had become an almost exclusively monastic practice. Later all priests took up the practice of praying the *divine office*, another term to describe the liturgy of the hours. Today, all Catholics are encouraged to pray the liturgy of the hours making it not only the official prayer of the Church, but truly a prayer for the entire people of God.

The praying of the liturgy of the hours is a way of being faithful to the instruction to pray constantly. It is structured primarily around the psalms—the most ancient prayer of the Church. All of the faithful are called to join in the celebration of the liturgy of the hours, to pray with one voice in praise and thanksgiving for the wonders God is working in our midst. Praying the liturgy of the hours makes our connection with the entire body of Christ grow stronger. Over time we will feel less and less conflict between what we want and what Christ wants for us.

Diversity Within the Unity of Liturgy

The liturgy is celebrated in every corner of the world in a variety of liturgical rites that reflect the diverse cultures from which they come. As the *Catechism* teaches, "The mystery of Christ is so unfathomably rich that it cannot be exhausted by any single liturgical tradition" (1201). Today, the Church approves of the following liturgical rites, all of which have equal dignity: Latin (principally the Roman rite, but also the rites of certain localchurches, such as the Ambrosian rite, or those of certain religious orders), Byzantine, Alexandrian or Coptic, Syriac, Armenian, Maronite, and Chaldeon.

How did these different liturgical traditions arise? The liturgical traditions arose due to the Church's mission of sharing the gospel with all people, all cultures, and in all places. The Church is open to adapting the liturgy to reflect the differences in culture, but only if attention is also paid to maintaining the unity of fidelity with Tradition, professing the same faith, receiving the same sacraments as derived from apostolic succession, and remaining obedient to the Pope.

There are certain parts of the liturgy that cannot be changed because they are divinely instituted. (For example, the words of institution of the Eucharist, spoken by Christ, cannot be changed.) The Church is the guardian of these parts.

Other parts of the liturgy can change, especially when change arises from the Church's participation in a local culture, particularly the culture of a recently evangelized people. But the degree and the pace of change in the liturgy are always measured by their fidelity to the faith and the impact they will have on the unity of the Church.

The Second Vatican Council said that the Church

respects and fosters the qualities and the talents of the various races and peoples. Anything in these peoples' way of life which is not indissolubly bound up with superstition and error, she studies with sympathy, and, if possible, preserves intact. Sometimes, in fact, she admits such things into the liturgy itself so long as they harmonize with its true and authentic spirit (Sacrosanctum Concilium, 37).

The Second Vatican Council's Constitution on the Sacred Liturgy points out the central role liturgy should have for our lives: "The liturgy in its turn inspires the faithful to become 'of one heart in love' when they have tasted to their full of the paschal mysteries. . ." (no. 10). In what ways does the Sunday Mass bring you together with people within and outside of your parish community?

Today no matter where you go in the world, if you join in the Sunday celebration of Eucharist in a Roman Catholic church, you will do essentially the same thing, say essentially the same prayers, and hear the same scripture readings.

This uniformity accomplishes two very important things. First, it ensures that over the course of time we will share in the unfolding of the entire Paschal mystery. Our lives will be shaped by the entire Christ event and not simply by those things which are favorites for our parish, pastor, or liturgy committee. Second, the uniformity of the liturgy helps to unite many and diverse people from all over the world. This uniformity allows us to be at home with one another in worship even if we have never met, and even if we do not speak the same language. The German bishops have said that Sunday breaks through the isolation from which so many people suffer today.

Other Liturgical Rites Within the Catholic Church

All of the lawfully recognized rites of the Church are of equal dignity. They celebrate the same mystery but in different ways. No one is in any way better than any of the others. These diverse rites exist as expressions of particular cultures. They make it possible for the people of those cultures to understand and participate more completely in the Paschal mystery. We call the Church "catholic" because it speaks to all people in all places in ways that they can understand. For this reason the Church works to integrate the local culture into its liturgical worship in a way that preserves that culture while at the same time ensuring that the universal faith of the Church will not be misunderstood in any way.

How do we know that there is unity amid this diversity? It is because the Churches that celebrate these rites adhere to the same faith as expressed in the Nicene Creed (which we recite at Mass), celebrate the same sacraments, and are led by bishops who are ordained by the valid successors of the apostles. The *Catechism* outlines it in this way:

> *The criterion that assures unity amid the diversity of liturgical traditions is fidelity to apostolic Tradition, i.e. the communion in faith and the sacraments received from the apostles, a communion that is both signified and guaranteed by apostolic succession (1209).*

Our worship shapes what we believe. It orchestrates much of our experience of God and prepares us to receive the grace that God is offering us. The elements which are part of our worship today are those which have been deemed necessary for accomplishing the work which God wants us to do. Each element of our liturgy has the power to shape us if we allow it to do so. Each piece of the liturgy is there to open a window into the mystery of God.

Research and report on one of the non-Roman Catholic rites for liturgy mentioned in this section.

Where Is the Liturgy Celebrated?

The liturgy is not tied to any one place. In many parts of the world, the absence of religious freedom prohibits the presence of churches. Similarly, in the first three centuries of the Church, Roman persecution prohibited the building of any places for divine worship. However, when religious liberty is not limited, Christians do construct buildings for worship. These churches signify and make visible the larger Church in this particular place. They also are a house of prayer:

- in which the Eucharist is celebrated and reserved;
- where the faithful assemble;
- and where Christ, our Savior, offered for us on a sacrificial altar is worshiped.

The inside of a Catholic church contains several elements that are key to liturgy. These include the following:

Altar. The altar is placed at the center of the sanctuary because this is where Christ's sacrifice of the Cross is made present. The altar is also the table of the Lord to which the community of faith is invited. The altar is symbolic of Christ's presence. The priest kisses the altar at the beginning of Mass.

Tabernacle. The tabernacle is the case or box that contains the Blessed Sacrament, the consecrated hosts. It is located in a place of great honor in the church. A tabernacle light burns near it as a sign of Jesus' real presence there.

Presider's chair. The chair of the bishop (*cathedra*) or priest is placed in the sanctuary to express his role in presiding over the assembly and directing the prayer.

Lectern (ambo). The proclamation of the Word of God requires a suitable place. The lectern may be of simple or elaborate design as long as the attention of the people may easily be directed there during the liturgy of the Word.

Holy oils. The holy oils which include the oil of catechumens, oil for the sacrament of the Anointing of the Sick, and the sacred chrism, which is used to consecrate a person in the Holy Spirit in the sacraments of Baptism, Confirmation, and Holy Orders are kept in a sacred place called the ambry.

Draw a map of the nave and sanctuary of your parish church including all of the elements listed on pages 57-58.

Baptistery. A parish church must have a place for the celebration of Baptism. The baptistery may be located in several different places in the church. In some churches it is near the entrance to symbolize the entrance of the person into the Church. In others it is near the altar. In still others it is in a separate place in the side of the church. The church must also have holy water fonts to allow Catholics to remember their baptismal promises.

Reconciliation Chapel. In previous times, places for the sacrament of Penance were known as "confessionals." Today, these are open areas to receive penitents that also offer the opportunity for private confessions.

A church must also be a space that lends itself to quiet and reflective prayer to accompany the Eucharist. A church also has an "other-world" significance. When we enter a church we symbolically pass from the world wounded by sin to the world of new Life in Christ that we are all called to.

Chapter 2
Review Questions

1. Explain the difference between signs and symbols.

2. How are sacraments connected with signs and symbols?

3. Who celebrates the liturgy?

4. What are two ways to participate in the one priesthood of Christ?

5. How is the liturgy celebrated?

6. What is the connection between the term sacraments and its Greek root *mysterion*, or "mystery"?

7. What did the Second Vatican Council teach about the importance of the Scriptures in liturgy?

8. What is an *icon*?

9. Why is Sunday the original feast day for Christians?

10. What are the requirements of Church law for Catholics regarding Sundays?

11. What is the focal point of the Church Year?

12. Name the threefold emphasis of Lent today.

13. Explain the two theories for Christmas being celebrated on December 25.

14. What are the two focuses of Advent?

15. What is the significance of the designation "Ordinary Time" as part of the Church year?

16. What is the liturgy of the hours?

17. Name two of the things the uniformity of the liturgy accomplishes.

18. Name several elements inside a Catholic church that are essential to liturgy.

Baptism

In Baptism You Died With Christ...

They were five separate occasions. Seven separate lives. But with each one the experience was much the same. With each one, there was wonder and hope, promise and comfort in that dancing flame of the large Paschal candle, the Easter candle. And if one's eyes moved away from the candle, its white and gold warmth and promise were echoed in the white and gold linen which covered the altar and the white and gold Easter vestments which the priest was wearing.

On all five occasions the priest held a bowl filled with the water of Baptism, the fresh clean water of new life. On all five occasions he dipped a branch into the water and pulled it out dripping. He shook it, sending droplets of hope and promise flying out into the air—and onto the coffins.

The coffin of a great-grandmother who died peacefully in her sleep at age ninety-one.

The coffin of a father who died at age sixty-one, in the middle of a life still full of plans, because a simple operation went wrong.

The coffin of a teenager who died because he and his friends were sniffing glue in a small closet in order to get high.

The coffins of a mother and her two daughters who were killed by a drunk driver in an intersection collision.

Describe or imagine a death of someone close to you that took you by surprise. What kind of questions did or would you ask God at the time of this death?

The coffin of a baby who lived for four months in the hospital after his birth but was never able to go home.

On each of these five occasions, as the droplets of water touched the coffin, the priest said, "In the waters of Baptism [you] died with Christ and rose with him to new life. May [you] now share with him eternal glory."

At the funeral of the great-grandmother the congregation was sad, but also ready to let her go. She had lived a long and good life. She had been ready to die, and her family had known that it was time. They had said their goodbyes. At each of the other funerals the congregation had been unprepared for the death. These deaths were too soon. They "shouldn't have happened." They seemed pointless, or stupid, or evil, or just plain unfair. They made people ask questions like,

"Where was God?"

"Why didn't God change things?"

"Why did it all end this way?"

"Why weren't our prayers enough to protect this person whom we loved?"

To all of these questions the Church responded quietly but clearly with the symbols of our Baptism, the symbols of life as God sees it.

Death has a way of making us think about life. Most of the time we take life for granted. We are busy with the day-to-day business of living and we don't stop to think about what life means or why people live. If we notice that life is going well, we rarely stop to ask why. When someone dies, however, we are often overwhelmed with questions. We wonder why something so precious must end. We question the purpose of life when life can be abruptly cut off before we have a chance to finish what we've started. We ask why life is so fragile, so easily destroyed. We wonder why the gift of life seems so unfairly distributed, why some live more years than they want to and others die long before they are ready. We demand to know why foolish mistakes can be "punished" by death, or why some people must die because others are filled with hate and evil.

Death raises the questions to which Baptism is the answer. Baptism is the sacrament that holds answers to the mystery of life. Life, in fact, is a mystery that we cannot fully grasp. The moments of our greatest awareness of its mystery are the moments of birth and death.

The Great Gift of Baptism

St. Gregory of Nazianzus called Baptism "God's most beautiful and magnificent gift." The word Baptism itself is taken from the Greek *baptizein*, meaning to "plunge" or "immerse." St. Gregory went on to explain the greatness of this sacrament:

(The Great Gift of Baptism cont.)

> *We call it gift, grace, anointing, enlightenment, garment of immortality, bath of rebirth, seal, and most precious gift. It is called gift because it is conferred on those who bring nothing of their own; grace since it is given even to the guilty; Baptism because sin is buried in the water; anointing for it is priestly and royal as are those who are anointed; enlightenment because it radiates light; clothing since it veils our shame; bath because it washes; and seal as it is our guard and the sign of God's Lordship* (Oratio 40, 3-4: PG 36, 361C).

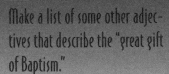

Make a list of some other adjectives that describe the "great gift of Baptism."

Baptism Overcomes Sin and Death

It is the sacrament of Baptism that brings about rebirth and initiates us into the Church, the Body of Christ. Baptism gives us the grace to live in the midst of a sinful world and our own sinfulness. As the *Catechism of the Catholic Church* defines:

> *Holy Baptism is the basis of the whole Christian life, the gateway to life in the Spirit, and the door which gives access to the other sacraments* (1213).

What are some bad habits you need to have washed away or overcome?

God is infinitely good and all of his works are good. Yet, certainly, evidence of sinfulness abounds. Terrorism and war occur in many places around the world. Disregard for human life is high: thousands of unborn babies are aborted each day, much of the world's population lives in poverty and despair, and older people and the ill live in a culture that debates the suitability of euthanasia.

In our own lives, sin is present. We face daily temptations. A "friend" asks to copy a homework assignment. Alcohol is offered at a party. We rage in anger at a parent. Sexual temptations are everywhere.

In Baptism, sin is overcome. Baptism forgives both original sin and personal sins. In doing so, Baptism is a sign that a community of the baptized can bring the Lord's presence to the world. The succeeding subsections examine more closely how this is so.

Original Sin

We are created by God in his image and in friendship with him. We can only live in friendship with God when we freely respond to him. This is God's plan for us.

Our understanding of God's plan also helps us to understand sin as "an abuse of the freedom" against God (*CCC*, 387). Original sin—the sin by which the first human beings disobeyed God's commands, choosing to follow their own will rather than God's will—is an essential truth of our faith. However, it is only through the long journey of revelation which culminates in the death and resurrection of Jesus

In your own words, explain this quotation as it relates to original sin: "We must know Christ as the source of grace in order to know Adam as the source of sin."

Christ, that original sin can be fully understood. As the *Catechism* points out, "We must know Christ as the source of grace in order to know Adam as the source of sin" (388).

Prior to the original sin of the first humans, the Church teaches that a fallen angel rejected God and his reign. This fallen angel—"Satan" or the "devil"—was the tempter who led our first parents to sin. Revelation also clearly tells that the entire human history has been marked by the original sin of Adam. With the original sin, death entered human history and the world has been inundated by sin since then.

The consequences of original sin affect all of us. St. Paul wrote in the letter to the Romans that "through one person sin entered the world, and through sin, death, and thus death came to all, inasmuch as all sinned" (Rom 5:12). How can one sin affect all of humanity? The Council of Trent explained that the whole human race is in Adam "as one body of one man." By this "unity of the human race" we are all share in Adam's sin, just as we all share in salvation through Christ. Because Adam's sin permanently wounded our human nature, it is transmitted to all generations—we are all born in this condition. Adam received original holiness and justice for him and all human nature. By his *personal sin*, all human nature was then affected and took on a fallen state.

Although we share in the original sin, it is not a sin that each one of us has committed personally. While we have lost the gift of original holiness and justice, our entire human nature has not been corrupted. While we are subject to ignorance, suffering, and death, and inclined to sin (known as *concupiscence*), Baptism grants the life of Christ's grace, erases original sin, and turns us back to God, albeit with a weakened nature that is inclined to evil.

By the sin of our first parents, Satan has acquired a certain domination over us. Life, complicated and filled with the consequences of original sin and all of the personal sins of men and women, is a constant battle with Satan and evil. Thankfully, the doctrine of original sin is closely connected with that of the redemption of Christ.

O Happy Fault!

After the original sin, God did not abandon the human race. Rather, God immediately detailed his plan for victory over evil and restoration from the fall to sin. This first announcement of the Messiah and Redeemer, of a battle between a serpent and the Woman, and of the final victory of her descendents comes in the book of Genesis, the first book of the Bible. God speaks to Satan about his temptation of Adam and Eve and about the Lord's ultimate victory over sin and evil. God said to the serpent:

> I will put enmity between you and the woman,
>   and between your offspring and hers;
> He will strike at your head,
>   while you strike at his heel (Gn 3:15).

The first letter of John tells us "the Son of God appeared that he might destroy the works of the devil" (3:8). Thus the passage from Genesis 3:15 is understood as God's first promise of a Redeemer for fallen mankind. The woman is understood to be Mary and her offspring is recognized as Jesus Christ.

The passage also helps us to understand Jesus as the "New Adam" who was freely obedient to God even to his death. On the cross Jesus' death won for us our redemption and was the atonement for our sins. His mother Mary was the first to benefit from his victory over sin: she was immaculately conceived without original sin and by God's special grace committed no sin of any kind while on earth.

You may have wondered many times why God simply did not prevent Adam from sinning. Wouldn't life for him and all of his descendents—including us—have been much easier? You have probably already witnessed how sometimes an even greater good can come from a bad situation. So, on the other hand, is the case here. As St. Thomas Aquinas offers:

> There is nothing to prevent human nature's being raised up to something greater, even after sin; God permits evil in order to draw forth some greater good. Thus St. Paul, says, "Where sin increased, grace abounded all the more"; and the Exultet sings, "O happy fault, . . . which gained for us so great a Redeemer!" (Summa Theologica III, 1, 3, ad 3; cf. Rom 5:20).

Dying and Rising With Christ

Christ's sacrifice on the cross was the source of our salvation. As the letter to the Romans also describes, "For just as through the disobedience of one person the many were made sinners, so through the obedience of one the many will be made righteous" (5:19). With Christ, we die in the sacrament of Baptism in order to live a new life. St. Paul explains further,

Do you agree or disagree with St. Thomas Aquinas's opinion on why God permits evil? Explain.

Answer the question posed in Romans 6:1-2. Will you persist in sin so that grace may abound? How can you who died to sin live in it?
How do you imagine eternal life? What are some glimpses of eternal life you have experienced in your life so far?

Or are you unaware that we who were baptized into Christ Jesus were baptized into his death? We were indeed buried with him through Baptism into death, so that, just as Christ was raised from the dead by the glory of the Father, we too might live in newness of life (6:3-4).

The element of death is one of the great mysteries in Baptism. In Baptism, we actually die with Christ sacramentally in order to rise with him. When we physically die later in life it is not something new; it is just the visible sign of what occurred when we were baptized.

Both the suffering we may encounter in life and our eventual death are experienced and dealt with in Baptism. In Baptism we actually die with Christ. More positively, all of the life, love, and hope which we experience after Baptism is a part of our eternal life. That is why when someone dies Christians do not despair. We do not despair because we have already seen a piece of the eternal life that will follow this physical death.

Like all sacraments, the extent to which we are able to recognize and feel the fruit of the sacrament is dependent upon our own faith. Following our Baptism we are already living eternal life. The meaning we long to find in the face of suffering and death has already been given to us. The devastating pain of suffering and death have already been taken from us. But without faith we will not notice.

More Grace and Effects of Baptism

St. Peter's words to the crowd gathered outside of the Upper Room on Pentecost summarize the grace and effects of baptism: "Repent and be baptized, every one of you, in the name of Jesus Christ for the forgiveness of sins; and you will receive the gift of the holy Spirit" (Acts 2:38). The principal grace and effects of the sacrament of Baptism remain the same: the forgiveness of sins and new life in the Holy Spirit.

Baptism is the first sacrament of Christian initiation, the beginning and foundation of Christian life. Baptism offers a sacramental bond of unity among all Christians, including those not in full communion with the Catholic Church. Baptism, then, becomes "a point of departure" (*Unitatis Redintegratio*, 22) for Christians from other denominations who are becoming Catholic. The Church accepts Baptisms as valid from Christian denominations that baptize using similar words and rituals, all the while orienting the convert toward a profession of the Catholic faith, incorporation into Catholic teaching and doctrine, and toward complete participation through the sacraments of Confirmation and Eucharist.

The effects of Baptism are signified by the main elements of the baptismal rite, including water, words, oil, white garment, and light.

Baptism Frees Us From Sin

The prime symbol of the sacrament of Baptism is water. The Church teaches that baptismal waters represent death to evil, sin, and selfishness. The early baptismal fonts were often understood as both symbols of a womb and a tomb. The image of the womb suggests the waters that surround the baby in the mother's womb. Emerging from this symbolic womb, the baptized is "born again" in Christ. He or she shares in the resurrection of Christ and enters a new life in Christ and the Holy Spirit. Likewise the image of the tomb suggested the tomb of Christ from which the newly baptized emerges with the risen Lord.

Baptism is an efficacious symbol that *actually* washes away sin, both original sin and personal sins. Some may ask, how can original sin be forgiven? Surely we cannot be found guilty for something we had no control over, so why do we need forgiveness? Sin is a rupture of our relationship with God, the forgiveness of sins is a restoration of that relationship. When we say that our sins are forgiven we are saying that there is no longer anything which separates us from God. Since both original sin and personal sin separate us from God, both need to be forgiven.

Baptism not only results in the forgiveness of sins, it also entails forgiveness of all punishment for sin. In other words, when we are baptized any punishment that God might have given us because of the things we have done is eliminated. (It is important to remember, however, that for Catholics the forgiveness of sins and the elimination of punishment are two separate things. Baptism forgives all sins and removes all punishment for sins. The sacrament of Penance forgives sins but does not necessarily remove all punishment.)

Baptism does not eliminate all of the consequences of sin, however. We will still experience illness, suffering, and death, but they will no longer have the power to separate us from God or from one another (unless we give that power to them). We may still have weaknesses in our character which make certain sins

A person who has been validly baptized into another Christian faith tradition is not "re-baptized" when converting to the Catholic faith. As our creeds state, "we believe in one Baptism for the forgiveness of sins." If there is some doubt as to the validity of a Baptism or if the person does not know if she or he were baptized, the person should be baptized conditionally with a formula like "If you have not been baptized, I baptize you...."

Make corresponding lists describing your character weaknesses contrasted by your character strengths. Write about a situation when your strengths won out over your weaknesses.

Baptism

seem attractive; and we will have an inclination to sin which makes it seem natural to think first of ourselves in many or most situations. However, neither our weaknesses nor our inclination to sin can separate us from God if we do not give in to them.

After being baptized, we can echo these words of St. Paul:

> *I am convinced that neither death, nor life, nor angels, nor principalities, nor present things, nor future things, nor powers, nor height, nor depth, nor any other creature will be able to separate us from the love of God in Christ Jesus our Lord (Rom 8:38-39).*

Baptism Makes Us New

Baptism not only cleanses us from our sins, but it remakes us into a new creation, imparting in us life in Christ. As Jesus explained to Nicodemus about how a person could be "born again":

> *"Amen, amen, I say to you, no one can enter the kingdom of God without being born of water and Spirit" (Jn 3:5).*

In the waters of Baptism our fundamental identity is changed. We are configured to Christ, becoming "a new creature" who comes to share the divine nature. We are a member of Christ and a co-heir with him. Baptism makes us children of God and temples of the Holy Spirit.

The words used in Baptism are "I baptize you in the name of the Father, and of the Son, and of the Holy Spirit." The use of the phrase "in the name of" in ancient Aramaic and Greek was a way to designate a personal relationship to the person named. Thus, Baptism in the name of the triune God relates us to the Blessed Trinity in several ways. The Blessed Trinity gives us sanctifying grace that:

- enables us to believe in, hope in, and love God;
- gives us the power to live and act under the guidance of the Holy Spirit through the gifts of the Holy Spirit;
- allows us to grow in goodness through the moral virtues.

As a way to symbolize new life in Christ, the celebrant puts on or over the newly baptized a white garment and says:

> *See in this white garment the outward sign of your Christian dignity. With your family and friends to help you by word and example, bring that dignity unstained into the everlasting life of heaven.*

The wearing of the Baptismal garment also is a reminder of the uniqueness of each person and a reminder to live a life of love worthy of our Christian identity.

Baptism Makes Us Members of the Church

Baptism incorporates us into the Church and makes us members of the Body of Christ. The *Catechism* explains that "[f]rom the Baptismal fonts is born the one

Ask your parents to explain the history and significance of a baptismal garment that is in your family.

People of God of the New Covenant, which transcends all natural or human limits of nations, cultures, races, and sexes" (1267).

Baptism has been described as "the embrace of God." In Baptism God reaches out to us and gives us his Spirit even though we are undeserving. Once we have received the Spirit, it is up to us to allow him to shape our lives. It is up to us to actually live as the children of God and not as the children of Adam and Eve. In Baptism the light of God *enters* us. We have the rest of our lives to learn to let that light shine from us out to the world.

All the baptized are members of the Body of Christ. We no longer belong to ourselves but to Christ. As members of the same body as all other Christians we have a responsibility for keeping their well-being in mind whenever we make a decision. We cannot ask, "What is best for me?" We must ask, "What is best for us?" We can live out our Baptism only if we put aside our selfishness and care for those whose need is greater than our own. We serve our brothers and sisters in need in communion with the Church and in obedience to the Church's teaching. When this seems impossible we should remember that in Baptism we received God's grace. This grace makes it possible for us to believe in, hope in, and love God. It also makes it possible for us to do what God calls us to do.

Our Baptism gives us a share in the common priesthood of all believers. Every person who has been baptized is responsible for doing the work of the Church, for participating in the sacraments, proclaiming the gospel, and caring for those in need. If we think that the Church is not making a difference in the world, then it is up to us to do more. We cannot wait for the priests and other dedicated leaders to do everything. All the baptized share in the priesthood of Christ. We have been anointed to bring God's transforming love to the world.

Name some ways you can or do work for the Church, participate in the sacraments, proclaim the gospel, and care for those in need.

Rites of Baptism

The rites of Baptism using essential words and symbols have quite a bit to do with understanding the meaning and grace of the sacrament. For typical Baptisms of infants, the sacrament ideally takes place on Sunday, the day of the Church's celebration of Christ's Paschal mystery. The sacrament may be held within Mass or outside of it, but always communally with other recently born children, friends, relatives, neighbors, and the community of faith. A description of some of the rites that make up the sacrament follow:

- *Welcome.* The celebrant asks the parents of each child these questions: "What name do you give your child?" and "What do you ask of God's Church for your child?" The child's name is important as he or she is

Describe the occasion of the last Baptism you attended. Write your impressions of any of the rites and symbols that stood out.

(Rites of Baptism cont.)

God's unique creation. The answer for the second question is "Baptism" or "faith" and is supplied by the parents. Baptism is the sacrament of faith.

- *Sign of the Cross.* The celebrant and then the parents and godparents trace the sign of the cross on the infant's forehead. This marks the person with the imprint of Christ and signifies the grace of Christ's redemption won for us by the cross.

- *Word of God.* One or two gospel passages are read. For example, Jesus' meeting with Nicodemus (Jn 3:1-6), the commissioning of the apostles to preach and baptize (Mt 28:18-20), or the baptism of Jesus (Mk 1:9-11). "The proclamation of the Word of God enlightens the candidates and the assembly with the revealed truth and elicits the response of faith, which is inseparable from Baptism" (*CCC*, 1236).

- *Exorcisms.* One or more exorcisms are pronounced to signify liberation from sin and the devil, and the child is anointed on the breast with the oil of catechumens.

- *Blessing of water and renunciation of sins.* The celebrant recalls the various roles of water in salvation history. Then he blesses the water by a prayer of epiclesis. The parents and godparents are asked questions in the name of the child to reject Satan, sin, and evil. Then they profess their faith in God the Father, Son, and Holy Spirit.

- *Baptism.* The essential rite of the sacrament follows. Baptism is performed with a triple immersion in the baptismal water or the pouring of water three times over the child's head accompanied by the minister's words: "Name, I baptize you in the name of the Father, and of the Son, and of the Holy Spirit."

- *Anointing with Chrism.* The celebrant anoints the child on the crown of the head, in silence. This signifies the child has received the gift of the Holy Spirit, anointed by the Holy Spirit and incorporated into Christ who is anointed priest, prophet, and king. In the Roman Catholic Church, this post-baptismal anointing announces a second anointing with chrism that will be conferred at a later time by the bishop—the sacrament of Confirmation which completes the baptismal anointing. (In the Eastern liturgies, the post-baptismal anointing *is* the sacrament of Confirmation.)

- *White garment.* The clothing with a white garment signifies that the child has become a new creation and has been clothed in Christ.

- *Lighted candle.* A candle lit by the father or godfather from the Easter candle signifies that Christ has "enlightened" the child and that he or she is to become "light of the world."

(Rites of Baptism cont.)

- *Approaching the Altar.* The child, clothed in the white garment of Christ, is readied to received the body and blood of Christ in Eucharist. In the Eastern Churches, Holy Communion is given to all the newly baptized and confirmed. In the Roman Church, First Holy Communion occurs later at the age of reason. To express the orientation of Baptism to Eucharist, the newly baptized child is brought to the altar for the praying of the Our Father.
- *Our Father.* As a child of God, the newly baptized participates in the prayer of the children of God, the Our Father.
- *Solemn blessing.* This is the conclusion of the celebration of Baptism. The celebrant first blesses the mother, who holds the child in her arms, then the father, and lastly the entire assembly.

Baptism Marks Us With the Seal of Eternal Life

Baptism is the seal of eternal life. "Baptism seals the Christian with the indelible spiritual mark (character) of his belonging to Christ" (*CCC*, 1272). Nothing—not even sin—can erase the mark of Baptism, though sin can prevent the person from gaining the rewards of salvation. Baptism is given one time only and cannot be repeated.

In earlier times a wax seal indicated documents were authentic and that nothing had been added to or taken away from them after they had been "sealed" shut. In Baptism Christians are marked by God as people who belong in the kingdom of heaven. If we "keep the seal" and remain faithful until the end we can be sure that God will recognize us and welcome us into his kingdom while we are on the earth and in body and spirit after our death.

Name some concrete ways you can "keep the seal" of Baptism.

The Biblical Roots of Baptism

The sacrament of Baptism was prefigured in the great events of the Old Testament. To say that Baptism was prefigured means that there were events which came before Baptism which can help us to understand Baptism and vice versa. These events are prefigured because their essential shape is similar to the essential shape of Baptism.

When Noah and his family were carried through the killing waters of the flood, they became a sign of the mystery of Baptism. The waters of Baptism are the waters which change the face of our world. They are the waters that erase the life of sin and death into which we were born. But just as God carried Noah through the waters of the flood and saved his life, so too God carries us through the waters of Baptism and gives us salvation.

When the people of Israel crossed the Red Sea to escape from slavery, that too was a sign of the Baptism that was to come. The crossing of the Red Sea and the liberation from Egypt is the event which gives identity to the Jewish community. It turns a group of slaves into a free nation. The crossing of the Red Sea is the sign of the true liberation from sin and death which was yet to come. The creation of the Jewish nation from scattered groups of slaves was the sign of God's plan to create one people from all the nations of the world. Baptism is the feast of freedom and unity for which the crossing of the Red Sea was only the appetizer.

Finally, the crossing of the Jordan River prefigured Baptism too. When the people crossed the Jordan they entered the Promised Land, a land which symbolized eternal life with God. In the years prior to this crossing the people were not faithful to God and they lost the Promised Land and were scattered throughout the world as an oppressed and persecuted people. Nonetheless, they continued to believe that Yahweh would one day return them to the Promised Land and allow them to live there forever. Jesus came to do just that. He came to restore the promise and the blessing to those who had lost it. He came to lead all people into a new Promised Land which cannot be taken from them. We enter this eternal Promised Land—God's Kingdom—by crossing through the waters of Baptism.

All of the events and all of the promises of the Old Testament find their fulfillment in Jesus. When we say that events are fulfilled in Jesus we are saying that the full meaning of those events can only be understood in light of what Jesus said and did. Jesus began his own public ministry by being baptized. In his person he repeats Noah's experience on the ark and the Israelites' journey across the Red Sea and across the Jordan. But while the Israelites were afraid and grumbled about God's way of doing things, Jesus trusted God completely and accepted whatever

Read the stories of the Great Flood (Gn 6:5—9:17), the crossing of the Red Sea (Ex 14:10-41), and the crossing of the Jordan River (Jos 3-4). Report on God's promise to his people in each of these events.

God put before him. Though sinless, he submitted to the baptism which John intended for sinners as a sign of his willingness to empty himself and to become one with us. When he came up from the waters, all that he had laid aside was returned to him as God said, "This is my beloved Son, with whom I am well pleased" (Mt 3:17).

The Spirit descending upon Jesus at his baptism is the sign that the new world, which the destruction of the flood hinted at, has finally come into being. The Spirit of God who hovers over the waters at Jesus' baptism is the same Spirit who hovered over the waters at the time of creation. The presence of the Spirit is the sign that something new is occurring. The waters of the flood wiped out creation, but they did not renew it. Sin reared its ugly head almost as soon as the ark landed (see Gn 9:20 ff). After the waters of Baptism wipe out the old world, the Spirit will create something new and sin will no longer be present.

It is not only Jesus' baptism by John which helps us to understand the meaning of Christian Baptism, it is also Jesus' baptism of suffering. Jesus refers to his passion as a baptism in a bath of pain (Mk 10:38). Because of this the Church has understood the water that flowed from Jesus' side when he hung on the cross to be the defining image for the waters of Baptism (Jn 19:34). The waters of our new life flow from Jesus' death. Baptism makes us partakers of that death so that we may be partakers of the resurrection. Unless we die, we cannot be reborn.

Jewish Baptisms

Baptism rituals existed in Judaism before the time of Jesus. There were two forms of Jewish baptism. The first was a ritual washing which was intended to purify persons or objects that were unclean according to Mosaic law. This person was somehow

When the Spirit came to the disciples at Pentecost they were given the gifts of conviction, determination, deep joy, and love for people. How do these gifts remain observable in the life of the Church? In your life?

unfit for contact with God and a ritual washing was intended to cleanse the person and restore unity with God.

John's baptism of repentance for sinners was a variation on this type of baptism. John's baptism offered cleansing but not a cleansing that would allow one to participate in religious ceremonies. Instead it was a prophetic sign of the divine cleansing that would accompany the coming of the messianic age. Those baptized by John were preparing themselves for the day of judgment—"the wrath to come." When Jesus accepts John's baptism, he indicates that Baptism is to be understood as a cleansing and purifying activity that prepares one for the end of time. Jesus says, "Allow it now, for thus it is fitting for us to fulfill all righteousness" (Mt 3:16). The term righteousness indicates Jesus' submission for the saving works of God the Father.

A second type of Jewish baptism was *proselyte baptism*. This was a ceremony for converts to Judaism. This washing of gentile converts was often accompanied by circumcision. Accompanying the ritual was the reading of the Torah; the law which the new converts were to follow. The conversion from a pagan religion to Judaism was understood as an entrance into new life. It seems evident that the Jewish-Christian writers of the New Testament saw similarities between Christian Baptism and Jewish proselyte baptism, particularly with respect to the new life which accompanied it.

As Jesus traveled around Galilee teaching and proclaiming the kingdom of God, his disciples, and perhaps Jesus too, baptized those who heard and believed (see Jn 3:22; 4:1-4). These baptisms were not baptisms in the Spirit. Rather, they were water baptisms like John's which had a strong emphasis on the initiation of the messianic era. They were also a sign that people were changing their lives and preparing for the new life which the Messiah would give. When the Spirit descended on Jesus' disciples at Pentecost these earlier baptisms were completed. They took on new meaning. At Pentecost Baptism with water and Baptism with the Spirit merge and it becomes possible for a person to be born again "of water and the spirit" (Jn 3:5). As Peter said to the crowds assembled below the window of the Upper Room: "Repent and be baptized, every one of you, in the name of Jesus Christ for the forgiveness of your sins; and you will receive the gift of the holy Spirit" (Acts 2:38).

Baptism in the Early Church

Following the coming of the Holy Spirit at Pentecost, Jesus' disciples began to carry out his command to "make disciples of all nations baptizing them in the name of the Father, and of the Son, and of the holy Spirit" (Mt 28:19). From the day of Pentecost onward, there are several steps that have always been essential to the process of becoming a Christian.

- First, one must hear the Word of God and be converted by it.

- Next those who wish to be Christian must profess their faith and their desire to live by that faith.
- Following this profession they are bathed in water with a triple immersion or triple pouring in the name of the Trinity.
- Finally they take up their new life as members of the Church which prays together and shares the Eucharist.

In the first century Jewish Christians were already familiar with the laws and faith tradition of God's original covenant. They understood the concept of one God and the concept of a faith which demanded a particular lifestyle. The period of preparation—especially for Jewish Christians—was short. As Christianity began to spread to people who were unfamiliar with Judaism, there was a need for a longer period of preparation between the first proclamation of the gospel and the Baptism of those who were moved by it. By the third century the Church had developed a fairly long and involved process (usually three years) for those who wished to become Christians. This long *catechumenate*—from a word meaning "to resound" or "echo"—gave people time to reshape their world view according to Christian beliefs.

In order to even enroll in the catechumenate a person had to demonstrate a willingness to change. Those who wanted to be Christians had to change—often radically—their way of life if they were involved in any activities which were opposed to the basic principles of Christianity. Careers like teachers of pagan philosophy, soldiers, and actors were forbidden. Once a person was enrolled in the catechumenate, he or she was expected to live in a manner befitting a Christian.

Each year at the beginning of Lent those catechumens who seemed most ready to become Christians would be publicly examined. Questions would be asked concerning how well they had been living out the faith. Had they honored widows, visited the sick and so forth? If a person was truly living as a Christian should live, he or she would be named one of the *elect* and would begin a final period of intense preparation for Baptism. The newly elect were given salt as a sign of the wisdom and the preaching of the word of God which would sustain and preserve them through the days ahead.

Throughout the season of Lent the elect would fast and pray, and come daily for a laying on of hands and an exorcism. On Sundays the elect would gather with the rest of the Church to hear the word of God and receive instructions. After the instructions the bishop, priest, or lay catechist laid hands upon them as a sign of the Church's prayers for them. Then they were dismissed to pray by themselves apart from the faithful.

On the fourth Sunday of Lent the elect were solemnly presented with the texts of the four gospels, the Creed, and the Lord's prayer. These treasures of the Church now belonged to them as well. The elect were expected to memorize the creed in order to be able to recite it on Holy Saturday morning.

By the sixth century, the bishop's acts of welcome were performed either in the baptistery or in a gathering hall. The bishop then processed into the church followed by the new Christians. (The procession itself was the public sign of belonging.) They were then allowed to join the Church in the prayers of the faithful and the celebration of the Eucharist for the very first time.

Read about the conversion and baptism of the Ethiopian by Philip in Acts 8:26-40. Tell which of the four steps described in the text are present in this incident.

Exorcism is from a Greek word that translates roughly "to drive away." The ritual itself originated in the actions of Jesus who drove out demons from many people he encountered. Minor exorcisms remain a part of Baptisms today, usually before the blessing of the catechumens. What is an evil that you wish Jesus to "drive away" from you?

On Holy Saturday the elect met one last time. They knelt before the bishop for a final exorcism. Any remaining attachment to their sinful way of life was broken. Then the bishop breathed on their faces and sealed their foreheads, ears, and nose with the sign of the cross. The bishop's breath was the sign of the life-giving air of the Church which they would now breathe. The sealing with oil and with the sign of the cross was the sign of the protection which the Church was giving them against the death-dealing forces of the world. In the early Church sealing with oil was seen as the mark of the shepherd on the sheep. Sealing with oil was also a way of strengthening a person for the struggle against evil, in much the same way that athletes rub oil on their bodies to prepare for a race or event.

The elect would spend the Holy Saturday night in vigil, listening to scripture and praying. In the morning following the night of vigil, the elect were led to the place of Baptism. When they arrived the waters were blessed. Then while the bishop prayed, the elect moved to another place to loosen their hair and strip off all clothing and jewelry, symbolizing a return to the primitive innocence of Adam and Eve.

When the elect stripped off their clothing they were abandoning any signs of evil which remained in their life. They were also indicating their intention to leave death behind them. The standard clothing of the day was made of wool. Because animals were dirty, they were viewed as a sign of death. They knew that when they came up from the water, the newly baptized would be clothed in linen. Because linen was made from plants, it was seen as a sign of life.

However before they descended into the waters of Baptism, the elect publicly renounced Satan and were anointed with the oil of exorcism. This second anointing from head to toe was an adaptation of the medical practices of the day. In the pagan world, sickness was considered to be the work of evil spirits. Those who were sick were anointed with oil to help them fight off their sickness. This baptismal anointing with oil was intended to cure spiritual sickness.

Following the second anointing the elect descended naked into the water down three steps (symbolizing the three days Christ spent in the tomb). The priest who was in the water with them laid his hand on their head and asked, "Do you believe in God the Father?" After a candidate said, "I believe," he or she was immersed in the water. The candidate was then asked, "Do you believe in God the Son?" Again the "I believe" was followed by an immersion. The candidate was asked a third time about belief in the Spirit and was once again immersed following his or her confession of faith. Then the candidate left the waters and was immediately anointed with the oil of thanksgiving as the presider prayed that the Spirit would descend upon the one being anointed. This anointing was what completed Christian initiation.

The newly baptized Christians were then dried and dressed in a white linen robe. They were to wear these robes for the entire Easter week. They were also given a candle as a sign of the light of Christ that lived within them. The bishop then led the newly baptized into the assembly while a litany was sung. The bishop went to the front of the sanctuary and the new Christians gathered around him. In the presence of the whole congregation the bishop prayed for them and anointed them once more. He then greeted the new Christians with the kiss of peace. By his actions the bishop publicly confirmed that these people now belonged in the Church.

The entry into the Church, and all the acts of hospitality which accompanied it, was the high point of the baptismal liturgy. If we wish to appreciate the full wonder of Baptism today we need to reflect upon the fact that Baptism allows us to work with one another in a way that would be impossible without it. Baptism is what makes individual persons into members of the Body of Christ.

Who Can Receive Baptism?

Christ himself taught that Baptism was necessary for salvation: "Amen, amen, I say to you, no one can enter the kingdom of God without being born of water and Spirit" (Jn 3:5). Jesus also commanded his disciples to "go to all nations and

Inscriptions From an Early Christian Baptistery

From this noble spring saving water gushes
which cleanses all human defilement,
Do you wish to know the benefits of the sacred water?
These streams give the faith that regenerates.

Here is to be found the source of life,
which washes the whole universe,
which gushes from the wound of Christ.
Sinner, plunge into the sacred fountain to wash your sin.
The water receives the old man, and in his place makes the
    new man arise. . . .[1]

Song From an Ancient Liturgy
This is the fountain of life that floods the entire world,
the water that took its beginning
from the pierced side of Christ.
You who are born again of this water,
place your hope in the kingdom of heaven.[2]

to baptize them" (see Mt 20:19-20). While God is not bound by his sacraments, he has bound salvation to the sacrament of Baptism. The Church does not know of any way to assure salvation other than Baptism. That is why the reception of the sacrament is so important and remains protected by the Church to this day.

God's love has been freely given to all people; therefore all people may be baptized. The ordinary minister of Baptism is the bishop, priest, or deacon, but in an emergency any person, even a non-Christian, can baptize. Catholics believe that God will honor every Baptism that is done in the name of the Trinity as long as the person administering the Baptism intends to do what the Church does. A person acting in a play or playing a practical joke cannot validly baptize someone else. On the other hand, a non-Christian who does not know exactly what Baptism is but who knows that it is important to Christians could administer a valid Baptism in an emergency. For example sometimes non-Christian nurses working in infant care baptize an infant in danger of death because they know it is important to the parents.

What about those who, for various reasons, are unable to be baptized? How are they able to be saved?

The Church holds that this same gift of salvation is given to all of those who specifically desired Baptism but who died before they received it. This is known as the *baptism of desire.* If catechumens die before Baptism the Church teaches that they still receive the gift of salvation. Likewise, any who are martyred for the faith, even though they are not baptized are given the salvation that comes with Baptism. This is known as the *baptism of blood.* Remember, God is not bound by the sacraments. He can act outside of them (see *CCC,* 1257).

The Church also believes that every person who does not know or understand the teachings of the Church but who "seeks the truth and does the will of God in accordance with his understanding of it can be saved." We assume that such a person would have chosen to be baptized if they had known that Baptism is what God desires (see *CCC,* 1260). All children who die without being baptized are entrusted to the love and mercy of God. God's tremendous love for all people and Jesus' tenderness for children allow us to believe that God will bring all children into his kingdom.

The very fact that Jesus became man tells us that God loves and values humanity. By becoming a human being,

> *the Son of God has in a certain way united himself with each [person]. . . . Since Christ died for all, and since all [people] are in fact called to one and the same destiny . . . we must hold that the Holy Spirit offers to all the possibility of being made partners, in a way known to God, in the Paschal mystery* (Gaudium et Spes, 22).

Church father Origen said, "Only the baptism of blood makes us more pure than the baptism of water." What do you think he meant by this statement?

Baptism of Adults

The Second Vatican Council reemphasized the connection between Baptism and an adult's "coming to faith" which was prevalent prior to the Middle Ages. The Council restored the catechumenate and made adult Baptism normative. When we say that adult Baptism is "normative," we do not mean that it is the form of Baptism used most often. The majority of Catholics are still baptized as infants. When we use the word "normative" we are saying that the full meaning of Baptism is most clearly revealed in the process of Christian initiation of adults. Baptism requires a conversion of the heart to God in order to bear fruit. In other words, Baptism requires the process of the catechumenate. This catechumenate does not just involve learning the facts of the faith. It involves learning to turn one's heart away from the evils of the world and toward God.

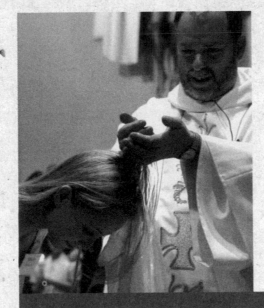

Church father Tertullian said that Christians are not born but made. The grace of Baptism is able to burst forth in those whose lives have been honed and shaped by the teaching, prayer, and discipline of the catechumenate, whether the catechumenate occurs before or after Baptism. The restored adult catechumenate can help us to understand all that is involved in making or truly becoming a Christian.

Today's catechumenate resembles the catechumenate of the early Church. Adults and unbaptized children over the age of seven (the age of reason) who wish to become Catholic Christians are publicly enrolled in the catechumenate. From the moment of their enrollment, catechumens are considered to be members of the Church, although not full members. If they were to die they would be entitled to a funeral Mass. The catechumens begin a period of regular prayer and study during which they are to develop an understanding of the Catholic faith. They will experience several minor exorcisms. These exorcisms are in the form of petitions to God:

> They draw the attention of the catechumens to the real nature of Christian life, the struggle between flesh and spirit, the importance of self-denial . . . and the unending need for God's help (Rite of Christian Initiation of Adults, 90).

They will also be formally blessed and anointed with the oil of catechumens. "The anointing with oil symbolizes their need for God's help and strength" so that they may break free of any unhealthy bonds in their past, overcome the "opposition

What is your experience with the adult catechumenate? Tell about the faith of someone you know who chose to be a member of the Catholic Church.

of the devil," and accept and live out the Christian faith (*Rite of Christian Initiation of Adults*, 99). At each Sunday liturgy the catechumens are called forward after the homily and before the prayers of the faithful. They are prayed for and then sent out to study the scripture more thoroughly.

The exorcisms, blessings, and anointings which are part of the catechumenate today are a reminder to the entire Church that we must constantly resist evil and seek to do the will of God. The fact that the catechumens leave before the prayers of the faithful and the Eucharist is a reminder of the awesome responsibility of prayer and of the awesome gift of the Eucharist.

At the beginning of Lent, those who are ready are named as the elect. In the presence of the whole Church, their godparents and teachers testify to the sincerity of their desire to become Christians and live the Christian life. The catechumens publicly express their desire to receive the sacraments. They then begin a period of more intense preparation for the three sacraments of initiation: Baptism, confirmation, and Eucharist. During the Sundays of Lent they will participate in several scrutinies and exorcisms. "The scrutinies are meant to uncover, then heal all that is weak, defective, or sinful in the hearts of the elect; [and] to bring out, then strengthen all that is upright, strong and good" (*Rite of Christian Initiation of Adults*, 141).

The Church also prays for their healing and conversion. The scrutinies serve as a reminder to all of us of the power of sin and the need for ongoing conversion. During the scrutinies the baptized pray among other things that the elect will "sincerely reject everything in their lives that is displeasing and contrary to Christ" and that the Holy Spirit will help them to overcome their weaknesses and teach them to know the things of God (*Rite of Christian Initiation of Adults*, 163).

Of all the things that the baptized can learn from observing adults who are joining the Church, none has as much power as the silent testimony of a truly changed heart. If we see the transforming power of the Holy Spirit during an adult Baptism we will never be the same. When an adult convert to Christianity has participated wholeheartedly in the conversion process of the catechumenate the transforming power of Baptism is hard to miss.

The Easter Vigil

Describe a time when you have witnessed the "flame of joy" alight in another.

The vigil didn't begin solemnly at all. In fact, for Chris, who was there to support her friend Hope, it began with a laugh that she almost couldn't suppress. The litany of the saints had been sung and the waters of the baptismal pool had been blessed and a sense of great anticipation seemed to hang over the congregation. Father Tom called the candidates for Baptism to come and stand around the font. They came forward barefooted and wrapped in gray-colored sheets. Chris noticed Father Tom staring at their bare feet. Then he looked down at his own feet. In a couple of minutes he was going to have to

(The Easter Vigil cont.)

walk down into the font with these candidates and he was still wearing his shoes and socks. As the candidates renounced their sins and professed their faith, Chris tried to guess what Father Tom would do.

"Do you believe in the Holy Spirit, the holy catholic Church, the communion of saints, the forgiveness of sins, the resurrection of the body, and the life everlasting?"

"I do!" seven voices called out in unison.

Then the pastoral associate responsible for RCIA stepped forward to lead Hope to the font. Father Tom stepped on the heels of his good leather shoes and forced them off his feet. Then he stepped into the font, socks and all! Chris wanted to laugh. She looked at her friend Hope to see if she was laughing, and then she noticed it: Hope's eyes were filled with a joy like none Chris had ever seen. Her face shone with the certainty that in this moment her life would change forever. Chris knew that Hope had not lived an easy life. She had experienced more than her share of pain. But now she was walking into this two foot deep pool and leaving her pain and the anger behind. Of course Father Tom had not taken off his socks. What difference did wet socks make in a moment as holy as this one?

Hope knelt and Father Tom put one hand on the back of her head. "I baptize you in the name of the Father." He gently pushed her forward until her head was under the water. "And of the Son," he pushed Hope down a second time. "And of the Holy Spirit." One final immersion and then Hope was standing, dripping with the water of Baptism and the tears that poured down her face. Hope's godmother handed her a towel and led her to a place where she could change from the gray sheet to a new white robe. When all of the candidates were baptized and dressed in the robes that symbolized their new life they were given candles to remind them to keep the flame of faith alive in their hearts. As Chris watched Hope mesmerized by her candle flame she knew that the flame of fire was nothing compared to the flame of joy which flashed in Hope's heart.

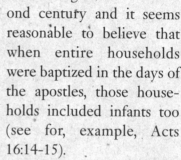

How is emphasis on the Baptism of infants and the forgiveness of sin in Baptism related?

What is the relationship between Baptism and conversion for Catholics who were baptized as infants?

Infant Baptism

The practice of baptizing infants has been with the Church since the beginning. Some other Christian denominations have questioned the practice, saying that adult commitment is needed in order to make the decision to live a Christian life.

The Church believes in infant Baptism for several reasons.

First, as we are all born with a fallen human nature and tainted by original sin, infants, too, need to be baptized in order to be freed from the power of darkness and brought into a life in which they live as children of God. Infant baptism is a grace and gift from God. If the Church and parents were to deny Baptism to an infant, they would be keeping the child from the true freedom which he or she deserves from as close to their birth as possible.

Second, infant Baptism has explicit roots in the Church dating back to the second century and it seems reasonable to believe that when entire households were baptized in the days of the apostles, those households included infants too (see for, example, Acts 16:14-15).

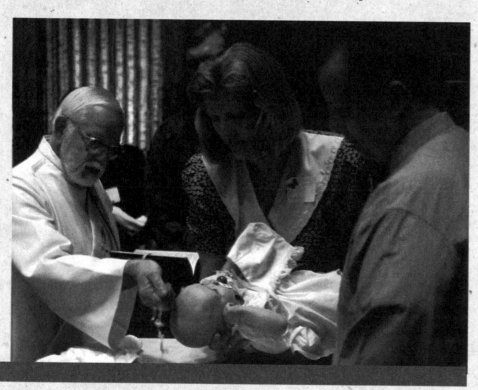

Third, having their child baptized as an infant is a sign of love of parent for child. At Baptism, parents, godparents, and others in the Church promise they will love the child and nurture his or her faith in a loving community. By being an example of Christ for them, parents, especially, encourage their children to accept Christ's love on their own as they grow into adulthood. As the *Rite of Baptism for Children* states:

> *To fulfill the true meaning of the sacrament, children must later be formed in the faith in which they have been baptized. The foundation of this formation will be the sacrament itself, which they have already received. Christian formation, which is their due, seeks to lead them gradually to learn God's plan in Christ, so that they may ultimately accept for themselves the faith in which they have been baptized (3).*

The sacrament of Baptism received at any age reminds us of God's unconditional love. God loves us simply because we are his creation, his children. It is God's grace and providence that brings us into the Church and offers us the gift of salvation.

Baptism is a free and unconditional gift. God calls us and makes us his own children because he loves us. But we will not experience the blessings of being God's children unless we allow that identity to be the most important thing in our lives. We will feel the full joy of Baptism only when our first heartfelt answer to the question, "Who are you?" is: "I am part of the family of God." We will experience the full joy of Baptism only when we have taken the words of St. Teresa of Avila to heart: "Let nothing trouble you, let nothing frighten you. The one who has God, lacks nothing." It takes a lifetime to grow into this kind of faith. Those who were baptized as infants need to learn to orient their lives to God in such a way that they can trust him completely. This does not happen without effort.

Chapter 3
Review Questions

1. Define original sin.

2. How do the consequences of original sin affect all of us?

3. Explain the meaning of the Easter proclamation: "O happy fault . . . which gained for us so great a Redeemer!"

4. What does death have to do with Baptism?

5. What are the principal grace and effects of the sacrament of Baptism?

6. As the primary symbol of Baptism, what does water represent?

7. What happens to our sin when we are baptized?

8. What is the white garment worn at Baptism a symbol of?

9. As members of the common priesthood of all believers, what are our responsibilities?

10. Describe the essential rite of Baptism.

11. Name three Old Testament events that prefigure Baptism.

12. Describe two forms of Jewish baptisms.

13. Name four essential steps that have always been a part of the Christian initiation process.

14. Who can receive Baptism?

15. On what day do the adult elect receive the sacraments of initiation?

16. Why does the Church believe in infant Baptism?

Endnotes

1.   Lucien Deiss, *Early Sources of the Liturgy* (Chicago: LTP, 1963), pp. 197, 198.

2.   *Rite of Christian Initiation of Adults*, 597.

4 Confirmation

The Mystery of God Within Us

All-powerful God, Father of our Lord Jesus Christ,
by water and the Holy Spirit
you freed your sons and daughters from sin
and gave them new life.
Send your Holy Spirit upon them
to be their Helper and Guide.
Give them the spirit of wisdom and understanding,
the spirit of right judgment and courage,
the spirit of knowledge and reverence.
Fill them with the spirit of wonder and awe in your
    presence.
We ask this through Christ our Lord (Rite of
    Confirmation, 25).

This is the prayer that the bishop says as he extends his hands to those he is to confirm. This is also the prayer that is answered when a person is confirmed. Through the sacrament of Confirmation, the confirmand (the person to be confirmed) does receive these particular gifts of the Holy Spirit: wisdom, understanding, right judgment, courage, knowledge, reverence, and wonder and awe in God's presence. These gifts become part of the identity of the confirmed.

☑

Name the seven traditional gifts of the Spirit and tell about something you associate with each gift.

The gifts of the Spirit help the confirmed to live more like Jesus. Unfortunately, although the majority of people who practice religion in North America are Christians, our society for the most part does not think that Jesus' way of doing things can "really work." We are constantly bombarded with the message that joy requires wealth, love requires beauty, and peace requires coercion. We are taught to doubt the power of the Holy Spirit who dwells within us, and to rely on force, money, or connections to bring about change.

The power of the Holy Spirit to give us strength, and to keep us close to God even in the midst of hardship, is not something we can explain to those without faith. The power of the Spirit to change the world through poverty, humility, trust, and gentle love is indeed part of the mystery of God. One way we can grasp that mystery is by sharing stories of the Spirit's power within the Church. As a starting point, reflect on the gift of courage as lived out in the following story of one teenage boy.

"Play Like A Champion Today"

In January of 2000 Scott Delgadillo was your average eighth grader living in San Diego. He was beginning to like girls, enjoyed hanging out with his friends, loved playing sports, and had a deep passion for his favorite team, the Notre Dame Fighting Irish. Scott was raised in a Catholic family, and grew to love Notre Dame at a very young age. He was rarely caught without wearing his Notre Dame hat or Notre Dame sweatshirt.

The winter flu that month seemed to take on a life of its own for Scott. He just couldn't shake it. Then one day the school nurse sent Scott home when she noticed he had swollen lymph nodes. Within a couple of days, the diagnosis was in: Scott had leukemia, a deadly form of blood cancer. The doctors started chemotherapy at once.

The local chapter of the Make-A-Wish Foundation (an organization that grants wishes to children with life-threatening illnesses) heard about Scott's situation and came to his home in February. "What can we do for you?" their representative asked.

Scott had his answer ready. "I want to go to Notre Dame," he said. "Can you guarantee my admission?"

Scott's request was met with silence. Then he laughed. He told them that he was just kidding and that what he really wanted was to spend a weekend at Notre Dame when the football team played a home game.

The game that was arranged was a September 16 contest with rival Purdue. When Scott and his family arrived on campus the Friday before the game, he was given first class treatment. He met with the University president and with the Notre Dame coach.

The men wondered what Scott had planned for that night. "Nothing, really," Scott answered.

"Good," said the Notre Dame coach. "I'd like you to speak at our pep rally."

Scott didn't hesitate. He said he would even though it meant getting up before a full arena of 12,000 fans. Scott cracked some tears during his talk. But the people watching, including the Notre Dame team, shed even more. With the arena completely hushed, Scott told everyone "as long as you have a positive attitude, you can do anything you want."

Then Scott made a promise. He said, "Some day I'm going to come back here and go to school." The arena erupted in cheers.

Notre Dame won the game against Purdue 23-21 on a last second field goal. Scott went into the locker room after the game and the team gave him plenty of gifts—their sweat bands, shorts, and caps. The gifts were fitting for another reason: the next day, September 17, was Scott's fourteenth birthday.

At the time of the game, Scott's cancer was in remission. Just two weeks later, in October, doctors discovered a relapse of the leukemia. Scott had to return to the hospital.

Meanwhile, the Notre Dame team didn't forget Scott. One of the players, 5'7" wide receiver Joey Getherall, sent Scott a photo of a winning touchdown he scored against Air Force. A letter Getherall wrote said, "I just wanted to let you know that I was playing for you on Saturday. I prayed to God and asked him for a little of your strength."

Notre Dame players have a tradition of touching a sign that is at the doorway leading from their locker room to the stadium tunnel as they head to the field. It reads: "Play Like A Champion Today." Someone gave Scott a replica of the sign and he put it over his bed.

In January 2001, when Scott was too weak for much of anything, he still mustered enough strength to slap his "Play Like A Champion Today" sign before he went to sleep at night.

Scott Delgadillo died on January 29, 2001. Exactly one week later his family had Scott's body flown to South Bend, Indiana, for a memorial service at Notre Dame. His mother explained, "Scott always said he was going back to Notre Dame. We wanted to grant him that wish."

Just before the bishop anoints the Confirmation candidate with chrism, the bishop and all of the assembled priests stand facing the candidate, extending their hands while the bishop prays the solemn prayer for the gifts of the spirit.

How did these gifts apply to the life of Scott Delgadillo (who was confirmed shortly before he died)?

Three of the gifts—wisdom, understanding, and knowledge—are different ways the Spirit helps us to see and know beyond the superficial layer of life down to its deeper meaning.

Imagine how Scott and his family's perspective of life changed on the day he found out he had cancer. Imagine how it changed again when he knew that he was going to die. Scott's positive thinking and attitude through it all allows us a glimpse of how the Holy Spirit was at work.

Two of the gifts—right judgment and courage—not only help a person to persevere through difficult times, but also to *do* what is good and right. Scott's courage through his illness was not only an inner courage, but also helped others. His mother's words—"he was an inspiration to many"—are proof of this.

The last two gifts—the gifts of reverence and wonder and awe—help us to relate intimately with God and his creation. The life of a single teenage boy helped wake many people up to the gift of life and the need to appreciate and thank God for each and every day.

Anointing and Other Symbols of Confirmation

It is nearly impossible to understand the sacrament of Confirmation without examining the rich symbolism oil has both in the Bible and in sacramental life. Anointing with chrism—a mixture of olive oil and perfume—is part of the essential rite of Confirmation.

In the Bible, oil is a sign of abundance and joy. For example, the Promised Land, unlike Egypt, overflowed with grain, wine, and oil due to the rains that began in autumn, continued through the winter, and became the showers of early spring (see Dt 11:14). The famous Psalm 23 likewise connects oil with God's goodness:

> You spread the table before me
>   in the sight of my foes;
> You anoint my head with oil;

> *my cup overflows.*
> *Only goodness and kindness follow me*
> *all the days of my life;*
> *And I shall dwell in the house of the Lord*
> *for years to come (23:5-6).*

The Bible also describes oil as a sign of healing; it offers soothing to bruises and wounds. In describing the sins of the nation Israel, the prophet Isaiah says the people's "wound, welt, and gaping gash" had not yet been "eased with salve" (Is 1:6). The Samaritan in Jesus' parable uses oil to heal the injured victim's wounds (see Lk 10:34).

According to other ancient symbolism, oil also signifies cleansing (oil is applied both before and after a bath), limbering of athletes prior to competition, as well as beauty, health, and strength.

Oil is associated with all of these meanings in sacramental life as well. For example:

- the pre-baptismal anointing with the oil of catechumens signifies cleansing and strengthening;
- the anointing of the sick is for healing and comfort;
- the post-baptismal anointing with the sacred chrism and the anointing with chrism in Confirmation and Holy Orders are signs of holiness and consecration.

With the anointing of Confirmation the confirmand receives the "mark" or "seal" of the Holy Spirit. A seal in this sense is much like the seal that masters marked their slaves with or the seal that leaders gave their soldiers prior to battle. The seal of the Holy Spirit received at Confirmation marks our total being to Christ as he belongs to the Father, our pledge to serve him, as well as his protection of us from now until the end of time. Given this seal, the person exudes the "aroma of Christ" in everything he or she says and does.

The sacred chrism is so important to the sacrament of Confirmation that the blessing of the chrism takes place apart from the celebration of the sacrament, yet is in a certain way still part of it. On Holy Thursday each year, the bishop consecrates the sacred chrism for his entire diocese at the cathedral. The chrism is then distributed to the local churches in the diocese and used throughout the entire year for both post-baptismal anointings, Confirmation, and Holy Orders.

 From the Bible, read the Scripture references to oil listed in this section. Make a list of adjectives that describe the use of oil in these verses.

Confirmation

Only since the early twentieth century did the reception of first Eucharist precede Confirmation. This created some misunderstanding as to Confirmation's role as a sacrament of initiation. In fact, Confirmation completes Baptism, while Eucharist completes both Baptism and Confirmation leading to full membership in the Church. What privileges do you associate with full membership in the Church? What responsibilities do you associate with full membership in the Church?

The Celebration of Confirmation

Confirmation, with Baptism and Eucharist, is one of the sacraments of Christian initiation. Confirmation bounds the Christian "more intimately" with the Church (see *Lumen Gentium*, 11). For Catholics, Confirmation is necessary for the completion of baptismal grace. As Pope Paul VI wrote:

> *In Baptism, the newly baptized receive forgiveness of sins, adoption as children of God, and the character of Christ. [In this way they are] made members of the Church and become sharers in the priesthood of [Christ]. . . . Through the sacrament of Confirmation those who have been born anew in Baptism receive the inexpressible Gift, the Holy Spirit himself, by whom "they are endowed . . . with special strength. . . . " Finally, Confirmation is so closely linked with the holy Eucharist that the faithful, after being signed by Baptism and Confirmation, are incorporated fully into the Body of Christ by participation in the Eucharist* (Apostolic Constitution on the Sacrament of Confirmation).

In the Roman Rite, Confirmation is celebrated separately from Baptism. Even so, the Church aims to make their unity with each other and with the Eucharist clear. When infants are baptized but not confirmed, they are anointed with chrism as a sign of the anointing by the bishop which is still to come. Then, in order to show the connection of Baptism with Eucharist they are brought to the altar for the praying of the Our Father. When Confirmation is separate from Baptism, the liturgy of Confirmation begins with a renewal of baptismal promises.

The Rite of Confirmation

In the Latin rite, the sacrament of Confirmation is conferred through the anointing with chrism on the forehead, which is done through the laying on of the hand, and through the words: "Be sealed with the Gift of the Holy Spirit." In the Eastern Churches of Byzantine rite, more parts of the body are anointed: forehead, eyes, nose, ears, lips, chest, back, hands, and feet.

The bishop is the ordinary minister of Confirmation in the Latin Rite. He is also the "original minister" (*Lumen Gentium*, 26). Ordinarily, Confirmation takes place within Mass in order to express its connection with the other two sacraments of Christian initiation. A person's initiation into the Church is culminated in receiving the Body and Blood of Christ. When Confirmation takes place within Eucharist, the following elements are included:

- *Liturgy of the Word.* The readings are taken either from the Mass of the day or from texts especially for Confirmation that have to do with the role of the Holy Spirit in the life of the Church and of individual Christians.

- *Presentation of the Candidates.* After the gospel, the pastor, another priest, deacon, or the catechist responsible for the instruction of the Confirmation candidates presents the candidates. This is usually done by calling their names and having them stand in place or come to the sanctuary.

- *Homily or Instruction.* The bishop gives the homily, explaining the readings, and leading the candidates, sponsors, and assembly to a greater understanding of the mystery of Confirmation.

- *Renewal of Baptismal Promises.* The candidates only stand and renew their baptismal promises in question and answer form (e.g., "Do you reject Satan and all his works and all his empty promise?" "Do you believe in God the Father almighty, creator of heaven and earth?" etc. with the answer: "I do").

- *The Laying on of Hands.* The pastor and other priests are encouraged to concelebrate the Eucharist with the bishop. The priests stand near the bishop as he lays a hand upon all the candidates. The bishop then sings or says the prayer for the gifts of the Holy Spirit found on page 87.

- *The Anointing with Chrism.* With the laying on of the hand, the anointing with chrism forms the essential rite of the sacrament of Confirmation. The bishop makes the sign of the cross on the forehead of the one to be confirmed. The dialogue which includes the sign of peace accompanies the anointing.

> **Bishop:** *Name, be sealed with the Gift of the Holy Spirit.*
> **Newly Confirmed:** *Amen.*
> **Bishop:** *Peace be with you.*
> **Newly Confirmed:** *And also with you.*

- *Liturgy of the Eucharist.* The Mass continues in the normal order. Sometimes the newly confirmed may join in bringing the gifts to the altar. The praying of the Our Father is especially meaningful because the Holy Spirit is the one who prays in us and allows us to address God as "Abba, Father."

- *Blessing.* A special blessing or prayer over the people is used at Confirmation. The bishop extends his hands over the people and sings or says words like these:

> *God our Father,*
> *complete the work you have begun*
> *and keep the gifts of your Holy Spirit*
> *active in the hearts of your people.*
> *Make them ready to live his Gospel*
> *and eager to do his will.*
> *May they never be ashamed*
> *to proclaim to all the world Christ crucified*
> *living and reigning for ever and ever.*

The following are among the gospel readings often chosen for the Rite of Confirmation: Matthew 16:24-27, Mark 1:9-11, Luke 4:16-22a, John 14:15-17. Read and tell what you think each has to do with the rite of Confirmation.

Confirmation

More on the Minister of Confirmation

Interview a priest. Ask him if he has ever administered the sacrament of Confirmation and, if so, to explain the situation.

The bishop is the "original minister" of Confirmation. Bishops are the successors of the apostles. They have received the fullness of the sacrament of Holy Orders. By administering Confirmation themselves, it is clearly demonstrated that the effect of the sacrament is to unite those who receive it more closely to the Church, to the apostles, and to the mission of bearing witness to Christ.

There are some situations when a priest may confer Confirmation. For example, when an adult is confirmed in the Roman Catholic Church (usually at the Easter vigil), a priest may confer Confirmation (using sacred chrism that was consecrated by the bishop). Also, if a person is in danger of death, any priest can give him or her Confirmation.

In situations where the needs of the Church require it, the bishop may appoint priests to administer the sacrament, and can also associate priests with himself to administer Confirmation (for example, if the number to be confirmed is quite large).

Confirmation in the Sacramental Economy

In Acts 2:3 the Spirit appeared to the apostles in "tongues as of fire." Compare this image of the Spirit with how God's presence is depicted in Exodus 19:18.

Confirmation is prefigured in the Old Testament, given its role in the economy of salvation. Many of the examples of this have to do with the coming of the Spirit to God's chosen ones.

The prophets of the Old Testament announced that the Spirit of the Lord would rest on the Messiah. Isaiah 11:1-2 says,

> A shoot shall sprout from the stump of Jesse, and from his roots a bud shall blossom. The spirit of the Lord shall rest upon him.

Also, the prophet Ezekiel declared that in the days of the Messiah God would send his Spirit upon all of the people:

> I will give you a new heart and place a new spirit within you . . . . I will put my spirit within you and make you live by my statutes, careful to observe my decrees (Ez 36:26-27).

In a similar way God spoke through the prophet Joel, announcing: "I will pour out my spirit upon all mankind" (Jl 3:1).

The Isaiah prophecy was fulfilled when Jesus was baptized. As he came up out of the water the Spirit of the Lord descended upon him in a visible manner as the sign that he was the Messiah. Jesus then assured his followers that just as the

prophecy which said that the Spirit would rest on the Messiah had been fulfilled, so too the prophecy which said that the Spirit would be given to *all the people* would be fulfilled. When his disciples were wor-
ried about the fact that he was going to leave them and they would no longer experience God's presence so clearly, Jesus told them, "It is much better for you that I go. For if I do not go, the Advocate (the Holy Spirit) will not come to you. But if I go, I will send him to you" (Jn 16:7). On another occasion he reassured his followers, "When they take you before synagogues and before rulers and authorities, do not worry about how or what your defense will be or about what you are to say. For the holy Spirit will teach you at that moment what you should say" (Lk 12:11-12).

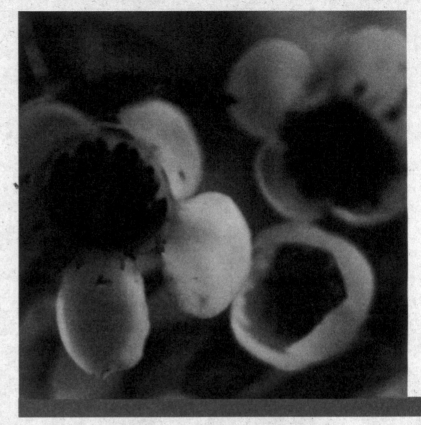

Following his resurrection Jesus breathed the Holy Spirit upon his apostles and gave them the power to forgive sins. At Pentecost he sent the Spirit in an even more striking manner (see Acts 2:1-41). The apostles who had been hiding in fear were suddenly filled with a new strength and courage. They began to proclaim all of the marvelous things that God had done culmi-
nating in the resurrection of Jesus and the coming of the Spirit. Peter assured the crowd who had gathered in the streets that the wonders they were witnessing were the sign that the messianic age had begun. He wanted the people to know that the coming of the Holy Spirit marked the beginning of the period when the world would be put to the test. The time had come for people to make one of two choices: Would they align themselves with God and share eternal life? Or, would they align themselves with all those things which would soon pass away?

Confirmation in the New Testament

Those who heard Peter's words on Pentecost understood the importance of the choice that was before them. "They were cut to the heart, and they asked Peter and the other apostles, 'What are we to do?'" (Acts 2:37). Peter explained that they must reform their lives and be baptized so that their sins would be forgiven. Then they would be given the gift of the Spirit so that they would be able to align themselves with the things of God.

From that day on the apostles baptized people and then laid hands upon them so that they would receive the Holy Spirit. There are three things which should be noted about the New Testament process of making new Christians:

First, the outpouring of the Spirit was an essential element of Christian Baptism from the beginning. Philip baptized many people in Samaria but Peter and John still went from Jerusalem to Samaria to lay lands on the new converts so that they would receive the Spirit (see Acts 8:14-17). This laying on of hands is recognized by the Church as the origins of the sacrament of Confirmation. It was the gift of the Spirit which made a person a Christian—that is, an "anointed one."

Second, a Baptism of water for forgiveness and not just a Baptism in the Holy Spirit was necessary if one was to become a Christian. Paul received a direct revelation from the Risen Christ. This was enough to make him an eyewitness to the resurrection. Nevertheless he still needed to be baptized by Ananias before he could carry out God's work. It seems that the water Baptism was necessary to unite Paul with the rest of the Church and allow him to live as a member of the Body of Christ.

Finally, the account of the first baptisms in Acts stresses the fact that after they had been baptized and had received the Spirit, the people devoted themselves to the teaching of the apostles, fellowship, prayers, and the breaking of the bread. In other words, the significant result of Baptism and the reception of the Spirit was that a person became part of the Church. Praying and sharing with one another was far more important than any of the signs and wonders that the Holy Spirit made possible. To put it another way: unity, and not any special ability, was the most important gift of the Spirit.

☑

What do each of the three acts associated with Christian initiation in the New Testament signify?

From the New Testament accounts we can see that from the earliest time there have been three distinct acts which were necessary for a person to be fully incorporated into the Church: a Baptism of water for the forgiveness of sins and for uniting one to the larger community of faith, a laying on of hands for the reception of the Spirit, and a sharing in the life of the Church, in particular a sharing in the prayers and the "breaking of the bread."

Confirmation Tradition and Practices Emerge

In the first centuries Confirmation generally was part of one single celebration with Baptism. St. Cyprian called it a "double sacrament." When Christianity was legalized in the fourth century in the Roman Empire, the number of Baptisms—including infant Baptisms—increased. Also, more and more rural parishes were founded and the number of dioceses increased. The sheer volume of persons (mostly infants) entering the Church prevented the bishop from being present at all Baptisms in order to complete Baptism with the anointing of Confirmation. At this time, two traditions for celebrating the sacrament of Confirmation emerged.

Explain why St. Cyprian called Confirmation a "double sacrament."

In the West (Roman Church), there was a desire to maintain the bishop's role in the sacrament. The bishop sustains and serves the Church's unity, catholicity, and its connection with the apostles. His presence at Confirmation expresses the unity of the new Christian with the bishop and these elements.

To maintain the connection with the Bishop, the practice of a double anointing with sacred chrism after Baptism arose. The first anointing was done by the priest at Baptism. It signified the participation of the new Christian in the Christ's office of priest, prophet, and king. This first anointing was "completed" by a second anointing by the bishop at Confirmation. This practice still continues today. If an adult is baptized there is only one post-baptismal anointing, that of Confirmation, and it is done by the priest.

In the Eastern Churches, following their ancient practice, Confirmation is conferred by the priest who baptizes. This practice gives greater emphasis to the unity of these sacraments of initiation, rather than separating Baptism and Confirmation by a period of years. The Eastern Churches maintain unity with the bishops by having the priest anoint only with *myron* (chrism) consecrated by the bishop.

Understanding More About the Sacrament

After the separation of Baptism and Confirmation, because of the difficulty of travel in the early centuries, many parents did not bring their children to receive Confirmation when the bishop was in the local area. Thus the period of time between Baptism and Confirmation grew longer and some never received the sacrament. By the sixteenth century, some of the Protestant reformers spoke

Read and report on some of the canons on Confirmation from the Council of Trent.

out against the sacramental character of Confirmation. The reformers felt that the importance of Baptism had been weakened by attributing too much to rites such as the laying on of hands and anointing.

The Council of Trent (1545-1563) defended the sacramental character of Confirmation while also emphasizing its necessity. The Council taught that all Catholics should be confirmed, and that Confirmation should take place after seven years of age, the age of reason, but no later than age twelve. At this time, First Communion took place at about age fourteen. Thus the traditional order of the sacraments of initiation was preserved: Baptism, Confirmation, Eucharist, though they were now spread out over many years. A Council of Trent canon reads as follows:

> If anyone says that the Confirmation of those who have been baptized is an idle ceremony, and not rather a true and proper sacrament; or that of old it was nothing more than a kind of catechism, whereby they who were near adolescence gave an account of their faith in the face of the Church; let him be anathema (Council of Trent, *Decree on the Sacraments, Canon I, Confirmation*).

Confirmation in Today's Church

In 1910, Pope Pius X permitted children to receive First Communion once they reached the age of reason. Pope Pius's intent was to increase devotion to the Eucharist as well as its frequent reception. He said that all the faithful should receive communion at least on Sundays and feast days, and even daily if possible. It was at this time that it became popular within the Roman rite to celebrate Eucharist, the last of the sacraments of initiation, before Confirmation. Many Eastern churches continued to baptize, confirm, and give First Communion to infants.

Today, the Church teaches that every baptized person not yet confirmed can receive the sacrament of Confirmation. The Church continues to abide the centuries old reference point of "the age of discretion" being the time to receive Confirmation. The Bishops of the United States have determined that the age of discretion may be any time between the ages of seven and eighteen.

There is diversity in the age for Confirmation from diocese to diocese and parish to parish within this window of age provided by the bishops. Part of this diversity comes from choosing different emphases on the theological understanding of the sacrament.

Those who place emphasis on the unity and order of the sacraments of initiation tend to support children being confirmed at the same time of First Eucharist to maintain the Baptism, Confirmation, Eucharist order. Another understanding connects Confirmation with Christian maturity, stressing the developing faith and chronological age of the person being confirmed.

The *Catechism of the Catholic Church* (see 1309) recognizes that though Confirmation is sometimes called the "sacrament of Christian maturity," adult faith and adult age should not be confused and that baptismal grace is freely given and does not need "ratification" to become effective.

To receive Confirmation, a person must be baptized and in a state of grace. He or she should receive the sacrament of Penance in order to be cleansed and prepared for the gift of the Holy Spirit. The person should also pray "intensely" to receive the strength and graces of the Holy Spirit and be prepared to take on the responsibilities of Christian life.

Most teenagers who are confirmed prepare for the sacrament in a parish-sponsored program. The preparation focuses on leading the candidate toward a deeper relationship with Christ as well as a greater familiarity with the Holy Spirit, including his actions, gifts, and callings. This preparation for Confirmation is designed to help the person become more capable of assuming the apostolic responsibilities of Christian life.

☑ Explain the requirements of a Confirmation program you personally experienced or one sponsored by a local parish.

Also helping a person prepare for Confirmation is his or her sponsor. The sponsor brings the candidate to the sacrament, presents him or her to the bishop for anointing, and later helps the person fulfill his or her baptismal promises faithfully under the influence of the Holy Spirit. A Confirmation sponsor is often the godparent from Baptism to help express the relationship between the two sacraments. The sponsor should also be someone who is spiritually mature, and a practicing Catholic who has received the three sacraments of initiation.

Any unbaptized person who is over the age of seven normally goes through the catechumenate in order to be baptized and join the Church. He or she then receives all three of the sacraments of initiation at the same time, usually at the Easter vigil. Also, a child who is in danger of death is able to receive Confirmation even if he or she has not reached the age of reason.

The Effects of Confirmation

Church father Tertullian who lived in the latter half of the second century wrote,

The body is washed that the soul may be cleansed; the body is anointed that the soul may be consecrated; the body is signed, that the soul too may be fortified; the body is overshadowed by the laying on of hands, that the soul may be enlightened by the Spirit; the body is fed on the body and blood of Christ, that the soul may be richly nourished by God (op. cit. Apostolic Constitution on the Sacrament of Confirmation).

☑

Tell how you have shared your faith with someone else or how someone else has shared his or her faith with you.

Each of the symbolic actions which is used during Confirmation signifies God's primary gift of the Holy Spirit. Those who are confirmed today receive the same gift of the Spirit that the apostles received at Pentecost. Through the sacrament of Confirmation we are more deeply rooted in our identity as children of God and we are more firmly united to Christ. This is what Tertullian was referring to when he wrote that our "soul may be consecrated." He also wrote that our souls are fortified (or strengthened) and enlightened. The sacrament of Confirmation *strengthens us by increasing the gifts of the Holy Spirit within us* beginning with the gifts of love and faith and including the gifts of wisdom, understanding, right judgment, courage, knowledge, reverence, and awe in the presence of the Lord. Confirmation also *gives us a special strength to share our faith in the Paschal mystery.* Finally Confirmation *enlightens us.* It makes our bond with the Church more perfect in part by helping us to understand and appreciate what the Church is and what the Church teaches.

Confirmation also "gives us a special strength:

- to spread and defend the faith by word and action as true witnesses of Christ,
- to confess the name of Christ boldly,
- and to never to be ashamed of the Cross" (*CCC*, 1303).

When we receive the gift of the Holy Spirit our identity and our relationships are changed forever. Like Baptism, Confirmation imprints an "indelible spiritual mark" on the person who is confirmed. This "character" given at Confirmation perfects the common priesthood of the faithful received in Baptism. Once the Holy Spirit has been given to a person, this gift cannot be taken away, nor will the gift ever go away. A person may choose not to listen to the Spirit dwelling within him or her, but that will not change the fact that the Spirit is there. For this reason Confirmation cannot be repeated.

Confirmation has several other effects; the main ones are described in the next sections.

Confirmation Commits Us to Prayer

Those who are anointed in the sacrament of Confirmation share more completely in the mission of Jesus. They are permanently enrolled in his service. One of the main thrusts of Jesus' mission was reconciliation. He came to reunite people to one another and to God. We participate in this reconciling work when we pray.

The prayer of the faithful which we pray during the liturgy is a particularly important form of prayer in the Church. In the early Church catechumens were not allowed to participate in this prayer because they were not yet prepared for the serious work which it entailed. After they were baptized, reciting the prayer of the faithful was their first act as members of the Church. It is only after Baptism that the Church believes they are finally ready to respond to the word of God in the prayer of the faithful and to join Christ in strengthening the bond of love among all people and between all people and God. After their Baptism the *neophytes*—as they are now called—are able to have a share in Christ's work of mediation.

Write three petitions for needs affecting the larger world community, your local city or region, and your personal family. Offer these with the other prayers of the faithful the next time you are at Mass.

The *General Instruction on the Roman Missal* says, "In the prayer of the faithful, the people exercise their priestly function by praying for all humanity" (#45). Through their prayers the people commit themselves to those who are in need within their community and throughout the world. Their attitude toward others is reshaped and the human community comes a step closer to full reconciliation. As scholar Lucien Deiss put it, "The prayer of the faithful is the mystery of love that binds [the praying] community to the universe."

The prayer of the faithful does more than express and strengthen our love for those around us. God responds to prayers prayed in faith. Each time we pray for the world, God acts to soften hearts and to remove some of the barriers which divide people from each other and from him.

Through the prayer of the faithful the people also bring the world for which they pray closer to God. At the heart of the petitions is an attitude of praise. We approach God with knowledge of and confidence in his ability and willingness to give us everything that is good. We accept his lordship over us and over all creation. We align ourselves with Jesus who surrendered everything, even his life, to God in love. Adam and Eve ate from the tree of knowledge in order to avoid total dependence on God. When we pray we express our willingness to be dependent upon God.

Confirmation Binds Us to the Church

Confirmation binds us more completely to the Church. Following Confirmation all of our actions should be actions which are suitable to one who is a member of the body of Christ. The more we respond to the Holy Spirit who is within us the more we will see the importance of consecrating every moment of our lives to God— of doing everything for the glory of God. The Church has established the *sacramentals* as one means of helping us consecrate various activities to God. A sacramental is a sacred sign that resembles the sacraments and signifies spiritual effects through the Church's intercession.

Blessings are the primary form of sacramental. When we bless events such as meals, people, objects, or places, we offer praise to God and acknowledge our dependence upon him. We then ask God to help us to orient our lives toward him.

Those blessings which permanently consecrate people or objects for the service of God are particularly important. Such blessings include the blessing of churches, altars, and holy oils, and the *rite of religious profession* (when a person becomes a religious brother or sister) (see *CCC*, 1671).

The rite of religious profession deserves special mention in our discussion of Confirmation. The post-baptismal anointing in Confirmation is the sign of consecration. Those who have been anointed share more completely in the mission of Christ. They are anointed with the Holy Spirit so that their lives may give off "the aroma of Christ" (*CCC*, 1294). Those who take permanent vows of poverty, chastity, and obedience in order to dedicate themselves wholeheartedly to the mission of Christ, give off this aroma in a very tangible way. They witness to the love and service which all the faithful are called to practice. The profession of religious vows is not a sacrament because it is not so much a new thing as it is an expression of the totality of the commitment made in Baptism and Confirmation. We refer to the life of religious brothers and sisters as "the consecrated life" because it is a sign of the full acceptance of the grace given in Baptism and Confirmation.

Sacramentals do not have the inherent power to pass on the grace of the Holy Spirit in the way that the sacraments do. However, as expressions of the Church's prayer, they prepare us to receive grace and cooperate with it. Sacraments confer grace every time they are performed, regardless of the goodness of the person who performs them. In contrast, the benefits which come from sacramentals depend on the inward disposition of the one who performs them.

Catholics also use a variety of prayers and special devotions to support and express their faith. These include the rosary, the stations of the cross, devotions to particular saints, pilgrimages, and fasts. Each helps us carry the liturgy of the Church into our daily lives. They help us to live out our Baptism and

Research and name several other objects, prayers, or blessings that are identified by the Church today as sacramentals.

Confirmation. These various forms of piety can support the sacramental life of the Church, but they are never to be seen as substitutes for it. The use of sacramentals and other forms of popular piety should always be in harmony with the liturgical seasons and the life of the Church as a whole.

Confirmation Commits Us to Action

Write your answer to the question posed at the end of this section, "What am I doing to carry the love of Christ into the world?"

Besides leading us to prayer, Confirmation also makes it possible for us to serve the world as Jesus did. The Holy Spirit gives us the gifts we need in order to respond to the needs of others; but we must choose to use those gifts.

In the early Church people had to demonstrate that they were prepared to live a life of service before they could even begin to prepare for Baptism, Confirmation, and Eucharist. Only people who were willing to care for those in need could become Christians. Lent developed as a time of intense preparation for the sacraments of initiation. The lenten fast was a way of making personal sacrifices in order to meet the needs of others. Even those who were already members of the Church participated in the lenten fast as a means of recalling and strengthening their own commitment to the work of Christ. Today, too, we need to regularly ask ourselves if we are living out our Baptism and Confirmation by helping others. Each one of us must ask, "What am I doing to carry the love of Christ into the world?"

Completion of Christian Initiation: The Funeral Liturgy

For Christians the day of death marks the end of the sacramental life of signs and symbols and the beginning of life lived in the unmediated presence of God. Death is the final fulfillment of the sacraments of initiation. In death we experience the completion of the new birth which was begun in Baptism. In death we are completely united with the Trinity. We live in full communion with the Father, Son, and Holy Spirit, a communion which was conferred when we were anointed with the Spirit at Confirmation. Finally, in death we participate in the feast of the kingdom which was anticipated in the Eucharist.

Death remains a mystery; but in the face of death there are two affirmations which Christians can make. First, death is a reality. Second, God is trustworthy and whatever lies beyond death was created by God and experienced by Jesus. The funeral liturgy makes these two affirmations clear. The function of a Christian funeral is to acknowledge the reality of death, to show God is love, to support the bereaved, and to commend the person who has died to God's care.

(The Funeral Liturgy cont.)

The Christian funeral is a liturgical celebration of the Church. The one who has died has passed beyond the world where God's love and presence are experienced through signs and symbols. The funeral liturgy *does* express and help us to experience the union of Christians which is not broken by death. It expresses and establishes our continued communion with the one who has died.

"The Christian meaning of death is revealed in the light of the Paschal mystery of the death and resurrection of Christ in whom resides our only hope. The Christian who dies in Christ Jesus is 'away from the body and at home with the Lord'" (CCC, 1681).

Give your impressions of a funeral that you attended. How did the funeral liturgy help you to grow in hope? If you've never been to a funeral, ask this question of someone you know who has been.

Chapter 4
Review Questions

1. Name the seven gifts of the Holy Spirit that come to us at Confirmation.

2. Tell at least one way the gifts of the Holy Spirit were present in the life of Scott Delgadillo.

3. Explain the meaning of the anointing with chrism in Confirmation.

4. How is the unity between Baptism, Confirmation, and Eucharist highlighted in the Roman Rite?

5. What is the essential rite of the sacrament of Confirmation?

6. Why is the bishop the "original minister" of Confirmation?

7. What are some Old Testament roots of the sacrament of Confirmation?

8. From the beginning of the Church, what are the three necessary acts for a person to be fully incorporated in the Church?

9. What led to the separation of Baptism and Confirmation?

10. What did the Council of Trent teach about Confirmation?

11. How did Pope Pius X's decision about moving First Communion to age seven affect Confirmation?

12. What are the some of the effects of Confirmation?

13. What is a sacramental?

14. How does Confirmation commit us to action?

15. Why do Christian funerals not confer a sacrament or sacramental character on the deceased?

Eucharist

Glimpses of the Mystery

How can we begin to describe something which the Second Vatican Council calls "the source and summit of the *Christian life*"? (*Lumen Gentium*, #11). The full wonder of the Eucharist is far beyond any words or descriptions that we can find. In the Eucharist God enters our lives in a way that is most clearly expressed by the act of eating and drinking. His body and blood pass into our body and blood. There is no other way to describe what happens. There is nothing else we can compare it to. But what does it mean? How does it affect us? While there are no adequate explanations, there are stories—stories which give us glimpses of what the Eucharist is.

A Gift of Inclusion

It was Easter Sunday morning in New Haven, Connecticut. Most of the people sitting out on the damp grass were huddled under blankets trying to ignore the predawn chill. The priest raised the bread and the cup, "Through Him, with Him, in Him. . . ." Despite the sounds of the birds and the distant rumble of traffic his voice could be heard clearly. The sloping hill acted like a natural amphitheater.

As he prayed the sun cleared the horizon. The voices of those gathered for the sunrise Mass rang out clearly with the words of the "Our Father." Then people were moving forward, ready to receive communion. The priest took the basket filled with consecrated hosts. But he did not walk toward the first person in line. Instead he began the long climb to the top of the hill where a woman sat in a wheelchair. The hill was steep and the priest was no longer young or particularly strong. Furthermore, the wind kept twisting his vestments about his legs, impeding his steps. At least twice he nearly tripped. When he reached the woman in the chair he was breathing hard. He offered her communion with a smile that filled his eyes, "The body of Christ."

"Amen."

Those who were close could hear the Easter joy in her voice. The priest began his slow descent. Several people quietly wiped tears from their eyes. Katie[1] could have gone into the neighboring building, taken the elevator to the lower level, and come out near where the altar had been set up for this Mass. That's what she would have done with most other priests. But Father Henri Nouwen, the great writer and preacher that all of these people had come before six in the morning to hear, had not waited for her to come down to him. He had made the difficult climb to her. That action may have been the most eloquent sermon on the Eucharist that anyone at Yale University ever heard.

The Strength to Survive

In a town in Michigan a retired couple and their adult son knelt side by side in a pew near the back of the Church. "Lord, I am not worthy to receive you . . . ." They spoke the words together with the rest of the congregation. Then they stood and began the long, slow walk to the front to receive communion. The son watched his parents walking in front of him. It was amazing really, the fact that they were still together after all these years and after so much pain and misunderstanding.

His father still drank too much. He said it was the Viet Nam war, the memories of horror that he couldn't shake. His mother still thought that life had treated everyone else better than it had treated her. She was angry so much of the time. And when she was angry her tongue wasn't kind. Mom had been sick when his dad came back from the war. Neither of them had been able to help or support the other. Both had felt abandoned and hurt. They'd never really gotten past that. He'd grown up in the middle of all that pain, longing for the day when he could leave home and escape it forever.

He *had* left and, to a large extent, he *did* escape. When he talked to them on the phone everyone behaved as if all was well. Living so many miles away, he could almost imagine that it was true. But now they had come to visit; and even though his dad wasn't drinking—wouldn't drink with grandchildren around—the son knew that nothing had really changed. Only a day after they had arrived he found himself looking forward to their leaving.

The occasion that brought them to church was the feast of the Ascension—a holy day of obligation. He and his parents agreed to go together to the evening Mass. Now he watched as each of his parents received the host. Then it was his turn. He looked at the small wafer resting in his palm—the body of Christ.

"The body of Christ," he repeated the words to himself. This was it. This was what had kept his family together all these years. This was why his parents loved each other through the pain. This is why he could have a healthy family even when he'd come from an unhealthy one. As he walked back to his pew, he watched his parents kneel side by side and bow their heads in prayer. He felt a flash of love for them. He was glad they had come to this Mass. He knelt beside them and offered his own silent prayer of thanksgiving.

A Chance for Peace

In the city of Kigali, Rwanda, a Tutsi man whose father had been brutally murdered by their Hutu neighbors was attending Mass with his family. He had not been in church very many times since his father's death. At first he had been in hiding and then he had been too bitter. His heart was filled with hate for the Hutus who had killed a man who had helped them more than once when they were in need. His heart was filled with anger at God who had let a man who had dedicated his life to prayer and peace die. But on this day his mother asked him to come and so he had.

During the homily, the priest spoke about the Eucharist. "When we eat it we become the body of Christ. We are united to everyone else who ever has or ever will eat this same holy food. We are even united to the Hutus who have hurt us and the Hutus who we have hurt. No army will ever make peace possible. But this food will."

The Tutsi man reflected on those words. He did not go forward to receive communion with the rest of his family. But as the last person in the communion

Describe a Mass when you were particularly overwhelmed by God's presence.

Write a story that may provide others with a glimpse of the meaning of Eucharist.

line passed him, he stepped in behind. As he walked back to join his family, they could see hope in his eyes for the first time in two years.

A Treasure Beyond Compare

On the feast of St. Nicholas in 1273, Dominican priest and theologian St. Thomas Aquinas said Mass. As he prayed the eucharistic prayer something happened which profoundly affected him. When the Mass was over he refused to write or dictate anything for the book he was writing. At the time, St. Thomas was working on the Third Part of the *Summa Theologiae*, one of the most complete theological works ever written. He was working on the section on Penance. Nonetheless, he put away all of his writing materials.

One of the other Dominicans asked him if he were really going to give up on this great work that he was doing, work which would enlighten all people and bring glory to God. Thomas replied, "All that I have written seems to me like straw compared with what has now been revealed to me."

Yes, the Eucharist is the source and summit of the Christian life. The rest of this chapter reveals more about the meaning of the Eucharist.

What Is the Eucharist?

The Eucharist is the "center and culmination of the entire life of the Christian community" (*Christus Dominus*, #30). All that we are and all that we strive to be as Christians can be found in the Eucharist. The Eucharist is the heart and soul of our lives as Christians. As St. Irenaeus wrote: "Our way of thinking is attuned to the Eucharist, and the Eucharist in turn confirms our way of thinking."

When a person participates in Eucharist and receives communion, he or she is entering the innermost life of the Church. This is why the Church calls the Eucharist the sacrament which completes Christian initiation (*CCC*, 1322).

A Catholic is baptized and confirmed only once. But he or she participates in Eucharist many times. Baptism and Confirmation make us participants in Christ's Paschal mystery. Each time the Church celebrates the Eucharist we enter these events once again. Through the Eucharist we recommit ourselves to our Baptism at every stage and every moment of our lives. We experience the life of God within us at Eucharist.

Name some other organizations or clubs that have initiation rituals. Describe a final rite of initiation in one of the organizations or clubs that you name.

If we understand a Christian to be someone who is part of the body of Christ, then we can see that it takes a lifetime to become Christian. It takes a lifetime for our actions to be in conformity with Christ. Each time we receive the body and blood of Christ we are reminded that we have not yet reached our goal; we are also brought one step closer to it. Each time we receive communion we are pulled into a more intimate union with Christ. Over the course of a lifetime the Eucharist initiates us into the life of the Trinity, until at last we are ready to share it completely in the kingdom of heaven.

The Eucharist reshapes our relationship with the Trinity because of what it is. The Eucharist is a blessing. In the Eucharist we experience God's absolute *transcendence*, that is the quality of God that lies beyond our normal perception. Through the Eucharist we acknowledge and accept that transcendence which Adam and Eve wanted to ignore or escape.

The Eucharist is a renewal of the covenant between God and his people; through the Eucharist God writes his law on our hearts. The Eucharist is the presence of Christ who promised to be with us always. The Eucharist is the perfect sacrifice which continually restores and energizes our relationship with God. The Eucharist is a meal which nourishes and sustains us and which provides us with an opportunity for fellowship and intimate sharing. The Eucharist is heaven on earth. Now, let us examine each of these parts of the eucharist more closely.

The Eucharist Is a Blessing

Recall from Chapter 1 that a blessing is a divine and life-giving action by God the Father. The blessings of liturgy are also a gift of God the Father to us. We respond to these blessings by responding to his grace. Christ, seated at the right hand of the Father, pours out the blessings of the Holy Spirit in the sacraments—most especially in the Eucharist.

A blessing is also a human act. We return thanks and adoration to God the Father for all that he has done. The Father blesses us by giving us life. We bless the Father by surrendering that life to him, as his son Jesus did. When we surrender our lives to God, the Holy Spirit is at work in us to enable us to praise and trust the Father in all situations. We believe in and accept his love for us and we love him in return.

St. Augustine said, "Thus if you wish to understand the body of Christ, listen to the Apostle, who says to the believers, 'You are the body of Christ and his members' (1 Cor 12:27). And thus, if you are the body of Christ and his members, it is your mystery which has been placed on the altar of the Lord; you receive your own mystery. You answer 'Amen' to what you are, and in answering it you accept it. For you hear, 'the body of Christ' and you answer 'Amen.' Be a member of Christ's body, so that your 'Amen' may be true" (Senno, 272).

How do you experience being the body of Christ at Mass?

Prayers of blessing are the most ancient and basic form of Jewish prayer and they are central to the liturgy. Prayers of blessing recall all that God has done. They marvel at an infinite God who cares enough to be involved in the day to day lives of human beings. In the liturgy of the Eucharist the Church praises and thanks the Father for all the wonders of creation. The Church recalls and gives thanks for the fact that even when we fail to appreciate what the Father has given us, even when we try to destroy it, God keeps on loving us and giving us more. We praise and thank the Father for offering us chance after chance to apologize and begin again. We also praise and thank the Father through Christ and in the Holy Spirit for his constant love and his constant efforts to help us experience that love more completely. The word *eucharist* means "thanksgiving."

In the Eucharist we proclaim the things that God has done, and in particular the things that God has done for us in Christ, and we are caught up in those things. When the Israelites commemorated Passover, they proclaimed God's greatness in freeing them from slavery and leading them to the Promised Land. As they proclaimed what God had done, they were caught up in that action. They became the people whom God had saved. They were the people to whom the Promised Land was given. They were not just people who knew what God had done for someone else; they were people for whom God had done everything that is good. A Jewish writer described Passover as "the festival of all times, in which the past deliverance blends with the future redemption in an eternal today." In the Passover celebration the time of liberation is now.

In the Eucharist, we offer a blessing just as Christ did through the gifts of his life, death, and resurrection. On the night before he died, Jesus anticipated his own passion and death and interpreted them in the terms of the Jewish Passover and its sacrifice. At the same time he gave the Eucharist to his followers as a means of remembering and actually making his passion and death present to them. Jesus made the Eucharist the new Passover. As the *Catechism* teaches:

> By celebrating the Last Supper with his apostles in the course of the Passover meal, Jesus gave the Jewish Passover its definitive meaning. Jesus' passing over to his Father by his death and Resurrection, the new Passover, is anticipated in the Supper and celebrated in the Eucharist, which fulfills the Jewish Passover and anticipates the final Passover of the Church in the glory of the kingdom (1340).

When the Church celebrates the Eucharist it blesses God for these great events of salvation: from creation to the Exodus, to the death and resurrection of Jesus and the coming of the Holy Spirit, to the second coming of Christ and the establishment of a new heaven and a new earth. As the Church proclaims these events, it is caught up in them. In Eucharist, God redeems us from sin and leads us to freedom. The Holy Spirit moves in our lives. In the Eucharist we are caught up in the new creation in which all tears are wiped away. In other words, when the Church celebrates the Eucharist, the entire Body of Christ—its head and its body—praises God for the life and salvation which he has given. And we experience that life and salvation in the present moment. In the Eucharist the time of liberation, the time of redemption, and the time of the new creation are all *now*.

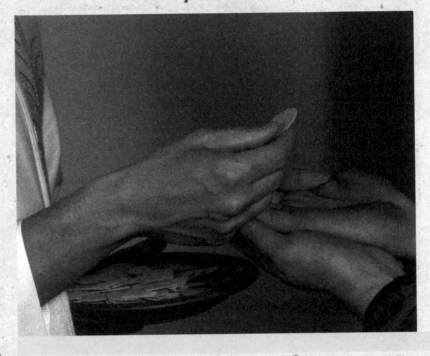

This does not mean that every time the Eucharist is offered we are conscious of these events. Nor does it mean that we always come away from the Eucharist feeling liberated, redeemed, energized, renewed, or anything else. What it does mean is that each time we take part in the Eucharist we are shaped in some way by the saving events in which we have participated. We are shaped by them because we are part of a Church which is shaped by them.

We are also shaped by them because they become part of our experience whether we are conscious of it or not. Even if we are completely oblivious to the saving events which we become a part of through the Eucharist, they still affect our relationship to the world. They still give us new options in life.

God the Father has done great things for his people through Christ and in the Holy Spirit. He has abundantly blessed them. When we participate in the Church's celebration of the Eucharist we proclaim those great things and give thanks and praise to the Father. We return blessing to him. As we proclaim and give thanks to God, he allows us to participate in the events which we are proclaiming. We are thereby blessed.

The Eucharist Is a Memorial

When Jesus gave the Eucharist to his apostles, he used the words "do this in memory of me." Taken in the context of the Old Testament, the word "memory" encompasses the whole relationship between God and his people. According to this understanding, if you gave people something to do "in memory of" an event, you were giving them a way of making that event part of their own experience. People who *remember* God's works of salvation are people who *experience* God's blessing and *respond* by doing God's will. The memory is an essential part of both experiencing the blessing and responding to it.

St. Gregory of Nazianzus wrote that "we must remember God more often than we draw breath." Describe some occasions in a typical day when you consciously make an effort to "remember God."

Eucharist

The prophets and religious leaders of the Old Testament were constantly trying to help the people remember God's actions so that the people would be faithful to him. More often than not, however, their words were ignored. The people learned what God had done for the Israelites of Moses' time. They knew what God had done for King David. But they did not believe that those events had been done for them, too. The book of Kings tells how time after time the Israelites abandoned God and accepted some of the pagan practices and pagan gods of their neighbors. The Israelites failed to remember the covenant. They turned away from it and felt the consequences of this inattentiveness.

Through the prophets, the Israelites were told of a new covenant which God would establish with them. This new

Understanding Covenant

A covenant is a binding agreement between two parties. This agreement may be between two equals, or a superior and an inferior. A covenant may oblige both parties to keep it, or only one.

The biblical understanding of covenant begins in the Old Testament (*testament* means "covenant") and is rooted in God's unconditional love for his people. Over and over, despite Israel's repeated infidelity, God promised to shower his mercy and love. He promised to do so by:

Tell of how you have experienced God's unconditional love in your own life.

- agreeing to continue life on earth (Noah; Gn 9:8-17);
- creating a special people and blessing them with land (Abraham; Gn 15–17);
- rescuing Israel from slavery and making them a holy nation (Moses; Ex 6:7);
- sending Israel a king and promising a Messiah (David; 2 Sm 7:14);
- writing his law on their hearts (Jer 31:33-34).

In the New Testament, Christ established a new and eternal covenant through his own sacrificial death and Resurrection. By giving us his Son, the Father faithfully and lovingly kept his covenant with us from now through eternity. The New Covenant is a law of love, grace, and freedom. Jesus, the supreme sign of God's love for us, draws us into his Body, showers us with gifts, relates to us as individuals, and invites us to share in his love by serving others.

covenant is one which the prophets explained would be "written in the hearts" of the people so that they will never be able to forget it completely. God imprints the great events of salvation history upon our memories even as the voice of a mother is imprinted upon the memory of her child before that child is born.

The Eucharist is the means by which God imprints these events on our memories. When Jesus took the cup at the Last Supper, he said, "This cup is the new covenant in my blood, which will be shed for you." Jesus' body and blood are the new covenant which the prophets foretold. When God establishes the new covenant through the Eucharist, it is truly written on our hearts.

The Eucharist Is the Presence of God Within and Among Us

One of the main truths that the Israelites recognized about their relationship with God was that he was present within and among the community. This presence was part of the essence of being God's chosen people. When the Temple was built in Jerusalem, God promised to be present there forever. But when the people of Israel were unfaithful to him, God allowed Israel to be overrun. He allowed the people to be dispersed throughout the world to places where they were far from God's presence. Through the prophets God made it clear that once he established the new covenant he would be present to his people wherever they were and forever. As the prophet Ezekiel says:

> *I will make with them a covenant of peace; it shall be an everlasting covenant with them, and I will multiply them, and* put my sanctuary among them forever. My dwelling shall be with them; *I will be their God, and they shall be my people (Ez 37:26-27; emphasis added).*

God is Present [handwritten margin note]

In the Eucharist God fulfills this pledge of a new covenant and makes his dwelling with us. Jesus is present in many ways in the celebration of the Eucharist:

> *He is present in the community which is gathered in his name.*
> *He is present in the Scripture which is his word.*
> *He is present in the person of the priest.*
> *And he is present in a unique way in the bread and wine which become his body and blood.*

The manner of Christ's presence in the eucharistic species (the bread and wine) is unique. This presence is called "real presence" because it is presence in the fullest sense. As the Council of Trent taught, in the consecrated bread and wine "the body and blood, together with the soul and divinity, of our Lord Jesus Christ and, therefore *the whole Christ is truly, really, and substantially* contained" (DS, 1651).

To better understand the presence of Christ in the Eucharistic species, it is necessary to understand what the Church teaches about the change that occurs in the species of bread and wine. It is during the consecration that the bread and wine become the body and blood of Christ while maintaining the appearance of bread and wine. The consecration occurs during the eucharistic prayer when the

Recount a story (either true or fictional) that you believe can help us understand some of the mystery of the change in the eucharistic species.

Look up more information on the Aristotelian understanding of the term transubstantiation.

What does it mean to you to say that in the Eucharist "you are what you eat"?

priest says and does what Christ said and did at the Last Supper. We express our faith in the real presence of Christ under the species of bread and wine at the time of consecration. The priest bows or genuflects as a sign of adoration. The assembly respectfully kneels in silence.

The term that the Church uses for this change from bread and wine to the body and blood of Christ is *transubstantiation*. Transubstantiation is a concept that has its roots in Greek philosophy, specifically in Aristotle's physics. Aristotle taught that every object could be defined by its substance and its accidents. The accidents were those things which could be perceived by human senses. The substance was what gave an object its true identity and formed its relationship to the world.

Following the consecration, the *accidents* of the bread and wine—those things which we can perceive—remain unchanged, but the *substance*—the true identity

of the bread and wine, and their relationship to the world—has changed completely. What was once bread and wine is now Christ and relates to the world as Christ. Those who treat the consecrated elements as bread and wine are being disrespectful whether they mean to be or not. Those who look beyond the bread and wine and recognize and respond to the presence of Christ in the elements perceive and respect the one who is really there.

When we eat and drink the consecrated bread and wine it changes us in a way that is unlike any other food. This is because the nourishment which the Eucharist gives us is the nourishment of Christ himself. When we eat ordinary food, it is incorporated into our bodies and we are changed because of its presence. When we eat and drink the Eucharist, Christ is incorporated into our bodies and we are changed because of his presence. (It is important to understand that the bread and wine become Christ, but Christ is not restricted in them.) There is an old saying, "you are what you eat." This is true in a very profound way in the Eucharist. We eat the body of Christ in order to become the body of Christ. If we are the body of Christ, then God is in our midst forever.

The Eucharistic presence of Christ endures as long as the Eucharistic species exist. Christ is wholly and entirely present in each of the parts (bread *and* wine). That is why the broken bread does not divide Christ. Nor does reception of only the Eucharistic bread or the Eucharistic wine somehow mean one has received only part of Christ. Also, the Church has always maintained the practice of venerating the consecrated hosts in solemn adoration outside of Mass, both communally and individually. The tabernacle is the place where the consecrated hosts are kept, and it should always be constructed and placed in a way that emphasizes the real presence of Christ in the Blessed Sacrament.

The Eucharist Is the Perfect Sacrifice

Play word association with the term <u>sacrifice</u>. What comes to mind?

Sacrifice comes from a Latin word that means "to make holy" or "to do something holy." Holiness refers to sharing in God's life and love. But only God can make us holy. Only God has the power to share his divine life with us.

Tracing the Meaning of Sacrifice

Sacrifice was a central concept for Jews of Jesus' time. In fact, sacrifice was the highest form of worship. Through their sacrifices, the people expressed their deepest feelings of gratitude for their unique relationship with God. They sacrificed objects of value to God as a sign of their desire to offer themselves to God. the giving of an animal or of the finest produce from the harvest was understood as giving of one's very self.

This gift-giving was what was really important in the Jewish understanding of sacrifice. The fact that the sacrifice was destroyed—usually burnt—was secondary. The intent was not to destroy something, but to give it to God. The altar within the Temple was understood as a symbol of the divine. When a gift was brought in contact with the altar it was a symbol that ownership had been transferred to God.

The more solemn the sacrifice, the more precious the gift that was brought. For the most solemn sacrifices people brought animals. The blood of the animal was seen as the most sacred part of the offering. When the blood of a sacrificial animal was poured on the altar, the life that had come from God was being returned to God. The rest of the offering was burnt so that its smoke would rise to

heaven, to the throne of God. When the sacrifice was an apology for sin, the destruction of the thing that was offered served a second purpose as well. The fact that its owner could no longer use or benefit from it was seen as a form of

(Tracing the Meaning of Sacrifice cont.)

compensation for the sin. As both a gift and a form of compensation offered for an offense, a sacrifice was understood to restore or strengthen the relationship between God and those who offered the sacrifice with sincere hearts.

When the prophet Isaiah spoke of the Suffering Servant he used the language of sacrifice. He described the Suffering Servant as giving "his life as an offering for sin" (Is 53:10). Isaiah said that the sins of the people had created a gulf between them and God (see Is 59:2, *New Jerusalem* translation). This gulf kept growing no matter how many sacrifices were offered because human gifts to God are always incomplete. We always hold something of ourselves back. Each time the people of Israel offered a sacrifice to God they held something back, therefore their relationship with God was not fully restored. There was a distance between them and God which grew greater with each sin and each imperfect sacrifice. Only a perfect sacrifice, a life truly given with nothing held back, could restore the broken relationship completely.

All four of the gospels report that Jesus used the Passover to insitute the Eucharist, saying, "This is my body, which is given for you. Do this in remembrance of me." And, after the meal, "This cup is the New Covenant in my Blood, that will be poured out for you" (Lk 22:19-20). It was through this action that Christ gave the Passover its ultimate meaning and anticipated the final Passover of the Church in the glory of his kingdom.

In the Eucharist, we both remember and proclaim the great works God has done for us. The events of our salvation become present and actual. In the Eucharist, Christ is now carrying out his sacrifice of the cross. The Eucharist is a sacrifice because in it Christ gives us the very body he gave up on the cross, and the very blood which he "poured out for the forgiveness of sins" (Mt 26:28)

The sacrifice of Christ on the cross and the sacrifice of Eucharist are one single sacrifice. as the Council of Trent taught: "the victim is one and the same: the same now offers through the ministry of priests, who then offered himself on the cross, on the manner of offering is different."

Jesus continues to offer the sacrifice of himself in the bread and wine each time the Eucharist is offered by bishops and priests ordained in the sacrament of Holy Orders. Each Eucharist is not a new sacrifice. Rather, each Eucharist is the presence in our midst of the *one eternal sacrifice* which Jesus made on the cross more than two thousand years ago. As the Catechism explains:

> In order to leave them a pledge of this love, in order to never depart from his own and make them sharers in his Passover, he instituted as the Eucharist as the memorial of his death and Resurrection, and commanded his apostles to celebrate it until his return; "thereby he constituted them priests of the New Testament" (1337).

Another word for sacrifice in the Jewish tradition is holocaust. Look up and report on the origins of that word.

The Eucharist is one way God makes us holy and shares his life with us. The Eucharist is a sacrifice instituted by the Lord at the Last Supper. It re-presents (makes present) Christ's sacrifice on the cross. The shedding of Christ's blood on the cross was the supreme sign of his love for us. In re-presenting the sacrifice of the cross, the Mass is the action that makes us holy and pleasing to God.

The Eucharist is a sacrifice of praise and thanksgiving for the work of creation. The eucharistic sacrifice thanks God for all he has accomplished through creation, redemption, and sanctification. The Eucharist also praises God in the name of all creation. This sacrifice of praise can only be made through Christ. Christ unites us to his praise and to his intercession so that the sacrifice of praise to the Father is offered *through* Christ and *with* him, and through the work of the Holy Spirit is accepted *in* Christ.

The Eucharist also makes Christ's sacrifice on the cross present, memorializing it and applying its fruits to the members of the Church. The same Christ who died for our sins is the one who continues to offer the Eucharist in an unbloody manner.

A Sacrifice of the Church

As the sacrifice of Christ and the sacrifice of the Eucharist are now one single sacrifice. Christ intended for this to be so. As the Council of Trent taught,

> *Because his priesthood was not to end with his death, at the Last Supper . . . he wanted to leave . . . the Church a visible sacrifice (as the nature of man demands) by which the bloody sacrifice which he was to accomplish once for all on the cross would be re-presented, its memory perpetuated until the end of the world, and its salutary power be applied to the forgiveness of the sins we daily commit (DS, 1743).*

The Eucharist is also the sacrifice of the entire Church. In the Eucharist, our praise, sufferings, prayer, and work are united with Christ and his total offering so that they take on new meaning and value. The Eucharist makes it possible for all generations of Christians to be united with his offering.

The whole Church is really united with the sacrifice of Christ. That is why the Eucharistic prayer always contains an aspect of intercession. We pray for:

Eucharistic Prayer I, the Roman canon, lists two specific times when the Church pauses to pray for the living and the dead. Locate these. Reflect on a person living and a person dead whom you will pray for the next time you participate at Eucharist.

- the Pope, who is a sign and servant of the Church's universal unity;
- the bishop, who is responsible for the Eucharist in his diocese, even when a priest is the presider;
- priests and deacons—the clergy—are remembered with their bishop;
- the faithful, especially the dead, are remembered.

Through the ministry of the priest the spiritual sacrifice of the entire Church is united with the sacrifice of Christ, which is "offered through the priests' hands in the name of the whole Church in an unbloody and sacramental manner until the Lord himself comes" (*Presbyterorum ordinis* 2 § 4).

Also, Christ's sacrificial offering is made for those already in heaven. The Church offers the Eucharist in communion with Mary and all the saints. The eucharistic sacrifice is also for the faithful who have died but who are not wholly purified. Prior to her death, St. Monica asked her son, St. Augustine, not to worry about where her body would be buried. Rather, she only wanted him to pray for her at Mass. She said to him, "Put this body anywhere! Don't trouble yourselves about it! I simply ask you to remember me at the Lord's altar wherever you are." The Church offers the sacrifice of the Mass for all so that the light and peace of Christ might fully embrace them.

The Eucharist Is a Sacred Family Meal–The Lord's Supper

The Mass is both a sacrifice and "the sacred banquet of communion with the Lord's body and blood" (*CCC*, 1382). The altar itself represents the two aspects of the same mystery: it is both an altar of sacrifice and the table of the Lord.

Jesus instituted the Eucharist in the context of a Jewish ritual meal. Because of its context within a meal, the Eucharist is both a sacrament of self-giving love and sacrifice, and also a sacrament of fellowship and of mutual exchange. When we examine all of the dynamics of people eating together we gain a better understanding of the meaning of the Eucharist.

Every Jewish meal in Jesus' time was a religious event which began and ended with a grace. The grace before meals involved a ritual with bread and a short prayer blessing the Creator. The grace after meals involved a ritual with wine and a prayer of blessing, thanksgiving, and petition. The Jewish people of Jesus' day saw their dependence upon food as a reminder of their dependence upon God. In the meal they recognized that they had been blessed. They then returned a blessing to God and were in turn blessed again. As they blessed God, God's life-giving love descended upon their table and upon their lives.

The following story, told by a man named Richard, illustrates the ritual significance of a meal that goes far beyond mere physical nourishment:

It was a sunny, late spring afternoon. The park was full of flowers and there was a light wind keeping the pollution at bay. You couldn't have asked for more perfect weather for a day trip to New York. Pat and I were having a great time. We spent the morning at the Metropolitan Museum of Art. Then we bought food for a fancy picnic lunch in Central Park.

We found a beautiful somewhat secluded place in the park and spread out our tablecloth. We each had a gourmet sandwich, one of those frothy, fruity drinks you can buy from a street vendor, and a slice of pie for dessert. I had just taken the first bite of my sandwich. It was delicious! A good pastrami sandwich is one of those things you need to go to New York for. I was about to take a second bite when a man who obviously lived on the streets came walking towards us. I was prepared to give him some change so that he would go away and leave us alone, but he didn't ask for any money. Instead he sat down across from me and pointed at my sandwich, "That looks delicious, could I have just a bite?"

What was I going to do? I pushed the sandwich toward him and told him to take the whole thing. I would go buy another as soon as this guy was gone. But he didn't leave.

"That's very kind of you," he said, "But I don't want to take all your food. I'll just take half." Then he proceeded to take my sandwich in his incredibly dirty hands and break it in two. He pushed one half back at me.

"That's okay," I said, "you need it more than I do." I tried to give him the second half, but he refused it.

"I wouldn't feel right eating in front of you. There's enough here for both of us."

I was thinking, "You don't have to eat in front of me. You could just take the sandwich and go away!" But he didn't go away. He sat with us and he ate. And he kept trying to get me to eat my half. Finally I took a bite. I was trying to do what Jesus would do. But I think I failed. I found it hard to swallow.

Meanwhile, Pat was eating her lunch, trying to behave as if this was perfectly normal. She had just taken the first bite of her pie when our guest asked, "Could I just have a bite of that pie? It looks mighty tasty." She passed him the whole plate; but he took three or four bites and then handed it back to her. She insisted that she really wasn't all that hungry and he should have it.

Name several meal rituals you have with your family. Name other rituals you have when you share a meal with friends.
What would you have done if you were in Richard's and Pat's situation?

Eucharist

What do you think St. Paul would say about our celebration of Eucharist today?

But he refused. "No thank you, Miss. I've appreciated your hospitality and I wouldn't want to take advantage of it."

After about five more minutes Pat and I looked at each other and then both of us started to make excuses for why we had to leave. But then we were hit with a dilemma—what to do with the food we hadn't eaten? There was no way we were going to eat it ourselves; but on the other hand to throw it out when this man obviously needed it would be an insult. Finally Pat just picked it up and set it on a nearby picnic bench. Then she folded up the tablecloth and we walked away as quickly as we could.

I have to admit, I felt like we had been given some sort of test of faith and had failed miserably.

How does this story give us new insight into the meaning of sharing the eucharistic meal? In the early Church the Eucharist was accompanied by a larger shared meal. In his first letter to the Corinthians (11:17-22), St. Paul chastised the community because the rich were sharing the Eucharist with the poor, but not sharing the rest of their food. If they were willing to share the body and blood of Christ, the most delicious and most nourishing food in the world, how could they not share everything else? If they were unwilling to share everything else it would seem that they had not really recognized the Eucharist for what it was. Their self-ishness was making a mockery of their faith.

The Church today must ask the same questions that Paul asked the Corinthians. How well do we understand the requirements that Eucharist calls us to in serving the needs of others?

The Eucharist Is a Holy Communion

At the church you attend, how is the Eucharist a sign of unity? What can be done to strengthen the unity of your parish community, both at Eucharist and outside of Eucharist?

In the early Church the Eucharist and the unity of the Christian community were understood as two parts of the same mystery. When he wrote to the Corinthians, Paul easily shifted between writing about the body of Christ as community and the body of Christ as Eucharist (see 1 Cor 11:17-33 and 12:12 ff). In the *Didache* we find this same connection in the prayer spoken by the priest over the bread:

*Even as this broken bread was scattered over the hill, and was gathered togeth-er becoming one, so let your Church be gathered together from the ends of the earth into your kingdom (*Didache, Chapter 14).

And Jesus himself said,

If you bring your gift to the altar, and there recall that your brother has any-thing against you, leave your gift there at the altar, go first and be reconciled with your brother, and then come and offer your gift (Mt 5:23-24).

The Eucharist is the sign and source of our unity. If there is anything which interferes in a significant way with that unity, it should be dealt with before we share the Eucharist. If it is not, we will be receiving the Eucharist unworthily. If there are obstacles to unity which we have no intention of removing, the pledge of unity which we make in the Eucharist will be a lie. Note that this is the reason the Catholic Church does not welcome non-Catholics to share the Eucharist with us except in very unusual circumstances. Until we are ready and able to heal the divisions between our denominations we will not be ready to share the sacrament of unity with one another.

In the early Church the Eucharist was seen as the most significant sign of the unity of the Christian community. Each Sunday, all of the Christians in a particular region would gather together for a single celebration of the Eucharist, presided at by the bishop. As the number of Christians under the care of each bishop grew, there was a need for more eucharistic services. These were presided over by priests who were understood as the bishop's surrogates.

As a sign that these separate celebrations were all part of the one celebration presided over by the bishop, the bishop would send a piece of the consecrated bread from the Mass at which he presided to each of the other churches within his region. The piece of eucharistic bread was dropped into the chalice. The Church continues this practice today as a sign of unity and a reminder of this ancient ceremony. It is also a reminder of the unity of the entire Church. The naming of the pope and the local bishop during the eucharistic prayer is also a sign of the unity of the universal Church.

Through the Eucharist we are united with those who have already joined Christ in heaven. The naming of the communion of saints in the eucharistic prayer is a reminder of this. When we eat the body and blood of Christ we are given a share in the intimate communion of the Trinity. Through the Eucharist, as through the gift of the Holy Spirit, Jesus fulfills the promise which he made to his disciples when he said, "On that day you will realize that I am in my Father and you are in me and I in you" (Jn 14:20).

Amen

The following is an excerpt from a sermon given by St. Augustine:

If you are the body of Christ and its members, it is the sacrament of what you are which is placed on the Lord's table: it is the sacrament of what you are which you receive. It is to what you are that you respond Amen. *This response is your signature. You hear: "Body of Christ." You respond: "Amen!" Be a member of the body of Christ so that your Amen may be true* (Sermo 272. PL38, 1247).

Use an artistic medium to describe your version of the kingdom of God. Draw, paint, write, or photograph a scene with your image of God's eternal kingdom.

The Eucharist Is Heaven on Earth

The Church calls the Eucharist a foretaste of the heavenly banquet (see *CCC*, 1090). In a sense it is the *hors d'oeuvres* before the main course. Just as *hors d'oeuvres* are small tastes intended to whet our appetite for the main course and sustain us until it comes, so the Eucharist is a small taste intended to whet our appetite for, and sustain us until, the feast of heaven. When we share in the Eucharist we participate in the heavenly banquet at which Christ is presiding. However, our participation is not yet the full participation of heaven. In the Eucharist we must experience the banquet through the signs of bread and wine. In heaven we will experience the banquet directly.

Jesus used images of feasts—particularly of a wedding feast—when he spoke about the kingdom of God. Regarding the Eucharist, Jesus said, "Whoever eats my flesh and drinks my blood has eternal life" (Jn 6:54). Eternal life is a future concept, something that belongs with heaven. But Jesus speaks in the present tense. The one who participates in the Eucharist already *has* eternal life. In the Eucharist the future and the present are the same. In the Eucharist God's great feast has begun.

Old Testament biblical tradition also used the image of a meal to talk about the day when the Messiah would come in triumph. The words of the prophet Isaiah expressed this most clearly when he described what would happen in the messianic age:

> *On this mountain the Lord of hosts will provide for all peoples a feast of rich food and choice wines, juicy, rich food and pure, choice wines.*
>
> *On this mountain he will destroy the veil that veils all peoples, the web that is woven over all nations; he will destroy death forever (Is 25:6-7).*

Historical Development of the Liturgy of the Eucharist

The ritual Jewish meal of Jesus' time was a model for the Eucharist. For example, the prayer which is spoken over the bread at a Jewish ritual meal is: "Blessed are you, Lord our God, King of the universe, you who have brought bread forth from the earth." Much of Jesus' ministry in the Gospels took place in the context of a meal where this blessing would have been offered. This blessing is the origin of the prayer which the priest speaks over the bread during the offertory:

> *Blessed are you, Lord, God of all creation.*
> *Through your goodness we have this bread to offer,*
> *which earth has given and human hands have made.*
> *It will become for us the bread of life.*

When the early Christian community celebrated the Eucharist, they did what Jesus did at the Last Supper. According to all of the New Testament accounts of the Eucharist Jesus followed the basic format of the Jewish meal:

1) taking the bread

2) speaking the prayer of blessing

3) breaking the bread

4) distributing the bread to those who were gathered

5) taking the cup

6) offering the prayer of blessing

7) sharing the cup with those who were present

All subsequent liturgies were built around these seven actions.

Justin Martyr (ca. AD 155) wrote the first surviving outline of the Mass. It began with a liturgy of the Word, the sharing of readings from the memoirs of the apostles (New Testament) or the writings of the prophets (Old Testament). These readings, which at times were quite lengthy, were followed by a sermon. After the sermon everyone stood for the prayers of the faithful. The prayers were followed by the kiss of peace. Then the people brought forward the bread and wine (and water on the occasion of baptism) which they had brought from home. The presider (bishop or priest) accepted these gifts and offered prayers of thanksgiving "at some length." When he finished praying the congregation gave their assent by saying, "Amen," the Hebrew for "so be it." The deacons were then called forward to distribute the consecrated elements to all who were present. Justin makes it clear that the bread and wine were no longer "common bread or common drink." He writes,

> *just as our Savior Jesus Christ . . . took flesh and blood for our salvation, so too we have been taught that the food over which thanks have been given by a word of prayer which is from him . . . is both the flesh and blood of that incarnate Jesus (Justin Martyr, First Apology).*

Many of the prayers which we use today at Eucharist date back to the time of Justin Martyr. The introductory dialogue of the liturgy of the Eucharist (e.g., "The Lord be with you. And also with you. Lift up your hearts. We lift them up to the Lord . . .") is all found in Justin's account.

The Apostolic Tradition, generally believed to have been written by Hippolytus around 215, outlines prayers and an order of worship that are even closer to today's liturgical style. Other eucharistic rites from the third century and early fourth century reflect the same basic structure. The only structural difference between the third century liturgy of the Eucharist and today's is that the liturgy

Research the form and ritual of the Jewish seder. Compare like elements with the Eucharist.

Justin Martyr was a Christian apologist, born about AD 100. He converted to Christianity about AD 130. He was martyred in Asia Minor about 165.

of the third century does not include the *Sanctus* ("Holy, holy") or the preface (the prayer which precedes the account of Christ's saving work). Both of these prayers entered the liturgy in the fourth century. Although the basic form of the liturgy was the same in most places in the early Church, the specific words of the prayers varied considerably from place to place.

The Celebration of the Eucharist Today

The *Catechism of the Catholic Church* says:

> The liturgy of the Eucharist unfolds according to a fundamental structure which has been preserved throughout the centuries down to our own day. It displays two great parts that form a fundamental unity:
>
> • the gathering, the liturgy of the Word, *with readings, homily, and general intercessions;*
> • the liturgy of the Eucharist, *with the presentation of the bread and wine, the consecratory thanksgiving, and communion.*

The liturgy of the Word and the liturgy of the Eucharist together form "one single act of worship;" the Eucharistic table set for us is the table both of the Word of God and of the Body of the Lord (1346).

Gathering Rites: The celebration of Eucharist begins as Christians come together in one place. Christ is at the head of the assembly, and he is the one who presides over every Eucharistic celebration. The bishop or priest acts *in the person of Christ the head,* presiding over the assembly, speaking after the readings, receiving the offerings, and saying the Eucharistic Prayer. Because Christ has chosen to act through his apostles and their successors, the presence of a bishop or priest is necessary for a valid eucharistic liturgy.

Once the people, including the priest, have gathered they take some time to prepare themselves to encounter the Lord. With one voice they offer prayers of praise, confession, and repentance. The gathering rites help people move from acting and praying as scattered individuals to acting and praying as a unified community.

The *Liturgy of the Word* follows the gathering rites. During the Liturgy of the Word, God speaks three times and the community responds three times. First we hear the word of God in the Old Testament (or in the book of Acts during the Easter season) and we respond with a psalm. Then we hear the word of God in the epistles. Finally we sing the "Alleluia," hear the word of God in the gospel, and we respond with the prayers of the faithful. Between the gospel and the prayers of the faithful the priest (or deacon) gives a homily. The purpose of the homily is to encourage the assembly *to accept* the Scripture readings as the Word of God and *to put* them into practice. The prayers of the faithful are the first step in accepting and acting on what we heard.

The *presentation of the offerings* (Offertory) follows the Liturgy of the Word. The bread and wine which we offer are both the gift of God and the work of human hands that cultivated them. We offer them to God as a sign of our gratitude for creation and as a sign of our desire to offer ourselves. When we bring them forward we are putting them and all that they represent into Christ's hands. He will take them just as he took the bread and wine at the Last Supper, and he will join them to his own sacrifice on the cross so that they will be perfected.

In Jesus' time the Jews had a practice of distributing a "bread of the poor" for the needy in their community. The early Christians continued this practice. When they brought the bread and wine for the Eucharist they also brought food to share with the poor. Beginning in the eleventh century the food was replaced with gifts of money.

The *Eucharistic Prayer* (also called the *anaphora*) is the heart and summit of the Mass. The eucharistic prayer is the prayer of thanksgiving and consecration. The prayer begins with the *preface* during which the Church gives thanks to the Father,

Look at the readings from a recent Sunday. What is the common theme between the first reading and the gospel? What is an important message of the second reading?
Read Eucharistic Prayer I, the Roman canon. Identify and name the exact wording of the preface, epiclesis, and anamnesis.

through Christ, in the Holy Spirit, for all his works: creation, redemption, and sanctification. The preface ends with the *Sanctus* (Holy, holy . . .), the unending hymn of praise of the angels and all the Church in heaven.

The *epiclesis* is the next part of the eucharistic prayer. The Church asks the Father to send the Holy Spirit onto the bread and wine. Through the power of the Spirit the bread and wine become the body and blood of Christ and those who receive them become one body and one spirit. The priest holds his hands palms down over the gift of bread and wine. The epiclesis is followed by the *institution narrative*. During the institution narrative the priest gives Christ his voice and his hands (see *Mediator Dei*, #69). The priest does not act out what Christ did. Instead he allows Christ to act through him. By the power of the words and actions of Christ and the power of the Holy Spirit, Christ's body and blood—his sacrifice offered on the cross—are made present.

The *anamnesis* follows the narrative of institution. The word "anamnesis" refers to active remembering, bringing the present into intimate contact with the past. During the anamnesis the Church calls to mind Christ's passion, death, and resurrection and his return in glory. The memorial acclamation is part of the anamnesis.

The offering follows next. After the Church recalls—and thereby makes present—what Christ has done, she offers his sacrifice to the Father. This offering is followed by intercessions (prayers) for the pastors of the Church and all the faithful both living and dead. The intercessions are a sign of the unity of the Church throughout the world and of the unity of the Church on earth and in heaven.

The eucharistic prayer concludes with a *doxology*, a prayer of praise.

> *Through him, with him, in him, in the unity of the Holy Spirit, all glory and honor is yours almighty Father for ever and ever.*

The congregation responds with the *great Amen*. This "Amen" is our response to and affirmation of the entire eucharistic prayer.

The last major portion of the liturgy of the eucharist is the *communion rite*. As the *Catechism* points out:

> *The faithful receive "the bread of heaven" and "the cup of salvation," the body and blood of Christ who offered himself "for the life of the world" (1355).*

Nourished by the body and blood of Christ the congregation is then sent out into the world to be Christ for others.

The Eucharist Sends Us Into the World

The word "Mass" comes from the Latin word for dismissal. In a sense, the aim of the Eucharist is to dismiss us, to send us out to be Christ for the world. The Eucharist does for our spiritual selves what ordinary food does for our bodies. It nourishes us and strengthens us so that we can live and so that we can do the other things we want and need to do. The Eucharist accomplishes this by deepening our union with Jesus. As Jesus himself said, "Whoever eats my flesh and drinks my blood remains in me and I in him" (Jn 6:56). When we are united with Jesus we are able to do God's will in the world.

Because the Eucharist unites us with Jesus, it separates us from sin. Sin causes and is caused by distance from God. When we were baptized all of our sins were washed away. Any distance between God and us was overcome and we were united with God. Over time, however, our own weakness causes us to drift away from God again, and the farther we drift the greater our tendency to sin.

The Eucharist continually draws us back to God. It fills us with Jesus' own love. By filling us with divine love, the Eucharist wipes away venial sin (*CCC*, 1394). Venial sins are those sins which weaken our love for God and for one another but which do not rupture or destroy that love. When we open our hearts to the love which is given to us in the Eucharist the weaknesses in our own ability to love are eliminated. The Eucharist also preserves us from future mortal sins—those sins which actually destroy love and break our relationship with God or with God's people. The mortal sins that we do commit need the sacrament of Reconciliation for healing.

The Eucharist sends us out into the world ready to love more completely. What is more, it sends us out not only as loving individuals, but also as a loving community. The Eucharist strengthens the bonds between all who receive and makes it possible for us to demonstrate among ourselves the love which we are to share with the world. The Eucharist makes us one body in Christ. When we recognize that we are one body, we will care for each other and the world will see what it means to be a disciple of Christ (see Jn 13:35). When we eat and drink the Eucharist without recognizing the body of Christ that we are both eating and becoming, we "eat and drink judgment upon [ourselves]" (1 Cor 11:29).

Finally, the Eucharist sends us out into the world to care for those who are most in need. Because we have received so much in the Eucharist we are expected also to give. As the *Didache* instructed the early Christians:

> Do not hesitate to give, nor complain when you give. . . . Do not turn away from him who is in want; rather, share all things with your brother, and do not say that they are your own. For if you are partakers in that which is immortal, how much more in things which are mortal?

Tell a way the Eucharist inspires your parish community to go out and serve those in need. How have you been inspired by the Eucharist to serve others?

How seriously do you keep the communion fast? What is your opinion of proper dress for men and women at Sunday Mass? What are some clothing items that you consider inappropriate?

Or as St. John Chrysostom put it:

> *You dishonor this [Eucharistic] table when you do not judge worthy of sharing your food someone judged worthy to take part in this meal. . . . God freed you from all your sins and invited you here, but you have not become more merciful"* (Chapter 4).

The Eucharist Requires Preparation

As with all the sacraments, the Eucharist imparts grace every time it is celebrated and every time it is received. This grace can only bear fruit, however, if those who receive it are properly prepared to act upon it and to allow it to shape their lives. In other words, although the Eucharist always gives us the ability to love more deeply and serve more generously, we must choose to use this ability. In order to prepare ourselves to receive the Eucharist we need to take time to reflect upon the current state of our relationship with God. We need to turn to God with love and ask him to fill us with an even deeper love. If we are aware of any mortal sin which we have committed we must receive the sacrament of Reconciliation before receiving communion.

Because we are physical as well as spiritual people, we must prepare for communion physically as well as spiritually. We are called to observe a period of fast before communion in order to allow ourselves to develop a hunger for it. In the United States this fast is one hour. We should also prepare ourselves physically as we would for any other important event. The Church challenges us to pay attention to our gestures, posture, and clothing so that we are saying with our bodies what we wish to be saying with our hearts.

All those who have prepared themselves to receive the body and blood of Christ into their hearts and lives as well as into their body are encouraged to receive communion each time they participate in the Mass. And in fact, Catholics are obliged to participate in the liturgy on Sundays and Holy Days of Obligation. They are also required to receive the Eucharist at least once a year, if possible during the Easter season (*CCC*, 1389).

The Eucharist Is the Pledge of Our Future Glory

At the Last Supper, Jesus told his disciples to look forward to the coming glory of God's kingdom. He said: "I shall not drink again the fruit of the vine until the day when I drink it new in the kingdom of God" (Mk 14:25). The Church never forgets this promise of Jesus' whenever Eucharist is celebrated. In prayer, the Church calls for Jesus' coming: "*Marana tha,*" which means, "Come, Lord Jesus!"

Jesus comes to the Church at Eucharist and is in our midst. However, his presence is veiled. Therefore the Church celebrates the Eucharist while awaiting Jesus' coming. In the Eucharist, we have a foretaste of heaven, and long for eternal life when we will be with the Church, Mary, and all the saints in heaven.

St. Pius X loved the Eucharist and encouraged the frequent reception of Holy Communion. He said,

> *Holy Communion is the shortest and safest way to heaven. There are others: innocence, but that is for little children; penance, but we are afraid of it; generous endurance of trials of life, but when they come we weep and ask to be spared. The surest, easiest, shortest way is the Eucharist.*

Do you agree with St. Pius X's words about frequent reception of Holy Communion? Why or why not?

Names for the Sacrament

The sacrament of Eucharist is expressed by many different names. It is called Eucharist because it is an action of thanksgiving to God. Each of these other names tells more about its meaning. Some of these names are:

- The *Lord's Supper* because of its connection with the Last Supper.
- The *Breaking of Bread* because Jesus used this ancient Jewish rite at the Last Supper. Also, it was in this action that Jesus' disciples recognized him after his resurrection.
- The *Eucharistic assembly* because the Eucharist is celebrated with the Church.
- The *memorial* because it remembers Christ's passion and resurrection.
- The *Holy Sacrifice* because it makes present the one sacrifice of Christ and includes the Church's offering.
- The *Holy and Divine Liturgy* because the Church's entire liturgy is centered in the celebration of this sacrament. In the same sense, it is also called the celebration of the *Sacred Mysteries*.
- *Holy Communion* because in this sacrament we united ourselves to Christ.
- *Holy Mass* because the liturgy concludes with our "sending forth" so that we can fulfill God's will in our daily lives.

Chapter 5
Review Questions

1. What act most clearly expresses how God enters our lives in Eucharist?

2. Why does the Church call the Eucharist the sacrament which completes Christian initiation?

3. How is the Eucharist a prayer of blessing?

4. What does the word *eucharist* mean?

5. How is memory an important part of the renewal of God's covenant in Eucharist?

6. Define *covenant*.

7. Explain how Jesus' presence at Eucharist can be described by the words *transubstantiation*, *accidents*, and *substance*.

8. In Jewish understanding, what was a sacrifice intended to do?

9. Is the sacrifice of Eucharist the same sacrifice as the one which Jesus made on the cross or a re-enactment of the crucifixion?

10. What did St. Paul say to the Christians at Corinth about their behavior at Eucharist?

11. What are two ways to understand Christian unity through the Eucharist?

12. Who are we united with at Eucharist?

13. How is the Eucharist the foretaste of the heavenly banquet?

14. On what is the ritual of the eucharistic meal modeled?

15. What are the two main parts of the Eucharist?

16. Define *anaphora*, *epiclesis*, and *anamnesis*.

17. What are the origins of the term "Mass"?

18. What are some requirements for participation in Eucharist?

19. Write at least three other names for the sacrament of Eucharist.

Endnotes

1.   Not her real name.

Penance

6

"Pray for Me" – A Story of Conversion

Three years ago Cameron came to the university from a small Catholic high school. He was one of those kids who chose college because he didn't know what else to do, and because college was the one place where his parents would still support him financially. He didn't want to be there and he had no intention of putting in any effort. Early in his freshman year Cameron started hanging around the Catholic Student Center, where he felt comfortable shooting the breeze with one of the staff members. John was a campus minister there.

John remembered those days well; most of the staff had tried to avoid Cameron as much as possible because Cameron only liked to talk about one issue—the horrible state of the world in general and how his life "sucked."

What are some other perplexing questions you have about life, God, evil, or suffering?

Share a time when you felt hopeful, even when the situation seemed dire.

Everything was bad now, and it was likely to get worse, according to Cameron. One thing everyone had learned quickly was never to ask Cameron how things were going unless they had the time and the energy to listen to at least half an hour of self-absorbed complaining.

Then something happened. Every spring the Catholic Student Center ran a weekend retreat. One afternoon about a week before the retreat, John was trying to talk several students into attending when Cameron came into the student lounge. John was trapped. He did not really want to invite Cameron to come along, but to do anything else would have been both unprofessional and unchari-table. So he asked and Cameron said he would come.

Cameron rode in John's car on the way to the retreat center. John was sure that by the time they arrived, the other two students who were also in the car were really regretting their decision to come. Cameron had complained about one thing after another for most of the drive.

The retreat began with a series of purposely silly activities aimed at helping students get to know each other. These were followed by the first talk of the weekend. A senior shared her faith story and spoke about listening for God's call. After her talk the students broke into small groups to discuss what it meant to be called by God. Then they all gathered together again for a time of prayer. The prayer time ended with the song that included lyrics "This is holy ground. You're standing on holy ground." John noticed that Cameron sat quietly for a long time after the song ended.

The following day three more students shared their faith stories. They reflected on faith, love, and forgiveness. In the evening there was a communal service of reconciliation. Father Mark gave a homily on God's promise to break our hearts of stone and give us hearts of flesh. When he finished speaking all of the students were invited to take time to pray in silence. Then those who want-ed to could receive the sacrament of reconciliation from Father Mark or Father Tom. John and two of the other non-ordained campus ministers were available for those students who wanted to talk but were not yet ready to receive the sacrament.

The room in which they held the service was filled with candles and quiet music was playing in the background. As the students prayed quietly, John prayed for them. He looked up in the middle of his prayers and noticed that Cameron was wiping his eyes. Cameron looked up at the same moment and saw John. He stood up and walked over. John thought he was probably embarrassed about the tears. He prepared himself for some kind of snide remark. But Cameron just sat down and said, "Pray for me. I need to change. I'm tired of being so negative and uptight." Then, before John could say anything, Cameron stood up again and walked away. A few minutes later he went to talk with Father Mark.

John prayed. He prayed that the Holy Spirit would fill Cameron's heart with faith, hope, and love. He prayed that God would wipe away Cameron's tears. He prayed that Cameron would find the ability to change. And he prayed that God would forgive him, John, for having wanted to leave Cameron behind.

John never knew what Cameron said to Father Mark or what Father Mark said to him. But during the last session of the retreat when the students were invited to talk about their experience, Cameron expressed thanks for the chance to "start again."

God has not chosen to remove all pain and sorrow from our world. He has not chosen to eliminate sin and its consequences. But he has refused to allow pain, sorrow, or sin to destroy what he has made. In the midst of negativity, sin, and evil God continually creates a path of love and he invites us to walk that path. Through the gift of the sacrament of Penance God makes it possible for us to recognize and turn away from sin, and draw closer to him in the process. There is an old story which says that each one of us is connected to God by a string. When we sin, we cut the string. When we seek forgiveness, God ties a knot in the string. Each time he ties a knot, the string gets shorter and we are drawn closer to God. Rather than taking away our freedom to choose, God has made it possible for us to turn even our worst choices into good.

When Cameron started college he was a selfish, angry, and despairing person. While he was on the student retreat he saw himself as he was and heard God's call to change. He turned toward God, and when he did, God used those things which had been negative to create something positive. Cameron had developed the habit of responding to everything with negative comments. Over time he replaced those comments with positive ones. In one sense Cameron changed completely, in another he did not change at all; he just found a new focus for his energy.

God did not take away all of the things that formed Cameron's personality. He still liked to talk. But from Cameron's brokenness God focused on Cameron's strengths. It was in talking and sharing that the wheels of forgiveness were put in motion.

It is important to remember that the sacrament of Penance is a sacrament of relationships. Sin wounds or breaks our relationship with God and with one another. When God helps us to overcome sin, he gives us what we need to repair those broken relationships. This has two important implications.

First, the sacrament of Penance involves a conversion process which takes time. Human relationships are not formed or healed in an instant. The sacrament of Penance involves more than a few minutes in a confessional.

Second, God does not turn our brokenness into strength for our sake alone. God uses individual brokenness to create strength within our relationships and strength within our community. God does not necessarily take away the things in our lives that led us to sin in the first place.

While God does not take away our freedom and force us to change he does continually call us to change. And, God does make it possible for us to change when we turn to him. God remains with us even when the darkness and hopelessness surround us, as the following poem expresses:

Write a short essay or journal entry describing a personal conversion experience or the conversion of another person whom you know.

I believe,
I believe in the sun,
even when it is not shining.
I believe in love
even when feeling it not.
I believe in God
even when God is silent.[1]

That poem was written on the wall in a cellar in Germany where Jews hid from the Nazis during the Second World War. In the midst of horrible brokenness, God blew a breath of hope which gave strength to the author of this poem. In the same way, the sacrament of Penance is also a breath of hope blown into the midst of a broken world. In the midst of sin, violence, hate, and suffering it can be difficult to see God's presence. The very existence of the sacrament of Penance assures us that no matter what happens in the world, God will not allow sin and evil to have the final word.

Conversion and the Story of the Prodigal Son

The term *conversion* indicates a radical reorientation of your life away from sin and evil, and toward God. Conversion is the central element of Jesus' preaching: "Repent, and believe in the gospel" (Mk 1:14), he said at the beginning of his ministry. Conversion is also a main element of the Church's ministry of evangelization ("preaching the gospel") and of the sacrament of Penance. In fact, the sacrament is called the "sacrament of conversion" because it makes Jesus' call to conversion sacramentally present. The sacrament of Penance can be the first step in returning to God our loving Father when we have strayed from him due to sin.

Conversion is illustrated in Jesus' parable of the prodigal son (Lk 15:11-32). When the younger son longed for the life that he had forsaken, he began the process of conversion. Reunion with his father became his goal. He said to himself,

I shall get up and go to my father and I shall say to him, "Father, I have sinned against heaven and against you. I no longer deserve to be called your son; treat me as you would treat one of your hired workers" (vv.18-19).

The process of conversion begins with a loathing for the place to which our sin has brought us or is bringing us. If we like where we are, if we are attached to the things which our sinfulness gives us, we will find it difficult or impossible to be converted. The prodigal son did not hear the call to conversion when he still

The reconciliation process is made up of an examination of conscience, contrition (sorrow), confession of sins, a commitment to change (accepting penance), forgiveness, and absolution. Read Jesus' famous parable of the Prodigal Son in Luke 15:11-32. How is each part of the reconciliation process present in the parable?

had lots of money and lots of friends. He liked where he was and he never took the time to think about where he was going. His choices were taking him to the pig sty; but he didn't notice.

The process of conversion also entails comparing our lives to the life of Christ. We must ask ourselves if our lives are directed toward complete union with God as Jesus' life was, or if our lives are directed toward some other goal. If we answer "some other goal," then we should think about the implications for ourselves and for those around us. What are we losing as we pursue that goal? Are we losing our ability to love and to accept love? Are we losing our ability to hope if things do not go our way? Are we losing our faith that God works good in all things? Are we losing our ability to cope with those things which we cannot control?

St. Paul tells us that there are only three things which really matter in the long run, even when everything else is taken away. Those three things are faith, hope, and love (1 Cor 13:13). When we direct our lives towards something other than God, we weaken or abandon our faith, our hope, and our love. When time takes away everything else, we will be left with nothing. We will be like the prodigal son on the pig farm:

And he longed to eat his fill of the pods on which the swine fed, but nobody gave him any (Lk 15:16).

When we loathe the emptiness in our lives or the emptiness looming ahead, when we long for the sense of purpose and joy which only God can give, we have taken the first step toward reconciliation. Part of the wonder of the sacrament of Penance is that God meets us in our emptiness and makes even that emptiness holy.

Ongoing Conversion of the Baptized

Two of the effects of the sacrament of Baptism are forgiveness of our sins and the gift of grace that makes us holy. This is also known as our justification. Baptism is the time and place of our first and main conversion. It is Jesus who calls us to this conversion. St. Peter implored the Jews gathered outside the Upper Room at Pentecost to

Create a poem or a symbolic drawing that depicts the struggle between evil and good.

Repent and be baptized, everyone of you, in the name of Jesus Christ for the forgiveness of your sins; and you will receive the gift of the holy Spirit (Acts 2:38).

Repentance is a change of mind and heart toward God that is reflected by the good words and actions of one's life. And what a gift Baptism is. As you recall from Chapter 3, in Baptism we renounce evil and gain God's gift of salvation, that is, the forgiveness of sins and new and eternal life.

In spite of the great gift of new life we receive in Christian initiation, our inclination to sin (called *concupiscence*) remains. It is the constant struggle of conversion directed towards holiness and eternal life that the Lord continues to call us. This "second conversion" is not only a work of our own lives. Rather, it is the work of our "contrite heart" that is "drawn and moved by grace to respond to the merciful love of God who loved us first" (*CCC*, 1428).

St. Peter, himself, lived a very public example of a second conversion. After Jesus' arrest, Peter three times denied knowing Jesus. When he realized what he had done, Peter "went out and began to weep bitterly" (Lk 22:62). St. Ambrose described these two conversions of Christians, saying, "there are water and tears: the water of Baptism and the tears of repentance."

Interior Conversion

Jesus preached against performing outward signs of penance absent from sincere interior conversion, or conversion of the heart. He said,

> *But take care not to perform righteous deeds in order that people may see them; otherwise, you will have no recompense from your heavenly Father (Mt 6:1).*

Interior conversion accompanied by interior repentance is a radical change of our whole lives, a return to God, an end of sin, a turning away from evil, and a repulsion of any evil we have already committed. It also involves a commitment to change our lives and sin no more, and a deep trust in God's infinite mercy and grace. This interior conversion is first a gift from the Holy Spirit who gives us the grace to return to the Lord and the courage to begin anew.

Acts of outward penance can and do accompany interior conversion. For example, both scripture and Tradition stress the importance of fasting, prayer, and almsgiving in relation to one's self, to God, and to others. Other ways to express interior conversion include reconciling with and praying for one's neighbors, the intercession of the saints, and works of charity.

Conversion is accomplished by:

- gestures of reconciliation;
- concern for the poor;
- the defense of justice and right;
- admitting one's faults;
- fraternal correction;

- changing the course of one's life;
- examining one's conscience;
- accepting spiritual direction;
- enduring suffering and persecution for the sake of righteousness.

The spirit of conversion is continually nourished by frequent participation in the Eucharist, reading the Bible, praying, and participating in the Church's seasons and days of penance (for example, Lent).

Share one practical way you can witness to your interior conversion, or conversion of the heart.

What Is This Sacrament Called?

The sacrament which the *Catechism of the Catholic Church* refers to as the sacrament of Penance is known by many names, each of which focuses on a particular dimension of the sacramental mystery.

- It is called the *sacrament of conversion* because it makes Jesus' call to conversion sacramentally present.
- It is called the *sacrament of penance* because it blesses the repentant sinner's efforts to change through the steps of conversion, penance and satisfaction, and it makes those efforts effective.
- It is called the *sacrament of confession* because the sinner confesses both his or her own sins and the infinite mercy and forgiveness of God.
- It is called the *sacrament of forgiveness*, because through this sacrament God forgives even the most serious sins.
- And it is called the *sacrament of reconciliation* because it fills us with God's reconciling love and restores our relationship with God and with God's people.

Sacramental Forgiveness and Reconciliation

Conversion is a primarily twofold process. First, it entails God's forgiveness of our sins. Only God can forgive sins. Second, our conversion involves reconciliation with the Church. Both of these elements of conversion are expressed and accomplished by the sacrament of Penance. To understand more about this process, we first have to examine the meaning of sin.

As the *Catechism of the Catholic Church* defines, "Sin is before all else an offense against God, a rupture of communion with him" (1440). Sin is an offense against reason, truth, and right conscience; it is a failure in our love for God and neighbor due to a misguided attachment to certain goods.

Sins are named and classified in several different ways. There are many kinds of sins; for example, the sins of the spirit and sins of the flesh listed in the letter

Consider the action of shoplifting. Describe two scenarios: one where shoplifting is a mortal sin, the other where it is not a sin at all.

to the Galatians (5:19-21). Another classification labels sins of thought, word, deed, or omission.

Sins are also distinguished between original sin and personal sin. Personal sin, also called "actual" sin, is any free and deliberate action, word, thought, or desire that turns us away from God and his law of love. A personal sin can weaken our relationship with God (venial sin) or destroy our relationship with him (mortal sin).

Venial sins weaken our love and attach us to created goods rather than God. Examples of venial sins are not praying regularly, making a sarcastic remark, or telling a small lie. While venial sins do not deprive us of sanctifying grace, God's friendship, love, or heaven, they do expose us to more opportunity for mortal sin.

Mortal sin kills our relation to God and others and destroys our capacity for love. Mortal sin results in the loss of love and sanctifying grace. If a person does not repent and receive Christ's forgiveness and dies in the state of mortal sin, he or she will be eternally separated from God, that is, in hell.

For a sin to be considered mortal three conditions must be met:

1. The matter of the sin must be serious. For example, murder, adultery, or any violation of the Ten Commandments is serious.
2. The sinner must be aware of the sinfulness of the act.
3. The decision to sin must be a deliberate and personal choice.

If a person is forced or pressured into doing something which he or she knows is wrong and wishes to avoid, that person is not guilty of a mortal sin. Likewise, if a person sins because of a mental illness, he or she does not bear the same responsibility as a person who is able to avoid sin but chooses not to. Mortal sin sets us in direct opposition to God, the source of love. After the person commits a mortal sin his or her relationship with God needs to be reestablished. The sacrament of Penance is the only sure way of reestablishing our relationship with God.

Who Can Forgive Sins?

When Jesus was preaching in a home in Capernaum, a paralytic was lifted down from the roof before Jesus. Jesus' first words to the paralytic were, "Child, your sins are forgiven." This bothered some of the religious leaders who observed the scene. "Who but God alone can forgive sins?" they asked themselves (see Mk 2:1-12).

The leaders were correct in the observation: Only God forgives sins. What they failed to believe, however, was that Jesus is the Son of God and he is able to exercise this divine power.

Also, by virtue of the authority given to him by God the Father, Jesus is able to give men the power to forgive sins in his name. The Risen Jesus told his disciples,

Receive the holy Spirit. Whose sins you forgive are forgiven them, and whose sins you retain are retained (Jn 21:22-23).

Jesus willed that *the whole Church* through its life and prayer would continue his ministry of forgiveness and reconciliation that he accomplished by his death and resurrection. But he gave the power of absolution ("to pronounce clear of blame or guilt") to the successors of the apostles, bishops and priests. In the sacrament of Penance, the formula for absolution spoken by the bishop or priest proclaims forgiveness for the sinner. In the Latin rite, it reads as follows:

> *God, the Father of mercies,*
> *through the death and the resurrection of his Son*
> *has reconciled the world to himself*
> *and sent the Holy Spirit among us*
> *for the forgiveness of sins;*
> *through the ministry of the Church*
> *may God give you pardon and peace,*
> *and I absolve you from your sins*
> *in the name of the Father, and of the Son, and of the Holy Spirit (*Ordo
> paenitentiae, *46).*

Explain how your call to forgive the sins of others is different from the mandate of priests and bishops to forgive sins.

Reconciling With One Another

In his ministry, Jesus not only forgave the sinner, but he welcomed back the forgiven sinner into the community of the People of God from which the sin had alienated or excluded him. Jesus' parables of the Lost Sheep, Lost Coin, and Prodigal Son (see Lk 15) each describe the rejoicing that accompanies the return to the community of the forgiven sinner.

When Jesus' gave the apostles the power to forgive sins, at the same time he gave them the authority to reconcile sinners with the Church. He said to St. Peter:

> *I will give you the keys to the kingdom of heaven. Whatever you bind on earth shall be bound in heaven; and whatever you loose on earth shall be loosed in heaven (Mt 16:19).*

The words *bind* and *loose* mean that whomever Peter, the apostles, and now the successors of the apostles, the bishops, include or exclude from communion with the Church is also bound or not bound in communion with God. For Christians, reconciliation with the Church is inseparable from reconciliation with God (*CCC,* 1445).

How do you feel when someone forgives you? How do you feel when you forgive someone else? How are the two feelings alike? different?

This does not mean that the Church somehow controls God's love or God's forgiveness. Even though forgiveness is expressed through the Church, recall that God alone can forgive sins. The Church is the body of Christ. Christ is the head. If Christ chooses something, the Church must do it. If Christ reestablishes a relationship with a sinner, then the Church must reestablish that same relationship. The Church is the sign of what God has done, and the instrument through which God acts. Remember that Jesus said, "Receive the holy Spirit." It is the Spirit of God who makes the decision to forgive. The Church simply acts upon that decision.

When Jesus gave the apostles the power to forgive sins, it was as if he designated them as his arms. Now, Christ, the head, makes the decision to embrace the sinner. In order to embrace the sinner he uses his arms, the successors of the apostles. The arms are the instruments of the embrace and the sign of the decision to embrace, but the arms did not make the decision nor do they have the power to change the decision (see *CCC*, 1446).

Each time a priest offers sinners God's forgiveness, he also welcomes them back into the life of the Church. The Church cannot reject anyone whom God has accepted. Thus both the repentant sinner and the Church find new wholeness in the sacrament. Each time the Church celebrates the sacrament of Penance, she becomes more Christ-like. The sacrament makes the Church a loving and forgiving Church. The sacrament also makes the Church truly one as God is one. The *Rite of Penance* makes it clear that the Church is wounded by sin and that through the sacrament of penance and reconciliation the Church renews itself (nos. 7 and 11). The Church is the instrument of God's healing love and mercy. The Church is also the sign of what that love and mercy can do to restore what has been broken.

Practice of the Sacrament of Penance

The practice of the sacrament of Penance began with Christ's institution of the sacrament, through his ministry of forgiveness and especially in his words recorded in John 20:21-23. Christ instituted the sacrament for all members of the Church, especially those who have committed mortal sin and have lost their baptismal grace and wounded the Church community. For these sinners, the sacrament of Penance offers a new chance at conversion as a way to recover the grace of justification. Church father Tertullian described Penance as "the second plank [of salvation] after the shipwreck which is the loss of grace" (*DePænetencia*).

As with all the sacraments, Penance is a liturgical action.

The sacrament may be celebrated in two ways: anonymously or face to face. In either way, typically, the penitent is greeted in a ritual manner by the priest and given a blessing. The scriptures are then read. It is the scriptures which call us to recognize our sins and to turn towards God. The scriptures also encourage us to have confidence in God's mercy.

Following the reading of Scripture, the penitent is invited to repent. He or she then offers a confession. If necessary the confessor may assist the penitent by asking questions. He then offers some practical advice for beginning a new life, helps the penitent resolve to make restitution in any situation in which harm has been done to someone else, and imposes a penance to atone for sin and to aid the person in starting a new life. When the penitent has accepted the penance and made an Act of Contrition (see page 148), the priest extends both hands or his right hand only over the head of the penitent and pronounces absolution (see page 145).

The priest then makes the sign of the cross over the penitent. This absolution is followed by a prayer of thanksgiving and praise and a dismissal with a blessing. Even if reconciliation involves only the priest and a single penitent it is a celebration of God and the Church and not simply the act of an isolated individual.

While individual confession remains the ordinary way for the sacrament of Penance, the Second Vatican Council also reintroduced a communal celebration of the sacrament in which all of the elements (greeting, blessing, scripture reading, homily) with the exception of the individual confession of sins and the granting of absolution take place in the presence of the whole community. Communal celebrations of the sacrament underscore the fact that reconciliation involves the whole Church and not just the individual and God.

On rare occasions when there is grave necessity for the sacrament and individual confession would not be possible, a communal celebration of the sacrament may include a general prayer of confession and general absolution. Grave necessity may include a situation where a person may die shortly without the opportunity for confession. Grave necessity can also exist when the ratio of penitents to confessors would deprive the penitents, through no fault of their own, to receive Holy Communion for a long time. Those who receive general absolution are still bound to confess their serious sins to a priest as soon as possible. It is up to the diocesan bishop to decide, based on Church law, what constitutes a significant need for general absolution.

How do you rate your level of comfort in going to face-to-face confession? Explain.

Write an act of contrition in your own words.

Over the centuries, the actual concrete form in which the Church has practiced the sacrament has varied. The feature "Sacrament of Penance in History" (pages 148-149) offers brief look at some of the historical development of the sacrament. Yet, throughout the changes in the practice of the sacrament over the centuries, the same fundamental structure has always been present. These two equally essential elements have always been present: first, the actions of the person (contrition, confession, and satisfaction) who undergoes conversion through the action of the Holy Spirit, and second, God's action through the intervention of the Church. The actions of the penitent and the role of the minister of the sacrament are described in the subsections that follow.

Act of Contrition

O my God, I am sorry for my sins with all my heart.
In choosing to do wrong and failing to do good, I have sinned against you whom I should love above all things.
I firmly intend, with your help, to do penance, to sin no more, and to avoid
whatever leads me to sin.
Our Savior Jesus Christ suffered and died for us.
In his name, my God, have mercy.
Amen.

Sacrament of Penance in History

In the first centuries, the reconciliation of Christians who had committed grave sins after Baptism (e.g., idolatry, murder, or adultery) was connected to very rigorous public penance, whereby the persons had to do penance for years before they could receive the sacrament and absolution.

During this time, the process often began with the sinner confessing to the bishop in private. The person was then enrolled into an "order of penitents." Because this process only concerned the gravest of sins, a person was rarely admitted into the order of penitents. In certain regions, a person could be admitted only once in a lifetime. The penitents could only participate in Eucharist through the Liturgy of the Word. Also, they wore sackcloth and ashes and knelt at the rear of the Church. Some of the penances assigned to them included fasting, prayer, abstaining from marriage and sexual intercourse, and the refusal to hold any public office.

(Sacrament of Penance in History cont.)

A second form of the sacrament was introduced in the seventh century by Irish missionaries who were inspired by the monastic tradition in the Eastern Church. This form involved private, individual, and devotional confession of sins to a priest. It did not require public or long works of penance before reconciliation was offered with God and the Church. This form opened the way for the sacrament to be performed in secret between the penitent and priest and is still celebrated that way today.

This practice also opened the possibility that the sacrament of Penance could be repeated often. It also allowed for the opportunity for mortal sins and venial sins to be confessed at one time.

Research and report on the practice and theology of the sacrament of Penance in a particular period of Church history.

Contrition

While the sacrament of Penance begins with the conversion of the person, conversion requires more than just a focus on a distant God. It requires a movement towards God. This movement begins with *contrition*. Contrition is defined as "heartfelt sorrow and aversion for the sin committed along with the intention of sinning no more" (*Rite of Penance*, 6a).

When we are contrite we accept responsibility for the things we have done. We also accept responsibility for our failure to love and we make a decision to be more loving. Contrition is not the same thing as shame. Shame directs our energy to ourselves and makes us long for perfection. Contrition focuses our minds and hearts on God and makes us long to draw closer to God. Contrition is rooted in faith and love for God. It needs the prayer and support of the Church in order to grow.

When we love God above all else we experience what is known as "perfect contrition." We willingly let go of all of those things which pull us away from God. When we experience perfect contrition God forgives all of our venial (lesser) sins. He also forgives our mortal (serious) sins as long as we intend to make a sacramental confession as soon as possible. Sacramental confession is a natural

Describe a time that you think you most closely approximated "perfect contrition" for something you had done.

part of perfect contrition. If we love God above all else we will want to be united with Christ by being united with his body on earth—the Church. Imperfect contrition is the result of love mixed with a fear of punishment or a dislike of the consequences of sin. It too can set us on the path to God and lead us to obtain forgiveness in the sacrament of Penance, but it is not sufficient to bring about the forgiveness of grave sins.

Also, in preparing for the sacrament of Penance, the penitent must examine his or her conscience in light of the Scriptures. Conscience is defined as a practical judgment of reason that enables us to discern whether an action or attitude is good or evil. Passages best suited to help in examining our conscience can be found in the Ten Commandments, the moral teachings such as the Beatitudes, and apostolic teachings in the Gospels and New Testament letters.

Preparing for the Sacrament

Because the sacrament of Penance entails conversion, it cannot happen without preparation and personal reflection. Before we can confess our sins we must become aware of them and we must choose to turn away from them. To prepare for the sacrament we need to take the time for a prayerful examination of conscience. We usually do this on our own prior to going to the sacrament.

A Christian conscience is both truthful and true. We must always obey the certain judgment of our conscience. The formation of our conscience is a lifelong task. Educating our conscience means focusing on the person and teaching of Jesus Christ, being attentive to the authoritative teaching of the Church, the guidance of the Holy Spirit, the gifts of the Spirit, and the advice of others.

Growth of our conscience is also accompanied by growth in the *virtues*. A virtue is "an habitual and firm disposition to do the good" (*CCC*, 1803). Human virtues govern our actions, help us control our passions, and guide our actions in light of faith and reason. We acquire human virtues through repeated effort of our good acts. The source of all the virtues are the four *cardinal virtues* (prudence, justice, fortitude, and temperance) which help to guide our intellects and wills, enabling us to live moral lives.

As Christians, we must take all the necessary steps to form a good conscience. The examination of conscience as part of our contrition in seeking out the sacrament of Penance is the perfect opportunity to pause and with the help of the Holy Spirit, take stock of our lives and the decisions that we have made or are about to make.

The following examination of conscience has been adapted from Appendix III of the *Rite of Penance*. Use this exercise to help you prepare for the sacrament of Penance.

(Preparing for the Sacrament cont.)

Find a quiet place and enter into a spirit of prayer. Ask yourself the following questions:

- What is my attitude toward this sacrament? Do I sincerely want to turn away from sin and draw closer to God? Do I see this as an opportunity to draw closer to God or as a chore that someone is forcing upon me?

- Are there serious sins which I have forgotten to mention or deliberately concealed during past confessions?

- Did I do the things that I committed myself to doing after my last confession?

Then examine your life in light of the word of God. God says: "You shall love the Lord your God with all your heart, and with all your soul and with all your mind and with all your strength." Ask yourself:

- Do I really love God and make faithfulness to God my priority? Or am I more concerned with the things of this world, whether friends, school, sports, my appearance, or something else?

- Is my faith in God firm and secure? Do I make an effort to grow in my understanding of faith? Do I listen to the word of God and the teachings of the Church? Am I willing to share my faith with others?

- Do I pray regularly and in all situations? Do I really turn my heart to God?

- Do I honor God's name? Have I used the name of God inappropriately? Have I sworn falsely or spoken ill of God?

- Do I keep the Lord's Day holy? Have I participated in the Mass on Sundays and feast days?

- Do I place my trust in any power other than God? Do I rely too much on money? Am I superstitious? Do I participate in occult practices?

Jesus says: "Love one another as I have loved you." Ask yourself:

- Do I genuinely love and care for those around me? Or do I use people for my own ends? Do I treat people with the respect with which I want to be treated?

- Do I contribute to the well-being and happiness of the rest of my family? Am I patient and loving within my family? Do I show respect for my parents and my brothers and sisters?

- Do I share my possessions with those who are less fortunate? Do I try to reach out to the poor, the sick, the elderly, and those who are outsiders? Or do I look down on or ignore those who are different from me?

- Do I see the mission of the Church as my own mission? Do I do what I can to share the Gospel and to work for peace and justice?

☑ Find a quiet spot and use this accompanying examination of conscience as a means of reflection on your own life right now.

(Preparing for the Sacrament cont.)

- Do I always try to give my best? Do I work hard? Am I fair to others? Am I honest?
- Do I show respect for those who have legitimate authority?
- Have I hurt another person in any way, either physically or emotionally?
- Have I refused to help a person in need?
- Have I tried to force others to do things my way?
- Have I damaged or stolen anyone else's property? Have I allowed jealousy or a desire for someone else's property to interfere with my relationships?
- Have I been ready to forgive those who have injured me or have I sought revenge?

Christ says: "Be perfect as your Father is perfect." Ask yourself:

- What are my goals? Am I really trying to live the way God wants me to live?
- How do I use my time, my health, my strength, and my talents? Do I use them to do God's will or do I squander them or behave as if they did not exist?
- Have I been patient in accepting the sorrows and disappointments of life?
- Have I taken care of the body which God has given me or have I mistreated it or dishonored it in some way? Have I engaged in pre-marital sex? Have I abused drugs, alcohol, cigarettes or food? Do I get enough rest and exercise? Do I work to develop my mind and my ability to think and reason? Have I filled my mind with unhealthy words and images by reading, watching, or listening to things which undermine human love and are offensive to God?
- Have I encouraged others to sin either actively or by my silence?
- Have I gone against my conscience?
- Do I choose to live as a child of God or am I a slave to my physical desires and emotions?

Pray for the Holy Spirit to be with you as you celebrate the sacrament of Penance.

Confession

True contrition results in confession or disclosure of our sins. Confession is the external expression of our sorrow and of our willingness to accept responsibility for our sins. Because we do not live purely interior lives, our contrition cannot remain purely within us. The outward form of contrition is confession. We tell our sins to the priest and we say we are sorry for them. Confession to a priest is an essential part of the sacrament of Penance.

Recall that God calls us to change and God will help us change, but God will not force us to change. Although God sees all of our sins, he will only free us from those we ask him to free us from. Confession is a request for such a healing.

Confession is also an expression of faith in God. When we confess our sins to God we are in fact proclaiming our belief in God's love and mercy. Sin is a failure to recognize God's love and generosity. Sin is rooted in the belief that we could "do better for ourselves" without God.

How often do you go to confession in a year? Name specific occasions when you go to confession.

When we sin we are acting like the prodigal son, taking what God has given us and trying to make it on our own. When we confess our sins, we are like the prodigal returning. When the prodigal son returned to his father and admitted his sin, he was expressing trust in his father's goodness. His action showed that he finally appreciated who his father was and all the blessings that came from life with his father. When we confess our sins, we are admitting our dependence upon God and our belief that life with God is the best life there is. An honest confession of who we are and of who God is forms the basis of our new life with God.

Confession not only forms the basis of our new life with God, it also forms the basis of our new life with the Church. When we confess our sins to a priest we are admitting the harm that we have caused to other people. We are admitting that our sin affected the entire body of Christ and we are asking that body of Christ to forgive us. When we confess our sins within the Church we are also expressing our belief in the goodness of the Church. We are looking at the Church through the eyes of God.

All Catholics are expected to confess their serious sins at least once a year. This expectation underscores the fact that there is nothing to be gained from putting off the sacrament, and much to be lost. Furthermore, any Catholic who is aware of having committed a serious sin may not receive communion without first receiving the sacrament of Penance. An exception is allowed if there is a serious reason for receiving communion and there is no possibility of going to confession first. Also, children must go to the sacrament of Penance before receiving Holy Communion for the first time. We cannot celebrate the sacrament of unity (Eucharist) when we have set ourselves apart from God and from God's people.

Finally, without being absolutely necessary, confession of venial sins is strongly recommended by the Church. Regular confession of our venial sins helps us form our conscience, fight against evil tendencies, let us be healed by Christ, and progress in the life of the Spirit (see *CCC*, 1458).

Satisfaction (Penance)

A person who is sorry for his or her sins and who confesses those sins to a priest must then work to build a new life with God and the Church. It is the effort to correct the mistakes of one's old life and to build a new life which completes the process of conversion. In order to begin building a new life, the repentant sinner must do everything possible to repair the damage which he or she has caused.

Correcting our sins is known as "giving satisfaction" or "doing penance." This means meeting the basic demands of justice: returning anything that has been taken, offering compensation for injuries, working to rebuild reputations which have been destroyed, and completing other like remedies. It also means making an effort to strengthen those things which have been weakened by sin. Our conversion is not complete until we do what we can to rebuild our relationships with God and with other people and to reinforce our own commitment to love.

When we confess our sins to a priest, he offers a penance. The penance may involve prayer, almsgiving, self-denial, or works of service. The purpose of the penance is to help us *begin* the process of correcting our past mistakes and building a new life with God. The act of penance gives us a starting point, not an ending point, for our new life.

Other than prayer, what would be some concrete penance ideas for teenagers who commit sins in each of the following areas: abusing drugs or alcohol, teasing a classmate, disobeying parents, misusing sex, cheating at school, missing Mass, swearing?

The Gift of Brokenness

In his book *Suffering*, Father Louis Evely tells the story of a Jesuit friend who was sent to a German concentration camp during World War II. During a long forced march the Jesuit and another man were walking arm in arm, holding each other up, helping each other forward. After a while the Jesuit felt the arm of the other man starting to slip. It slipped once. Then it slipped again and then it was no longer there. The second man fell. Like so many others he could go no further. He would die on the road. The Jesuit stopped for a second, looked back at his fallen companion, and then carried on marching.

(The Gift of Brokenness cont.)

Father Evely says that his friend carried that experience with him his whole life. It taught him how weak he really was. It showed him that he could never deserve God's love. God's love was a fabulous gift; it was not something he had earned. That Jesuit was given the soul of a poor man. He learned to claim nothing as his own and to take nothing for granted.[2]

In our brokenness we can see what we may have missed before: life is not something that we have earned or something that we need to earn, but something that God gives to us out of love. When we understand this truth we will be free to live in joy. We will be able to approach each moment of life with the wonder and exuberance of a young child opening gifts on Christmas morning.

What does it mean to be broken as a person? How can brokenness be a gift to help you be more contrite?

Absolution

The sacrament of Penance begins in the actions of the penitent who seeks conversion. The sacrament is completed in the actions of the priest who grants absolution. The Church assigns such importance to this ministry and has so much respect for the penitent, that every priest who hears confessions is bound to keep absolute secrecy of the sins confessed to him. This secret is known as the "sacramental seal."

When a priest celebrates the sacrament of Penance, he is fulfilling the ministry of Jesus, the Good Shepherd who seeks out lost sheep, the Good Samaritan who heals, the Father who awaits his prodigal son, and the fair and impartial judge whose judgment is just and merciful. When the priest sees that a person's conversion is genuine, he extends his hands on that person and pronounces God's forgiveness. As the *Catechism* reminds us: "The priest is the sign and instrument of God's merciful love for the sinner" (1465). Through the imposition of hands he restores the sinner to the community in which the Holy Spirit is active. In the words and gestures of the priest who gives absolution, God renews the broken relationship with the sinner and reconnects the sinner to the Paschal mystery.

The priest is "not the master of God's forgiveness, but its servant" (*CCC*, 1466). The priest unites himself to the intention and love of Christ. To function in his role of confessor, the priest should,

* have a proven knowledge of Christian behavior;
* have experience in human affairs;
* respect and be sensitive toward the sinner;
* have a love of the truth;
* be faithful to the Magisterium of the Church;
* lead the penitent with patience toward healing and full maturity.

Describe how you feel when you complete the sacrament of Penance.

Penance

The priest must also pray and do penance for the penitent, entrusting him to the Lord's mercy. Priests must take every opportunity to encourage Catholics to confess their sins in the sacrament of Penance and they must offer regularly scheduled times or make themselves reasonably available whenever they are asked for the sacrament.

The Effects of the Sacrament of Penance

When the sins of the penitent are absolved, all the obstacles to a complete union with God and with the Church are removed. The person's own efforts to love will be effective because they are united to Christ's love. Through the sacrament of Penance we are reconciled with God, with our neighbor, with ourselves, and with all of creation. Those who approach the sacrament of Penance with a contrite heart and an openness to God usually experience peace, serenity of conscience, and a deep sense of God's love after they have completed the sacrament.

The sacrament of Penance reopens the path to complete union with God. The sacrament brings about a true spiritual resurrection and a restoration of the dignity and blessings due to God's children—especially friendship with God. It does not, however, guarantee that we will be faithful or that we will be completely united to God. The sacrament of Penance, like the sacrament of Baptism which precedes it, only achieves its true purpose of uniting us to God if we allow the grace of the sacrament to permeate our entire life. It is only when our efforts at penance move beyond a desire to "get us out of trouble" and move us to more fervent service of God and of our neighbor that we will experience the true wonder of the sacrament.

The sacrament also reconciles us with the Church. Sin damages or breaks our communion with others. The sacrament of Penance repairs or restores that communion. The reconciled sinner is made even stronger by the exchange of "spiritual goods" among all members of the Body of Christ, both those on earth and in heaven.

Finally, because we submit ourselves to God's mercy, the sacrament of Penance anticipates our final judgment when we meet the Lord at death. It helps us to repent and teaches us penance and faith in God's loving mercy. By God's grace, these virtues will help us pass from death to an eternal life of joy in heaven.

The Meaning of Indulgences

The doctrine and practice of indulgences have a close connection with the effects of the sacrament of Penance. Indulgence is defined as "a partial or total wiping away of punishments due for sins that have been forgiven."

In the sacrament we are forgiven for our sins and welcomed back to communion with God. This does not mean, however, that we are freed from all of the consequences of sin. When a parent forgives a child for something that the child

What attitude must a penitent take towards his or her penance in order to fully experience the wonder of the sacrament?

has done, the parent stops being angry with the child, but the parent may not remove all of the consequences which result from the child's behavior. For example, the fact that a parent forgives a child for spilling something or breaking something does not imply that the child does not have to clean up what has been spilled or broken. The same is true in our relationship with God. The fact that we have been forgiven does not mean that we do not have to repair the harm which we have caused.

Unfortunately, each sin causes harm that extends far beyond what we can see. If you are unkind to one person, that person may react by being unkind to someone else who may in turn be unkind to someone else, and so on. Even if you repair your relationship with the person you hurt, you will not be undoing all of the harm that you have done. Sometimes our sins are so great that no matter how sorry we are we cannot even repair the harm that we have done. If we cannot repair the harm that we have done, then we at least have a responsibility to make up for it in some way, that is, to balance it out with good.

The Church teaches that we must make amends for the harm which we have caused before we die or we will need to make amends after death. We do not know exactly how this is accomplished after death, we simply believe that God expects us to "clean up the mess we have made" and provides us with a way to do it.

This expectation does not fall to us as isolated individuals, however. We are all members of the one body of Christ. Our sins injure the entire body and our acts of love benefit the entire body. It is possible for the other members of the body of Christ to assist us in our efforts to undo or make amends for the harm which we have done. When we are completely united with the Church we can request that the loving acts of Christ and of his holy people be considered as our own effort to undo the harm of our sin. When the Church grants an indulgence she is effectively saying, "this person is truly united with us and we offer the love of the body of Christ in payment for his or her sins."

The practice of granting indulgences is part of the Church's understanding of the unity of the Body of Christ. It is the Catholic belief that God does not save us as isolated individuals, but as members of the Church. When we are fully united to the community of the Church, our actions become the actions of the Church and the actions of other members of the Church become our actions. When we have undergone a sincere conversion and have participated in the sacrament of reconciliation and in the Eucharist, the Church offers us her assistance in making amends for our sins. We indicate that we wish this assistance by performing specific acts. This process of asking for and receiving the Church's assistance is what is entailed in the granting of indulgences.

There are names for different kinds of indulgences. A *partial indulgence* frees us from some of the remaining responsibility which we have for our sins. A *plenary indulgence* frees us from any remaining responsibility which we have for our sins. In order to receive a plenary indulgence a person must truly love God, detest sin, place their trust in the power of the Paschal mystery, and believe in the mutual

Recent understanding of indulgences asks that anyone in the Church should prayerfully intervene on behalf of a sinner who seeks an indulgence. What are some voluntary works of charity and prayerful penances you can undertake to help a repentant sinner?

assistance which can be given by the communion of saints (*Indulgentiarum Doctrina,* 10). A person must then do four things. He or she must

1. make a sacramental confession,
2. participate in the Eucharist,
3. pray for the intentions of the Holy Father (by saying an Our Father and a Hail Mary or by offering a prayer in his or her own words), and
4. perform the specific act to which the indulgence is attached, for example offer prayers in a specific pilgrimage site.

Indulgences are not about "collecting points." They are about uniting our efforts to love and to be faithful with the efforts of the whole Church, including the faithful who have died and are now in purgatory. By saying prayers and performing actions approved by the church, we can help those now being "purified" to gain indulgences, thus taking away some of the temporal punishment due for the sins they committed while on earth.

Chapter 6
Review Questions

1. Explain how the old story of people being connected to God by a string is related to the sacrament of Penance.

2. What is indicated by the term conversion?

3. If our sins are forgiven in Baptism, why do we need a sacrament of Penance?

4. Name some outward acts of penance that accompany interior conversion.

5. What are some other names for the sacrament of Penance?

6. What are the two parts of the conversion process?

7. Differentiate between mortal and venial sins.

8. In the sacrament of Penance, who can forgive sins?

9. What does the sacrament of Penance do for the Church?

10. What are the two ways individual confessions are typically celebrated?

11. When did private, individual, and devotional confessions come into practice?

12. Define *contrition*.

13. How does a person typically prepare for the sacrament of penance?

14. How often are Catholics expected to confess their sins?

15. What does a penance usually involve?

16. What are the effects of the sacrament of Penance?

17. Define *indulgence*.

Endnotes

1.   Eugene J. Fisher, Leon Klenicki, *From Desolation to Hope: An Interreligious Holocaust Memorial Service* (Chicago: Liturgical Training Publications, 1990), p. 23.

2.   Louis Evely, *Suffering* (New York: Herder and Herder, 1967), pp. 65-66.

Anointing of the Sick

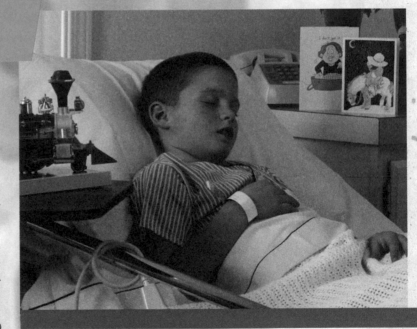

The Mystery of Suffering

Carlos is ten. He is in the hospital dying of a degenerative muscle disease. Jackie is wearing a wig to her senior prom because her hair fell out during radiation treatments. Terry has a stroke at age thirty. Bev has had blinding migraines at least once a week since she was eleven. Jason will never run again after the car accident. Elaine's joints are in constant pain. Margaret can no longer control her bladder. Michelle. . . .

"Out of the depths [we] cry to you, O Lord . . ." (Ps 130:1).

Suffering and illness are part of the reality of our world. Sometimes we know what causes them. Sometimes we know why this person is afflicted and not that one; but most of the time we have no idea. Why does cancer strike a teenager, a toddler, a mother of six? Why would a dancer's muscles suddenly start to degenerate? Why should one seventy-year-old woman lose control of her bladder while

Share some questions you have about suffering.

How have you witnessed God's presence in your or another's suffering?

another does not? Why would a fifteen-year-old break his neck in a freak accident? Why? Why? Why? For thousands of years people have asked this question— why suffering?—but we have not found an answer.

When the Messiah came, many expected him to provide an answer to the question about suffering. People asked Jesus whose fault illness was. They challenged him to "heal himself" and to prove himself by putting an end to all suffering (see Lk 4:23). They called him to "come down off the cross," to show that he could and would eliminate all suffering, and then, they said, "we will believe" (Mt 27:42). But Jesus did not come to explain suffering or to take it away. He came to be with people as they suffered and to teach them how to respond to suffering.

There have always been those who say that suffering is just the way of the world; we need to accept it and move on. They say, "it is God's will," as if those words should be enough to take away the pain or stop the tears. Jesus taught us that this type of stoicism is not what God wants from us. When Jesus' friend Lazarus died, Jesus cried. On the night before his crucifixion Jesus said, "my soul is sorrowful even to death" (Mt 26:38), and his anguish was so great that his sweat became like drops of blood. And Jesus himself prayed, "*Abba* (Father), you have the power to do all things. Take this cup away from me" (Mk 14:36).

No matter how great our faith is, suffering is real and it hurts. We want it to go away. What is more, suffering is something we can and should try to eliminate, *if and only if* we can eliminate it without eliminating or diminishing love.

Jesus asked God to release him from the suffering that loomed ahead, but he also said, "still, not my will but yours be done" (Lk 22:42). Jesus accepted arrest, torture, and crucifixion because to do anything else would have been to deny his relationship with God or his love for those in need.

The Church's document *Pastoral Care of the Sick: Rites of Anointing and Viaticum* reminds us that we are called to follow Jesus' example: "We should fight strenuously against all sickness and carefully seek the blessings of good health, so that we may fulfill our role in human society and in the Church." At the same time we should be prepared to accept the suffering that does come our way and move through it with love and trust for God.

Lessons of Suffering

Jesus taught that suffering should not lead us into despair or revolt against God. The fact that we are suffering does not mean that God is not there or that God does not care. Whenever we suffer God suffers with us. Elie Wiesel, a Jewish writer who endured the concentration camps as a boy, tells a story that captures the Catholic understanding of God's place in our suffering.

> *One morning all of the prisoners were called out to watch the execution of three people, two adults and a young boy. All three were to be hung. The ropes were placed around their necks and the supports were kicked out from under*

Name any lessons you have learned from a time you have suffered or from witnessing the suffering of another.

their feet. As the two adults fell their necks were broken and they died instantly. But the child was too light. The rope did not break his neck. Instead he hung there struggling and kicking, trying to get air into his lungs. The other prisoners were forced to stand and watch as he slowly suffocated to death. Elie Wiesel recalls hearing someone behind him ask the question, "Where is God? Where is God now?" And when he heard the question Wiesel knew the answer, God was there in front of them, hanging from that rope.[1]

We believe that God is present in all of our suffering. Jesus comes to us when we suffer and he suffers with us. He shares our pain, and if we allow him to, he will make that pain bearable. God's love for us only intensifies when we are suffering.

Jesus Healed Body and Soul

When Jesus encountered the sick and suffering he healed them. His compassion for the sick was so great that he identified himself with them. He said, "I was . . . ill and you cared for me" (Mt 25:36). He then taught that one of the requirements of discipleship was to care for those who are sick. When we care for "one of the least ones" we do so for Jesus (see Mt 25:36).

Jesus showed a preferential love for people who were suffering. He spent more time with them than with people whose lives were going well. He shared his love for the suffering in a unique way. Because of their suffering they were invited to participate in the kingdom in ways that those who were healthy could not. Because they understood brokenness and isolation, because they were acutely aware of their own mortality, they were able to experience the wonder of wholeness, inclusion, and new life. They understood the significance of healing as a sign of the coming kingdom in a way that the healthy could not.

There is an award-winning photograph taken at an orphanage in Mexico that makes this point clearly. The photograph shows two young children who had just been given wrapped Christmas presents. One child's eyes are alight with anticipation. The other child's face is almost expressionless. The photographer explained that the first child had received a present the year before, but the second child had never received a present and had no idea what to expect. He had been told about presents but he could not imagine what it would be like to receive one.

The same was true for those who encountered Jesus. Those people he healed and restored to life in the community had some understanding of what it meant

to be granted new life. Those who had never experienced healing or renewal did not really know what to expect. Like the child who could not experience the wonder of the gift in front of him, they could not experience the wonder of Jesus' presence and healing actions.

Jesus instructed his disciples to heal the sick as he did. After his resurrection, Jesus commissioned the eleven apostles to "Go into the whole world and proclaim the gospel to every creature." As one of the signs of this ministry, Jesus told them that "They will lay hands on the sick, and they will recover" (Mk 16:15, 18).

As a Church, we are responsible for offering healing to the sick in our midst. In order to carry out our responsibility we must take into account the many aspects of true healing as it was offered by Jesus. As part of his healing, Jesus forgave sins and welcomed the sick back into the community. Jesus not only healed bodies, he also healed relationships and souls.

When he healed the man who was paralyzed, he began by forgiving his sins (Mk 2:1-12). When he healed the ten lepers, he sent them to the priest so that they might be officially reintegrated into society (Lk 17:14). The young girl who everyone thought was dead was treated the same way by Jesus. After she was healed, Jesus said she should be given something to eat (Mk 5:43). Illness often isolates people and turns them in on themselves. Disease does not just attack the body, it attacks the spirit. Sometimes it is the spirit that needs the most healing.

All of the people that Jesus healed eventually died. And it seems likely that at least some of them got ill again before they died. Bodily healing in this life is never permanent. But the spiritual healing which Jesus gave may well have been permanent. Although we do not know what happened to any of the people that Jesus healed, it seems likely that at least some of them were among the early Christian disciples, and maybe some among the first martyrs. No matter what was done to the martyrs' bodies, their spirits could not be broken. They understood that neither suffering nor death would last because God would take away both.

How do you feel distant from your community (family, school, church, etc.) when you are ill? In what ways do you feel welcomed back into the community when you are well?

Read the story of the healing of Jairus's daughter and the woman with the hemorrhage from Mark 5:21-43. Compare the two healings. How are they different?

Jesus Gave Meaning to Suffering

Illness and suffering have often led to varying feelings towards God. On one extreme, illness and suffering can lead to revolt against God. Differently, very often illness and suffering can lead the person to search for God and return to him.

The Church teaches of a developing understanding of the meaning and purpose of suffering in the economy of salvation. In the Old Testament, man lives his sickness in the presence of God. He both laments his illness and implores God to heal him. The person's illness is also connected to sin; it becomes an avenue to conversion and forgiveness. As the psalmist prays,

> From all my sins deliver me;
> a fool's taunt let me not suffer (Ps 39:9).

The linkage of illness, sin, and evil with God's forgiveness and healing of the individual also lead to the connection between suffering and the redemption of sin of others. The book of Isaiah says as much in the last of the four Suffering Servant prophesies—prophesies whose message of suffering and glorification is fulfilled in the Paschal mystery of Jesus Christ:

> Because of his affliction he shall see
> the light in fullness of days;
> Through his suffering, my servant
> shall justify many, and their
> guilt he shall bear (Is 53:11).

Also, Isaiah announces a time when God will forgive every sin and heal every illness (see Is 33:24).

Jesus' suffering and the meaning he brought to it was the culmination of the Old Testament understanding. Jesus' suffering was *redemptive*, meaning that it brought humanity back into the fullness of relationship with God the Father. Jesus suffered because of his love for God and for God's people. Jesus' suffering was the price he paid to give his gift of love. He could have avoided suffering, but only by denying his love for God or for God's people. Because Jesus was willing to give himself for love, because he was willing to suffer for love, his suffering changed the relationship between God and all of humanity. His total generosity, his willingness to give his very self, undid the damage caused by Adam and Eve's selfishness. Jesus' suffering redeemed humanity from isolation and reconnected us with God.

Those who were ill in Jesus' day had a unique opportunity to participate in Jesus' initiation of God's kingdom. In a similar way, those who are ill today have

Read the Lord's response to Job on the question of "Why is there suffering?" from Job 38–41. What is your reaction to this text? How did Job react (see Job 42)?

a unique opportunity to love as Jesus loved and so to participate in his saving work. Illness, suffering, and death came into the world because of sin. They were not part of God's original plan for creation and they are not good. Nevertheless, our faith tells us that God uses everything, even those things which appear to be bad, to accomplish good. As the letter to the Romans expresses:

We know that all things work for good for those who love God, who are called according to his purpose (Rom 8:28).

In illness we experience our powerlessness and our limitations. "Every illness can make us glimpse death" (*CCC*, 1500). When we are ill we have an opportunity to surrender ourselves completely to God. When we are healthy it may be difficult to know whether or not we are trusting God. When a person is ill, trust in God becomes much easier to define. Illness can also provide a person with an opportunity to prioritize and choose those things which are truly important.

People who are seriously ill may not be able to do the things the world thinks are important, but they can still do what God thinks is important. Suffering can free people to embrace love with the wholeheartedness of Jesus, because suffering can reveal the insignificance of everything else. This is why Jesus says, "blessed are the poor in spirit," and "blessed are those who mourn" (Mt 5:3, 4). Those who are not filled with the things of the world can be filled with the blessings of God which are so much greater.

We Share in the Work of Redemption

As God invites us to share in the work of creation, he also invites us to share in the work of redemption. God the Father does not just give things to us, he gives us the ability to give to others. Suffering is an opportunity to love as Jesus loved. When we love through our suffering, we are united with Christ and our suffering becomes part of Christ's suffering. It becomes a gift of love which will help to change the world. Suffering gives us an extraordinary power to make a difference.

From the moment of our Baptism our goal is to be like Christ. When we are ill or suffering, we become like Christ in a very special and profound way. That is a beautiful gift which should not be despised. In the letter to the Colossians St. Paul says that in his own physical suffering he is "filling up what is lacking in the afflictions of Christ" (Col 1:24). We know that Jesus' gift of love, Jesus' acceptance of suffering, was sufficient to bridge the gulf between God and humanity. God the Father does not ask for any more than what Jesus has already given. So what does Paul mean when he speaks of "filling up what is lacking"? It is true that Jesus' love is all that is needed to reconcile people to God, but in order for any person to benefit from that love he or she must first become aware of it. Jesus' love can only be made visible through the actions of his body, the Church. It is made visible in a particularly profound way through the actions of those members of his body who love through suffering even as he did. What Paul is saying is that through his own suffering he is able to make Jesus' love and Jesus' sacrifice present to others. In our suffering we have an opportunity to do the same.

When the disciples asked Jesus why a certain man had been born blind, Jesus told them that he was blind so that the glory of God might be made manifest in him. Jesus said, "Neither he nor his parents sinned; it is so that the works of God might be made visible through him" (Jn 9:3). But before the works of God could be made visible in him, the man had to live in blindness for many years. Our suffering may last for a very long time, but we believe that in that suffering there is a hidden promise, a hidden meaning which will be made clear to us on the last day.

The Sacrament of Anointing

Father Louis Evely wrote that "Since Christ . . . the meaning of suffering is no longer a distressing problem, but merely a resemblance, a staggering election."[2] The call to suffering is a call as significant as the election to be an apostle.

Nevertheless, it is impossible for a person to answer that call alone. Without the help of the Holy Spirit, suffering will not free a person to love. Instead it can break a person's spirit and weaken his or her faith. Suffering can make a person selfish, angry, irritable, demanding, and impatient. Suffering can cause an unbearable loneliness that leads to despair. Jesus has given the Church the sacrament of Anointing in order to aid those who are seriously ill and help them use their illness in service to Christ.

In the words of the Second Vatican Council:

> By the sacred anointing of the sick and the prayer of the priests the whole Church commends those who are ill to the suffering and glorified Lord so that he may raise them up and save them. . . . And indeed she exhorts them to contribute to the good of the People of God by freely uniting themselves to the passion and death of Christ (Lumen Gentium, 11).

Explain the paradox in your own words: Christ's suffering completes the work of redemption yet we "fill up what is lacking in the afflictions of Christ."

The sacrament of Anointing of the Sick instructs all of the faith community to come to the aid of sick people in our midst. There are several ways you can show that you care. You can pray for the sick of your community. You can visit them in person. You can write them a letter telling about yourself and inquiring of them. What are some other ways you can care for the sick? Share your ideas. Initiate one of the ideas mentioned above or your own idea.

Look up a gospel passage you feel would be appropriate to read at the time of the anointing of the sick. Write a brief homily connecting the passage with the meaning of suffering or the care of the sick in your community today.

Rite of Anointing

Examining the rite of the sacrament can help us to understand more of the ways the Church discerns suffering, especially the way that it unites a person to the sufferings of Christ.

The priest, as representative of the Church, is the minister of the sacrament. The introduction to the Church's instruction on the sacrament, the *Pastoral Care of the Sick: Rites of Anointing and Viaticum*, asks that the priest care for the sick through visits and personal acts of kindness.

The sacrament itself is for any person who is seriously ill. The sacrament may be repeated if the sick person recovers from the illness after the anointing or if the same or another illness becomes more threatening. A sick person should also be anointed before surgery whenever a serious illness is the reason for the surgery. Old people may be anointed if they are in a weak condition, even if no illness is present. Also, younger people who are sick, including children, may be anointed if there is sufficient reason to be comforted by the sacrament.

The rite of anointing can take place in three situations: within Mass, outside of Mass, or in a hospital or other institutional setting.

For each of these situations, the matter for the sacrament is the same: olive oil blessed by the bishop. The oil for the sick is usually blessed for his diocese by the bishop at the Mass on Holy Thursday evening.

The sacrament is conferred by anointing the sick person on the forehead and the hands, saying:

> Through this holy anointing
> may the Lord in his love and mercy help you
> with the grace of the Holy Spirit.
> May the Lord who frees you from sin
> save you and raise you up.

The person responds "Amen."

When the sacrament takes place outside of Mass, the priest greets the sick person and the others present and sprinkles them with holy water. He instructs them about the need to pray for the sick, to forgive sins, and to anoint with oil. A penitential rite follows.

Also, prior to the anointing, the liturgy of the Word takes place with a scripture reading that details the many times and ways God has healed. After the anointing, the priest prays the following:

> Lord Jesus Christ, our Redeemer,
> by the power of the Holy Spirit,
> ease the sufferings of our sick brother (sister)

and make him (her) well again in mind and body.
In your loving kindness forgive his (her) sins
and grant him (her) full health
so that he (she) may be restored to your service.
You are Lord for ever and ever.

The priest then introduces the Lord's Prayer and those gathered join in. If the sick person will receive communion, this takes place after the Lord's Prayer.

In whatever setting the sacrament is celebrated, the communal nature and responsibility of all the faithful to care for the sick is stressed. This is a more recent emphasis of the sacrament especially since the time of the Second Vatican Council. Briefly tracing the effects of the sacrament and the history of the sacrament sheds more light on this development.

Effects of the Sacrament of Anointing

The sacrament of the Anointing of the Sick unites the one who is sick or older in age with the passion of Christ. When a person is anointed he or she is in a sense "consecrated" to participate in the saving work of Jesus and to help make Christ's redemptive suffering present to the world (see *CCC*, 1521). Anointing completes a person's conformity to the death and resurrection of Christ which began in baptism. In the sacrament of Anointing any sins which still separate a person from Christ are forgiven if the person has not been able to obtain forgiveness through the sacrament of Penance.

Through the sacrament of Anointing, those who are ill or old receive a special grace of the Holy Spirit. This grace strengthens them and gives them the peace and the courage to overcome the difficulties that go with serious illness and old age. This particular gift of the Holy Spirit heals the soul and, if God so wills, also heals the body. It strengthens those who receive it against temptation and anxiety and makes it possible for them to bear suffering bravely and even fight against it (see *CCC*, 1520. Also, *Pastoral Care of the Sick: Rites of Anointing and Viaticum*, 6).

"When the Church cares for the sick, it serves Christ himself" (*Decree on the Pastoral Care of the Sick*). When the Church cares for the sick it also participates in the ministry of Christ. Through the sacrament of Anointing the Church intercedes for the benefit of the sick person. The sick person in turn assists the Church. By uniting himself or herself to

The Council of Trent taught that the three effects of the sacrament of Anointing are:
- It wipes away sin and the remnants of sin.
- It brings about spiritual healing.
- It restores physical healing when this will help the person in his or her condition before God.

Christ's suffering the one who is sick helps the Church itself become more Christ-like. He or she makes it possible for the Church to be the body of Christ, the body of the one who suffers with us, in the world.

Finally, the person who receives the sacrament of Anointing and viaticum (see below) shortly before death has the nourishment necessary for the passover from this life to eternity with the Triune God. The Anointing of the Sick completes our conformity to the death and resurrection of Christ, begun in Baptism. It completes the holy anointings of Baptism and Confirmation which sealed and strengthened our new life in Christ. As the *Catechism* describes, "This last anointing fortifies the end of our earthly life like a solid rampart for the final struggles before entering the Father's house" (1523).

Viaticum

The sacrament of Anointing is for all who are seriously ill. Viaticum is the liturgical rite for the dying. Viaticum means "food for the journey." It is a person's last reception of Eucharist.

As the sacrament of Christ's Passover, the Eucharist is the fitting sacrament with which to mark the end of this life and the passing over into the next. Whenever possible, the dying person should receive viaticum within the Mass in order that as death draws close he or she may share fully in the eucharistic sacrifice which "proclaims the Lord's own passing through death to life" (*Pastoral Care of the Sick: Rites of Anointing and Viaticum*, 177). The distinctive feature of the reception of the Eucharist as viaticum is the renewal of baptismal vows by the one who is dying.

Before a person receives viaticum, he or she should participate in the sacrament of Penance, if possible, and in the sacrament of Anointing. Just as the sacraments of Baptism, Confirmation, and Eucharist mark the beginning of our Christian pilgrimage, the sacraments of Penance, Anointing, and the Eucharist as viaticum mark the end of our earthly pilgrimage and prepare us to enter eternal life (see *CCC*, 1525).

The Historical Development of the Sacrament of Anointing

Jesus instituted the sacrament of the Anointing of the Sick in his own healing ministry. The earliest actual reference to a Christian sacrament of Anointing occurs in the letter of James:

> *Is anyone among you sick? He should summon the presbyters of the church, and they should pray over him and anoint [him] with oil in the name of the Lord, and the prayer of faith will save the sick person, and the Lord will raise him up. If he has committed any sins, he will be forgiven (5:14-15).*

☑

Imagine that you know that this is your final day on earth. Rank, in order of importance, five things you would want to do before you die.

Both while Jesus was alive and after he had ascended into heaven his followers anointed and laid hands on those who were sick in order to heal them. When prayers were not sufficient to heal a person, however, sickness was viewed as problematic. Incurable illnesses were believed to be related to persistent sin although there was no particular understanding of how or why this was true.

Nevertheless, a seriously ill person was believed to be in some way separated from the healing love of God. Certain illnesses or physical disorders that caused undo attention (e.g., epilepsy or other disorders with symptoms of uncontrolled motion or speech) were considered so bothersome that the person was not allowed to receive the Eucharist. Like the catechumens, people with these types of illnesses were prayed over at Eucharist and dismissed following the liturgy of the Word.

From the second through the seventh century prayer for healing was considered part of the overall ministry of the Church. Whenever a person was seriously ill, other Christians would gather around and pray for him or her and then rub oil which had been blessed by the bishop on whatever parts of the body were in need of healing. It was necessary that the oil be blessed by the bishop, but any Christian could administer it.

During the Middle Ages there was increasing concern with who actually did the anointing. Over time the sacrament had come to be associated with death. According to the popular view, it became necessary to have a priest at the deathbed to insure a safe departure and to carry a person into the afterlife. The sacrament of Anointing came to be seen as something that accompanied a final reception of the sacraments of Reconciliation and Eucharist, which—according to the Council of Trent—could be offered only by a priest.

During the twelfth century the sacrament was given the name *extreme unction* ("last anointing") and was viewed as a form of insurance against hell. When Thomas Aquinas wrote of the sacrament he mentioned its power to forgive sins, but added nothing about physical healing. The monastic anointing rite of the Middle Ages actually concluded with the clothing of the anointed in a penitential hair shirt. If a person did recover after being anointed he or she was expected to live out the rest of his or her life in penitence. Among other things, this meant that single people could not marry and those who were married were

Interview a family member who lived prior to the Second Vatican Council. Ask the person to share his or her remembrances on the sacrament of extreme unction. For example, attitudes about when to call the priest for the sacrament as well as the form of the sacrament itself.

expected to abstain from sexual relations. It is no wonder that the sacrament became associated more with dying than healing.

In 1439 the Council of Florence declared that sacramental anointing was *only* for those who were in danger of death. In the first draft of the *Doctrine on the Sacrament of Extreme Unction,* the Council of Trent repeated this limitation. The final draft, however, said that the sacrament was for the sick, but *especially* those who seemed about to die. From the time of the Council of Trent until the Second Vatican Council, the sacrament of extreme unction was associated with "last rites" and took the following form:

> *The person to be anointed was sprinkled with holy water.*
>
> *This was followed by three short prayers as well as the confiteor and absolution.*
>
> *Next came a scripture reading followed by a litany of petitions.*
>
> *The priest then laid his hands on the head of the one who was sick and offered a prayer and a blessing.*
>
> *The sick person's body was anointed on each of the senses and a prayer was said to accompany each anointing.*
>
> *More prayers were said, and the priest blessed the person one final time. A final communion or* viaticum *was usually offered at the same time.*

The Sacrament of Anointing Today

The Second Vatican Council refocused certain aspects of the sacrament of extreme unction so that it is now more fittingly called the sacrament of the Anointing of the Sick. Today, the sacrament is not for those only who are at the point of death. The Council taught that "as soon as any one of the faithful begins to be in danger of death from sickness or old age, the appropriate time for him to receive this sacrament has certainly already arrived" (*Sacrosanctum Concilium,* 73).

This means that when a person is old enough that the reality of death is frequently part of his or her thoughts, when a person is diagnosed with an illness which may be terminal, when a person is suffering from a debilitating disease and his or her life is not what it once was—all of these are appropriate times for the sacrament of Anointing. If the illness and suffering continues over a period of time and the person's relationship with God or with the Church is affected, the sacrament may be repeated.

Since the Second Vatican Council the Church has once again begun to think of anointing as part of the mission of everyone in the Church. *The Pastoral Care of the Sick: Rites of Anointing and Viaticum* says,

> *If one member suffers in the Body of Christ, which is the Church, all members suffer. . . . For this reason, kindness shown toward the sick and works of charity and mutual help for the relief of every kind of human want are held in special honor. Every scientific effort to prolong life[3] and every act of care for the sick, on the part of any person, may be considered a preparation for the Gospel and a sharing in Christ's healing ministry.*

Research the Church's latest teachings on the prolongation of life using both ordinary and extraordinary medical means.

It is thus especially fitting that all baptized Christians share in this ministry of mutual charity within the Body of Christ by doing all that they can to help the sick return to health, by showing love for the sick, and by celebrating the sacraments with them (32-33).

Priests are still the only ministers of the sacrament; however, the sacrament is no longer viewed as something that is between the priest, the person who is ill, and God. The priest prays for the sick person as the spokesperson of the whole Church. Through the sacrament, the whole Church recommits itself to the one who is ill and the one who is ill offers his or her suffering for the sake of the Church. Too often the sick and elderly feel as if they have been cut off from the rest of the world. The sacrament of Anointing strengthens the connection between the one who is ill and the rest of the body of Christ. It also gives those who feel that they have nothing left the grace to continue giving of themselves.

Today we recognize that the grace given in the sacrament of Anointing is always a healing grace. Sometimes the healing is physical. Sometimes the healing is a forgiveness of sins which a person has succumbed to because of his or her illness. And sometimes the healing is a spiritual healing which turns seemingly meaningless suffering into a deeper relationship with Christ.

Sacrament of Anointing: A Practical Application

I was twenty-eight years old, newly married, and pregnant with my first child. My legs started to swell. That can happen in pregnancy, but the swelling wouldn't go away. I couldn't wear stockings or socks because the pressure was excruciatingly painful. I couldn't stand for more than a minute or two and I couldn't climb stairs at all. If I did the blood vessels in my legs would burst. My husband had to carry me up and down the stairs to our apartment every day. I traveled back and forth to the rheumatoid clinic in the city several times a week.

Toward the end of my pregnancy things started to get a bit better, and when Becca was born I thought everything would be fine. But then I got a phone call from the clinic. Would I please come in to the cancer clinic? They didn't want me to worry, but they thought that I might have a blood disease and the cancer clinic was equipped to do the necessary tests. I had a new baby. I was feeling better. Yes, I was tired a lot, but what new mother isn't? I wasn't really worried. What difference did it make to me which clinic did the blood tests?

We were in the process of moving into a new house. My husband was spending a lot of time doing renovations. My dad was helping him. One Friday afternoon while they were at the house I went back to the apartment with the baby to take a nap. While I was there I received a phone call. "You have a type of cancer called lymphoma. You need to wean the baby by Monday so that you can begin chemo." That was it. There I was, all alone and someone gives me this news on the phone. Couldn't they at least have made sure that someone was around?

Why do you think people are hesitant or afraid to ask for the sacrament of the Anointing of the Sick? What can be done to help change those attitudes?

I was on medication for six months. I was off for two weeks and then I felt the lumps in my neck coming back. It's hard when that happens the first time. It is so much harder the second time. This second time I became aware of so many other people who were sick. I thought that I should reach out to them but I was afraid. I was afraid of getting too close to someone and having them die.

Up until then my Bible was one of those books that was always around but that I rarely read. I started reading it all the time. Whenever I couldn't sleep, I would get up and read the Bible. I especially loved the passage, "don't worry about tomorrow, today has problems enough of its own." I would read it and then I would feel God's peace and I would be able to sleep. My doctor kept asking me if I needed anything to help me sleep, but I never did.

It was also during my second round of treatment when I first met with Brenda. She was a hospital chaplain and now she works as a pastoral associate in our church. I saw her every week. We cried together, we prayed together. She encouraged me to share everything with her. I knew it wouldn't go any farther so I told her things I couldn't tell anyone else. I told how hard this was on my marriage. Gerry is someone who just closes in on himself when he's really upset. I wanted to talk about what was happening, but he just couldn't. And then I felt hurt.

When I wasn't angry with him I was angry with myself. I felt like this was something I was doing to Gerry and to Becca. I thought maybe God was punishing me for things I had done. I thought maybe he was punishing me because I got pregnant a month before my wedding.

Brenda helped me see that God is a loving God. He doesn't punish people with horrible illnesses. Illness just happens. She encouraged me to go to the sacrament of Reconciliation and ask for forgiveness if I felt that I needed it. I did. I was starting to feel more at peace with myself and with my family. Brenda kept praying with me and for me. Every week she would put her hands on my head or my shoulders or the lymph nodes on my neck where the cancer kept appearing, and she would pray that God would heal me. That touch was so important. I never realized before how much being touched meant.

The second time I was on medication for a year. I was off for a month and the cancer came back. Brenda asked me if I would like to receive the sacrament of Anointing again. A priest had administered it to me the first time I was in the hospital, but I barely realized what was happening to me.

This time I was more afraid. I was afraid to ask people to take time to come and pray with me and pray for me. I didn't feel worthy. In the end I did ask a few people to come: Gerry, my parents, Brenda, and Father Paul. We sang together. Then Father Paul sprinkled me and everyone else with holy water. He explained the sacrament of Anointing to my parents and to Gerry. He told them about what it says in the letter to James about the Church praying with and for the sick. He reassured my parents that we weren't doing this because we thought I was going to die, but because we wanted to ask God to heal me.

We all prayed together for forgiveness. It was the same prayer that we say every Sunday at Mass, but somehow it was different this time. We were saying "I'm sorry" to each other. In that prayer my parents and Gerry and I said all the things that we had been unable to say for the past year-and-a-half.

Mom, Dad, and Gerry also each read a passage from the Bible. And then they all prayed for me. Father Paul invited them to stand around me as they prayed, and put a hand on me if they wanted to. They all did. They prayed that I would have strength. They prayed that I would be protected from sin and temptation. They prayed that I would be healed. As they prayed I felt a peace and comfort unlike anything else I have ever felt. I could feel God's presence.

Then Father Paul put his hands on my head and said a prayer. He anointed my forehead and my hands with oil and said a prayer. Then because of my illness he anointed my neck. I was about to start very intensive radiation. The doctors said I would probably loose my saliva glands. Father Paul said that he would anoint my neck as a special prayer that I would not lose those glands. After the anointing we all prayed the Lord's Prayer together and sang one final song. I was closer to my parents and to Gerry than I have ever been.

I began radiation the next day. I didn't lose my saliva glands. I didn't even wake up thirsty in the middle of the night. The doctors were very surprised, to say the least. Three months after the treatments were done I was scheduled to go in for tests. Up until then I had been at peace. But the thought of the tests terrified me. It brought everything crashing back down on me.

Father Paul offered to anoint me again. This time we did it during Mass and the whole congregation prayed for me. I could feel all the weight of my illness and my fear being lifted off. I can't really describe it. But it was real. During the week between when they took the blood and when I got the results I wasn't afraid. God gave me the strength I needed.

Anointing of the Sick

I've been cancer free for three years now. I believe the cancer is really gone, but with my kind of cancer you never really know. The doctors will only say I'm in remission. Things may change tomorrow or in two years. But even if the cancer does come back, I'm not as afraid. God has healed my soul. I'm not afraid of dying any more.

Chapter 7
Review Questions

1. How did Jesus respond to the common thought that because suffering is "God's will" we should accept it and move on?

2. How are we called to follow Jesus' example regarding suffering?

3. Where do Catholics believe God is when we suffer?

4. What are some reasons that Jesus showed a preferential love for those who were suffering?

5. What did Jesus teach about being responsible for the sick in our midst?

6. How is Jesus' suffering redemptive?

7. How do we share in the work of redemption?

8. Who is the minister of the sacrament of the Anointing of the Sick?

9. Who is the sacrament for?

10. In what three situations can the rite of anointing take place?

11. What is the matter used in the sacrament?

12. How is the sacrament conferred?

13. What are the effects of the sacrament of Anointing?

14. Define *viaticum*.

15. What is the earliest reference to the sacrament of the Anointing of the Sick?

16. How was the sacrament considered part of the overall ministry of the Church from the second to seventh centuries?

17. What is the meaning of *extreme unction*? When did this understanding of the sacrament come about?

18. How is the sacrament today viewed as an action of the whole Church?

Endnotes

1. Elie Wiesel, *Night* (New York: Hill and Wang, 1987), pp. 70-72.

2. *Suffering* (New York: Herder and Herder, 1967), p. 29.

3. As the *Catechism* teaches: "Discontinuing medical procedures that are burdensome, dangerous, extraordinary, or disproportionate to the expected outcome can be legitimate" (2278). Aggressive medical treatment that is disproportionate to any expected results or impose excessive burden on the patient and his or her family may be refused.

Holy Orders

Sharing in the Priesthood of Christ

The sacraments of initiation—Baptism, Confirmation, and Eucharist—confer a common vocation on all Catholics, a vocation to holiness and to the task of evangelizing the world. Two other sacraments—Holy Orders and Matrimony—are directed to the salvation of others. They also contribute to a person's own salvation, but they do so through their service to others.

The subject of this chapter is the sacrament of Holy Orders. Those who receive this sacrament are sent in Christ's name to "feed the Church by the word and grace of God" (*Lumen Gentium* 11 § 2). It is through the sacrament of Holy Orders that Christ continues the ministry he entrusted to the apostles. Through the service of the ordained ministers—especially bishops and priests—Christ himself becomes visibly present to the Church as its head and high priest.

From your own experience, tell what it means to say that priests "feed the Church by the word and grace of God."

Father Theodore Hesburgh, CSC, President Emeritus of the University of Notre Dame once explained how the role and function of the ordained is connected to the ministry established by Jesus:

> *His role today is the same as it was when Jesus chose his disciples. He told them to go out and teach, baptize, and bring people the grace of salvation. That task doesn't change in any basic way and is relevant to every society, culture, and geography.*
>
> *When the Holy Father came to the United States, he came not as a diplomat but as a priest. He said Masses for thousands, preached to them, blessed them, talked to the United Nations about human rights, peace, and freedom.*
>
> *The world today needs those functions of the priesthood just as they did in the time of Jesus* (Extraordinary Lives, p. 264).

As you recall from Chapter 2, there are two ways for Christians to participate in the one priesthood of Jesus Christ: the ministerial or hierarchical priesthood of bishops and priests, and the common priesthood of all the faithful. The ministerial priesthood differs from the common priesthood in that it is at the service of the common priesthood. It is directed at unfolding the baptismal grace of all Christians. The ordained minister serves the Church by teaching, leading worship, and governing.

This chapter focuses especially on the ministerial priesthood, established in the sacrament of Holy Orders which consecrates certain men to one of three degrees of sacred order: episcopacy (bishops), presbyterate (priests), and diaconate (deacons). The sacrament of Holy Orders confers a gift of the Holy Spirit that allows those ordained to exercise a "sacred power" on behalf of Christ for his Church (see *CCC*, 1538).

Necessity of the Ministerial Priesthood

The priestly work of Christ remains essential to God's plan for the world. That is why Jesus gave the Church the sacrament of Holy Orders in order to ensure that the priestly work which is necessary to the life of the Church is never forgotten or distorted.

Through the sacrament of Holy Orders and the ministerial priesthood which arises from it, Christ continues to lead and build up his Church (*CCC*, 1547). The existence of the ordained ministry, especially bishops and priests, insures that Christ as head of the Church is made visible in the midst of the entire community of believers.

The ministerial priesthood enables the Church to celebrate the sacraments; and as long as the Church celebrates the sacraments she does what Christ does. Each time the Church baptizes, she gives life. Each time the Church confirms she gives strength. Each time the Church celebrates the Eucharist, she gives sustenance and nourishment. Likewise each time the Church celebrates the sacraments of Penance or Anointing, she brings forgiveness and healing.

Also, when the Church joins in the celebration of a marriage, she reflects Christ's love; and when she ordains someone she continues the process of consecrating the world to God. Each time the Church celebrates a sacrament she calls all those present to the priestly work which they should be doing in the world. She reminds them of what Jesus has done for them and what they must do for others.

The ordained minister (especially bishops and priests), by the sacred duty he has received, molds and rules the priestly people. Acting in the person of Christ, he brings about the eucharistic sacrifice and offers it to God in the name of all the people. Bishops, priests, and deacons must proclaim and teach God's word to all people, lead the Church in worship, and guide and rule God's people by imitating Christ's model of humble service.

Now, the same Lord has established certain ministers among the faithful in order to join them together in one body where "all the members have not the same function" (Rom 12:4). These ministers in the society of the faithful would be able by the sacred power of their order to offer sacrifice and remit sins. They would perform their priestly office publicly for [people] in the name of Christ (Decree on the Ministry and Life of Priests, No. 2).

From Prairie Farm to Archbishop

In the story below, the Archbishop of Vancouver, Canada, Adam Exner, OMI shares how as a teenager God came calling while doing chores on his family's farm and how he eventually listened and responded, setting the wheels in motion for a vocation to the priesthood and eventually the episcopate.

Though I and my family held the priesthood in high regard, the idea of becoming a priest just didn't take root in me. I had my heart set on being a farmer. I loved farming and looked forward to the day when the home farm would become mine. According to family tradition, I, the youngest, was to inherit the home farm.

One blistering hot day towards the end of July 1946, two of my older brothers and I were working in the bush, cutting down trees by hand with axes, thus preparing the bush to be ploughed under in order to make more arable land.

At noon we went home for lunch. During the meal, my mother advised us not to go back to the bush right after lunch, because it was so hot and she was concerned that we could suffer from sun stroke. "Wait until about three o'clock before returning to work," she said and then added, "I will make dinner later tonight, so you can still get in a full day's work." My two brothers followed Mother's advice. I didn't. I went back to the bush immediately after lunch. Why? Because I was ambitious! I wanted as much land cleared as possible. After all, the home farm would one day be mine.

Write a short story telling about a time you have brought the presence of God to another.

(From Prairie Farm to Archbishop cont.)

Back in the bush alone, I worked hard. At a given point I had just cut down a beautiful young poplar tree in the prime of its youth. Hot and drenched in sweat, I sat down on the tree stump for a rest. As I sat there looking at the tree I had just cut down, an unexpected and unsettling interior dialogue emerged in my soul. It began with a deep feeling of sorrow for the young tree I had just cut down.

An inner voice spoke to the tree, "You were in the prime of your youth, healthy, strong, and full of potential, and here I have cut you down. Soon I will lop off your branches, throw you on the pile from where you will be taken home to be cut up and used for firewood. What a way to go!"

Then another inner voice said, "Don't feel bad. When this tree appears before its Maker, it will be able to say, 'I have fulfilled the plan you had in mind for me.' What about you? Will you be able to say that too when you meet your Maker face to face?" the inner voice asked. I knew then and there that I couldn't.

Until that point in my life I hadn't really thought of what plan God might have for me. I had made my own plans and was feathering my own nest. Relentlessly the inner voice persisted, "Like this tree, you are in the prime of your youth, healthy, strong, and full of potential. Some day you too will be cut down and will meet your Creator. He will ask you, 'What have you done with the gift of life I have given you?' When that moment comes, as surely it will, what would you want to be able to say?"

After some serious thought, I decided that I would like to be able to say, "God I have tried as best I could to use the gift of life you gave me to serve you and to serve my brothers and sisters." Though I was absolutely sure that this is what I would like to say to God at the end of my life, I was deeply shaken by the realization that to become capable of saying that, my life would have to change radically. I would have to give up my dreams and say "yes" to God's plan for me. Then and there, deep within me, in my heart of hearts, I knew what God was asking of me. Then and there, I knew that I would never be at peace until I was ready to dedicate my life to the service of God and his people. Though I knew what I had to do, I was far from ready to do so. My whole interior rebelled and I began a vigorous battle against the idea of giving up my life dreams.

For the rest of the afternoon I worked feverishly in the hope that the pesty, unsettling thoughts that had invaded my soul would go away. They didn't. That evening I was very quiet at dinner and went for a walk afterwards, hoping for relief. No relief came. I went back into the house and picked up a Catholic magazine with the intention of reading the joke section on the last page, again seeking relief. The joke page was there, but the opposite page was filled with pictures and a strong pitch for vocations to the Missionary Oblates of Mary Immaculate! That was the last thing I needed! I threw the magazine

(From Prairie Farm to Archbishop cont.)

away and went to the cupboard where the newspapers were kept with the idea of reading the comic section. That would help.

As I was about to open the drawer, an inner voice said, "This is really bothering you; maybe you should ask some questions or seek some advice." I quickly decided that I wasn't ready to do so and opened the drawer. The newspapers were there, but for some unexplainable reason there was a prayer book on top of the newspapers. I had never seen it there before. The prayer book was open and in big bold print glaring at me were the words from the gospel of St. Luke (11:9), "Ask and you will receive, seek and you will find, knock and it will be opened to you." This was just too much. I'd had it. I slammed the drawer shut and went to bed. Needless to say, I couldn't sleep.

For the next two weeks, I slept very little. The little sleep I did get was broken and fitful. Due to lack of sleep and rest, I was beginning to look more and more tired and haggard. Towards the end of these two weeks, one mid-afternoon, while hard at work, I dropped into the house for a drink of water. As I came in, my mother looked at me and said, "What's the matter with you? You look sick." At that moment I surprised myself by blurting out, "Mom, I have to leave home." "My God," my mother exclaimed, "You are sick. Sit down and tell me what is going on." I sat down and told her my story.

She listened intently and then, with tears rolling down her cheeks, said, "I want to tell you something that I have never told to anyone before. Ever since I was a little girl, I have said a prayer to God every day, asking God to give me a good husband and children and asking God to take at least one of my children for his service. When you, the youngest, dropped out of school, my heart sank, but I didn't stop praying; I only changed my intention, saying to God, 'If you don't want one of my children for your service, that is all right, but in answer to my prayers, please give a vocation to a child from another family.' Then quietly and with a look that reflected deep inner joy and gratitude, she added, "Maybe God wants one of my children after all."

At this point, all resistance within me melted away and I could say, "Be it done to me according to Your word." I had just taken the first step, a big one, in my faith adventure. I was now at peace with myself and with God and I could sleep again. But in subsequent days, every so often tempting inner voices tried to frighten me, "What have I done? Am I fooling myself? Am I worthy? Am I capable? Is it worth it? Will I be happy?" Whenever these disturbing thoughts emerged, another inner and stronger voice would reassure me saying, "Do not be afraid. I will be with you. Trust me. I will make you worthy and capable. Just cross one bridge at a time. Walk in faith. With my help, there is nothing you cannot do."

Story quoted from www.vocationsvancouver.com.

The Importance of Apostolic Succession

We cannot speak of the sacrament of Holy Orders without identifying and understanding the importance of the apostles and apostolic succession. The word apostle means "one sent." Jesus himself was the Father's apostle, sent to preach the good news and bring salvation to all. All of the Gospels record that Jesus chose a special group of twelve of his followers who were charged by him to be his apostles. The gospel of Mark tells us, "He appointed twelve [whom he also named apostles] that they might be with him and he might send them forth to preach" (Mk 3:14). The Greek word that the evangelist Mark used was *apostoloi*, which can also be translated "emissaries."

Christ gave the apostles a share in the work he was given by his Father. He said to them: "As the Father has sent me, even so I send you" (Jn 20:21), and "He who receives you receives me" (Mt 10:40). The twelve apostles were witnesses to Christ's public ministry and to his resurrection.

The apostles not only received a mandate from Jesus to carry out his mission, but the power to accomplish it as well. Giving them a share in the mission he received from his Father, he promised to be with them always through the gift of his Holy Spirit. Thus the mission he gave to the twelve is a permanent one, still carried out by the church today.

The apostles were the foundation upon which Christ built the Church. They in turn appointed others to continue their work. They did this by handing on to them the gospel they received from Christ and by means of a laying on of hands. The term "apostolic succession" refers to the continuous and uninterrupted transfer of the preaching and authority that Christ gave to his apostles and which they passed on to their successors, the bishops.

In the early Church there were some who claimed to be apostles who were not. Not all of them, however, were teaching what Christ taught. Some were actually teaching things that were antithetical to Christ's teachings. For example, one group known as the *gnostics* claimed to have "secret knowledge" of Christ. One of the lessons of their so-called secret knowledge was that the physical world had not been created by God. The gnostics taught that the physical world was either evil or irrelevant.

In response to the gnostics the Church began to formalize some of its beliefs. A universally accepted list of scriptures—the canon of the scriptures—was formed. The Apostles' Creed which outlines the fundamental truths of Christianity was also developed.

But the real issue between the Church and the gnostics could not be settled with a canon of scripture or a creed. The real issue had to do with who had the authority to speak in Christ's name. The Church insisted that Christ had given his apostles the authority to speak in his name. Whatever knowledge he wished to pass on, he would have given to those apostles. They in turn would have passed it on to their successors, the bishops. And, since all of the successors of the apostles rejected the notion of a group possessing secret knowledge, such secret knowledge must not exist.

From that point on it became important for any person or group who wished to speak in Christ's name to demonstrate their direct connection to the apostles. Those bishops who did not have written records connecting them directly to the apostles were still considered to be successors of the apostles and authentic interpreters of Christ if they were in agreement with the rest of the bishops. The most fundamental concept of apostolic succession was solidified, that is, that only those who are direct successors of the apostles have the authority to interpret and teach the message of Christ.

Holy Orders is the sacrament instituted by Christ as the means of handing on his mission and mandate to his apostles and future generations. From Christ, bishops and priests receive the mission and sacred power (faculty) to act in the person of Christ; deacons receive the strength to serve the Church in liturgy, word, and charity in communion with the bishop and priests. Apostolic succession, preserved through the sacrament of Holy Orders, thus protects the Church against an influx of ideas that would undermine Jesus' message.

Apostolic succession not only protects the teaching ministry of the Church, it also protects her sacramental ministry. A person can only act in Jesus' name if he or she has received the grace to do so. That grace is not something the person can bestow on himself or herself. It is something that must be given. Furthermore it can only be given by one who has the authority to give it (see *CCC*, 875).

Apostolic succession ensures that the priests who act as ministers of God's grace have the authority to do so. Jesus gave his apostles the authority to act in his name in the performance of certain sacramental acts. They in turn passed that authority on to their successors. Only the apostles and their successors have received the authority to act in the person of Christ during the celebration of the sacraments.

According to Catholic teaching, the effectiveness of the sacraments is not dependent upon the goodness of the minister, but it is dependent upon the minister's connection to Jesus from whom the sacraments come. Apostolic succession ensures that the faithful will not be left in doubt as to whether God's grace has been given. If the minister is validly ordained, he has the authority to act in Christ's name and grace will be given. If the minister is not validly ordained, he does not have the authority to act in Christ's name and we cannot presume that grace has been given.

The first Christian community in Jerusalem was made up of the apostles chosen by Jesus—excluding only Judas Iscariot, the one who betrayed him. Read Acts 1:12-26, detailing the story of their experience after Jesus' ascension and their choosing of an apostle to replace Judas.

Holy Orders

Finally, in addition to the sacramental nature of the ministry of the ordained, apostolic succession also guarantees the ruling nature of the ministry. Christ himself instituted the apostles as "the seeds of the new Israel and the beginning of the sacred hierarchy" (*Ad gentes*, 5). This ministry has a "collegial character," that is, every bishop exercises his rule within the college of bishops in communion with the bishop of Rome, the Pope, who is the head of the college. Priests, too, exercise this ministry from within their diocese under the direction of their bishop.

The Gifts of Ordination

Today the word "ordination" is used to describe the sacramental act which integrates a man into the order of bishops, priests, or deacons. The word *order* has roots in the Roman Empire. It was originally used to refer to an established organization that had a particular purpose or set of responsibilities. Within the Church there have always been established groupings of people which Tradition refers to as orders: the order of bishops, the order of priests and the order of deacons, as well as the order of catechumens, the order of virgins, and the order of widows, to name a few more. In the early Church, official integration into any of these orders involved a rite called ordination. An ordination was a religious blessing or consecration for a specific task.

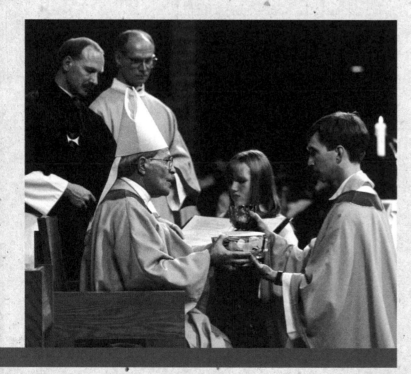

Today the word ordination is reserved for describing sacramental ordination. Sacramental ordination confers a gift of the Holy Spirit which permits the exercise of a sacred power. This sacred power comes from Christ through the Church and consists of the ability to act in the person of Christ offering God's grace to others through the sacraments and also in the offices of teaching and ruling. (The fullness of this sacred power is in the consecration of a bishop in the sacrament of Holy Orders.)

When we say that a bishop and his priest designate acts in the person of Christ, we are not saying that he pretends to be Christ, nor are we saying that he is some sort of substitute for Christ. What the Church holds is that Christ works through him in such a way that when the bishop or priest celebrates the sacraments, it is not he who is acting, but Christ who is acting. It is Christ himself who baptizes, who confirms, who offers himself to God the Father during the Mass, who forgives and anoints, who witnesses and blesses a couple's marriage vows, and who, in the case of a bishop, ordains. Also, when the bishop offers the Church a teaching or ruling, he is acting as a representative of Christ who was himself teacher, shepherd, and priest.

The personality of the bishop or priest and the manner in which he behaves during a sacramental celebration may affect how others perceive the sacrament, but they cannot affect the sacrament itself. When he celebrates the sacraments he is a slave to Christ in the truest sense of the word "slave." He is a possession of Christ and his own person is for the most part irrelevant. In his let-ter to the Philippians Paul wrote that Jesus "emptied himself, taking the form of a slave" (2:7). During the celebration of the sacraments, a bishop or priest, through the power of God's grace, does the same. Whenever a bishop or priest celebrates the sacraments, he "empties" himself of himself and is "filled" with Christ. This self-emptying occurs because of the grace given in ordination. It does not depend on his willingness to be emptied in any particular sacramental celebration.

Sometimes we think of the position of the bishops and the priests within the Church as a position of power, but in fact it is a position of complete power-lessness. The one who is ordained surrenders his own power to act so that Christ may act through him. When James and John asked Jesus if they could have seats of honor next to him in the kingdom, Jesus asked them if they could drink from the cup from which he had to drink. He was asking them if they could empty themselves completely in the same way that he was about to empty him-self (see Mk 10:35-45). It is this same self-emptying which Jesus requires of those who would hold leadership positions within the Church today. A vocation to the priesthood is a vocation to become insignificant so that Christ may be all impor-tant. Think of it this way:

> *When you go into a Catholic Church, you know that Christ is present in the Blessed Sacrament, contained in the tabernacle. This is true because of the actions of a priest. Who that priest was and what he was like were of no importance. All that mattered was that he was a priest, and Christ had worked through him in order to transform the bread into Christ's own body. Without*

that priest you would not have been able to be in Christ's presence in the same way; and yet the individual identity of the priest was irrelevant. He had left no mark of himself. This is why we say that a priest is a slave of Christ.

Because Christ acts through the priest in the sacraments, the Church also acts through the priest in the sacraments. The Church is the body of Christ; therefore whatever is done in the name of Christ is done in the name of the Church as well. When the priest gives his voice to Christ, his voice becomes the voice of Christ's body, the Church. When the priest baptizes it is Christ who baptizes. Because it is Christ who baptizes, it is the whole Church—the body of Christ—who baptizes. When the priest forgives someone in the sacrament of Reconciliation, it is Christ who forgives. Because it is Christ who forgives, it is also the Church—the body of Christ—who forgives. When the priest offers the body of Christ to God during the Eucharist, it is Christ who is offering himself. Because Christ is offering himself, the whole Church—the whole body of Christ—also offers itself "through him, with him and in him, in the unity of the Holy Spirit" (see *CCC*, 1553).

The presence of Christ acting through the minister does not preserve the minister from all human weaknesses, errors, or sins. The sacrament of Holy Orders does not guarantee that the minister will always empty himself so that he is able to act in the person of Christ. Ordination does not even guarantee that the minister will not harm the Church. There may be times when the minister's own infidelity to the gospel weakens the faith of others or even leads them astray. What the sacrament of ordination does guarantee is that in the celebration of the sacraments the minister will not hinder Christ's grace. The sacrament of Holy Orders changes the character of the minister in such a way that he cannot avoid emptying himself and being filled with Christ when he celebrates the sacraments.

☑ Do you associate the positions of bishop and priest more as positions of power or powerlessness? Explain.

More on Priestly Character

☑ Speaking of the effects of ordination and how Christ acts through people who may be unworthy, St. Augustine wrote: "The spiritual power of the sacrament is indeed comparable to light: those to be enlightened receive it in its purity, and if it should pass through defiled beings, it is not itself defiled" (In. Jo, ev. 5, 15: PL 35, 1422). Develop your own image to describe the spiritual power of ordination.

When we talk of someone's "character," we are talking of those attitudes and behaviors which are automatic. We are referring to those things which a person does without thinking whenever he or she is faced with a particular situation. If we say, "it is in her character to teach," we are saying that whenever the opportunity presents itself, she will teach even if she does not particularly feel like teaching. If we say that "it is in his character to be honest," we are saying that he will tell the truth even when telling the truth is uncomfortable or risky. When we say that ordination gives the person who is ordained a new character, we are saying that, in certain situations, ordination changes the automatic response of the one who is ordained. Specifically, ordination changes his automatic behavior during the sacraments.

The Communal and Personal Dimensions of the Sacrament of Holy Orders

The sacrament of Holy Orders gives the person who is ordained a new spiritual character. He is configured to Christ so that he can serve as Christ's instrument within the Church. The sacrament of Holy Orders is not for the benefit of the one who receives it, but rather for the benefit and salvation of others (see *CCC*, 1534). The bishop, priest, or deacon benefits from ordination only because ordination enables him to serve others, and in serving others he will draw closer to God himself.

Just as the sacrament of Holy Orders is intended for the Church as a whole and not just for the one who receives it, so too the power and authority which is given in the sacrament must be exercised within the Church as a whole and not in isolation. The bishops of the Church exercise their ministry in communion with other bishops and in union with the Pope, not on their own. This "college" or body of bishops receives its authority from its head, the Roman Pontiff, or Pope, in the same way the apostles received authority from St. Peter who was the head of the apostles. The word Pope traces to the Latin and Greek words for "Papa." Due to the virtue of his office as "shepherd of the whole flock" (see Jn 21:15 ff.), the Pope is pastor of the whole Church and has "full, supreme, and universal power over the Church" (*Lumen Gentium*, 22). The Pope can always exercise his power freely.

Priests exercise their ministry within the *presbyterium* ("priesthood") of the diocese and under the direction of the diocesan bishop, not on their own. Bishops have the authority to teach in the name of Christ, but only when they teach in union with one another and with the Pope. Likewise, priests have the authority to proclaim and interpret the gospel within the local Church when they depend on and are in communion with the bishop.

Even in the celebration of the sacraments, bishops and priests must act in a manner that is in keeping with the Church as a whole. If in celebrating a sacrament a priest or bishop intends to do something other than what the Church normally intends within that sacrament, he is not acting in the person of Christ or with the authority of Christ. Thus, although many of the early Anabaptists were

The liturgy of the hours is also called the divine office. It is the official prayer of the Church and a response to St. Paul's request to "pray without ceasing" (1 Thes 5:17). It is recited seven times over the course of 24 hours and includes psalms, hymns, scripture readings, responses, intercessory prayers, canticles, and other spiritual writings. In years past, the divine office was prayed mainly by priests and religious. Now, it is a prayer all the Church is encouraged to pray as often as possible.

priests, they were not (according to Catholic teaching) acting in the person of Christ when they rebaptized adults who had been baptized as infants. This is because even though they were celebrating a sacrament, they were not intending to do what the Church normally does in baptism.[1]

Although ministry within the Church is always exercised with others, it still has a personal character. Each person who is ordained is called to bear personal witness to the common mission of the Church. He is to practice in his personal life what he proclaims in his public life. Because the one who is ordained has a leadership position in the Church, others will look to him as an example of how to live as Christians. This means that ordination comes with an enormous responsibility to live faithfully. It is for this reason that the Church insists that those who are ordained must shape their life around prayer, especially by praying the liturgy of the hours daily.

The Three Degrees of the Sacrament of Holy Orders

There are three degrees of the sacrament of Holy Orders: the ministries of bishops, priests, and deacons. The three degrees are a ministerial participation in the priesthood of Christ. The orders of bishop and priest enable the one who is ordained to act in the person of Christ, the head of the body, in the celebration of the sacraments. Deacons are ordained to help and serve the priests and bishops

in their work. While priests and bishops are configured to Christ in order that they might act as the head of Christ's body, deacons are configured to Christ in order that they might serve as he served.

The fullness of the sacrament of Holy Orders is found in *episcopal ordination*—the ordination of bishops. The Pope is the successor to St. Peter as the Bishop of Rome and, because of this, the Supreme Pontiff of the Catholic Church. He and his fellow bishops are the ones who receive the grace of the Holy Spirit to be the visible presence of Christ the teacher, shepherd, and priest. As covered previously, bishops not only have the responsibility for making the grace of God available through the sacraments, they are also responsible for teaching in the name of Christ and ensuring that the teachings of Christ are understood and applied appropriately within the modern world.

The teaching of the Pope and bishops is authentic, as they are endowed with the authority of Christ. This supreme participation in the authority of Christ is ensured by the gift of *infallibility*. This gift of infallibility has three dimensions. It refers first to the Church as a whole. The Second Vatican Council taught: "The whole body of the faithful ... cannot err in matters of belief. This characteristic is shown in the supernatural appreciation of faith (*sensus fidei*) on the part of the whole people, when, from the bishops to the last of the faithful, they manifest a universal consent in matters of faith and morals" (*Lumen Gentium*, 12). The second dimension of infallibility refers to the teaching of the college of bishops. The *Catechism* states: "The infallibility promised to the Church is also present in the body of bishop when, together with Peter's successor, they exercise the supreme Magisterium, above all in an Ecumenical Council" (891). The third

dimension of infallibility refers to the exercise of this gift by the Pope when he makes a particular pronouncement on matters of faith or morals. Again, the language of the *Catechism* helps us to understand this: "The Roman Pontiff, head of the college of bishops, enjoys this infallibility in virtue of his office, when, as supreme pastor and teacher of all the faithful—who confirms his brethren in the faith—he proclaims by a definitive act a doctrine pertaining to faith or morals" (891). Thus we believe that the teaching of the Pope and bishops in union with him in the matter of faith and morals is protected from error.

The bishop is usually the "proper" or "ordinary" pastor within a diocese. For that reason he is sometimes called the "ordinary" of the diocese. (A bishop appointed to help the ordinary in a diocese is called an auxiliary bishop.) The word bishop itself comes from the Greek *episcopoi* meaning "overseer." Each ordinary is responsible for ensuring that the work of Christ is being done in his diocese. Furthermore, the bishop is the visible source and sign of the unity within his diocese.

All of the bishops together are responsible for ensuring that the work begun by Christ is continuing in all regions of the world. The unity of all of the bishops within the college of bishops under the authority of the Pope is the sign of the unity of the Church throughout the world. When a bishop is ordained he receives the grace of strength from the Holy Spirit. He is given the grace to guide and defend the Church and to show particular love for the poor, the sick, and the needy.

Research:

- The name and background of your local bishop.
- How many Popes there have been.
- Details about the ministry of a deacon in your parish or neighboring parish.
- How many years and the course of study it takes to be a priest.

The bishop, as a function of the "sanctifying office," is also the leader in the celebration of divine worship. Through the gift of ordination he provides, he is the "steward of the grace of the supreme priesthood" (*Lumen Gentium*, 26) which his priests offer and he offers personally. The Eucharist is center of the particular diocesan and parish Church. The bishop and his priests make the Church holy by their prayer and work, and by their ministry of the word and of the sacraments.

From his governing office, the Pope and bishops (along with their helpers, priests and deacons) have ruling authority in the Church. All institutions have need of a governing structure so that the work can be done. The ruling office of the Church has one purpose: the growth of faith and holiness. Church law—called "canon law"—includes precepts and rules that regulate the Church. These laws along with other legitimate commands of the Pope and bishops must be respectfully obeyed by all Catholics.

Priests are ordained to be co-workers of the bishops. The word priest comes from the Greek *presbyteroi*, a name for the elders in the early Church. In a sense priests are the representatives of the bishop in the local congregation. Priests are consecrated to preach the gospel and to act in the person of Christ in the celebration of the Eucharist. Priests are also ordained to baptize, to bless marriages, and to anoint the sick. Priests share in the bishop's ministry of forgiving sins in the sacrament of Penance, and under special circumstances they may also confirm those who have been baptized.

When priests are in union with their bishop they share his authority to act in the person of Christ. The spiritual gift which priests receive in ordination prepares them to preach the gospel everywhere and to participate in the universal mission of salvation; nonetheless, they must be given permission by the local bishop to exercise these gifts. Occasionally a priest is released from the obligations (or even forbidden) to exercise the gifts received in ordination. He may at the same time be released from the bonds of priestly celibacy and be allowed to marry. He cannot, however, become a true layman again. This is because the sacramental character which he received in ordination and the grace of the Spirit which enables him to act in the person of Christ in the sacraments still remains.

Deacons are ordained to assist the priests and the bishop in their work within the Church. The word deacon comes from *diakonoi*, the word which means to serve or specifically "to wait on tables." Through their ordination deacons are configured to Christ who washed the feet of his disciples and made himself the servant of all. Deacons are ordained to read the gospel and to preach at liturgy, to assist the priest during the celebration of the Eucharist in other ways, to assist at and bless marriages, and to preside over funerals. In the Latin Rite deacons also act as ministers of baptism. Deacons have a special responsibility for participating in the Church's works of charity.

There are two types of deacons. There are those who are ordained as deacons as a step toward priestly ordination and there are those who are ordained to the permanent diaconate. The permanent diaconate is the only degree of the sacrament of orders which may be conferred upon a married man in the Latin rite.

The Rite of Ordination

The ordination of a bishop, a priest, or a deacon is very significant to the life of the Church. Therefore it normally takes place in the cathedral (the main church of the diocese) at a Sunday celebration of the Eucharist. The essential rite for all three degrees of ordination consists in the bishop imposing his hand on the head of the ordinand and offering a prayer of consecration which is specific to the degree of ordination. In the prayer the Church asks God to pour out his Spirit on the one being ordained and to give him those gifts which he will need in order to serve the Church well in his new role. Since the sacrament of Holy Orders is the sacrament of the apostolic ministry, only validly ordained bishops—those who are in the line of apostolic succession—can validly confer the three degrees of the sacrament of Holy Orders.

Only a baptized man may validly receive ordination (see the feature "Only Men Can Be Priests," pages 200-202). The Church teaches that it cannot ordain women since Jesus, who chose only male apostles, did not ordain women though he stressed their dignity against many repressive laws of his day. Also, as the *Catechism* teaches, paraphrasing the words of Pope John Paul II, "No one has a *right* to receive the sacrament of Holy Orders. Indeed no one claims this office for himself; he is called to it by God" (1578). It is the Church that has the right and responsibility to call someone to receive orders. Normally, all ordained ministers in the Latin Church (with the exception of permanent deacons) are chosen from men of faith who live a celibate life and intend to remain celibate "for the sake of the kingdom of heaven" (Mt 19:12).

In the Latin Church before the candidate is ordained he is presented to the bishop and the bishop and the community are assured that he has received the necessary training and been chosen for ordination in accordance with the teaching and practice of the Church. The candidate then is ordained by a bishop who is validly ordained himself. In other words, the bishop officially proclaims him as a man who has been chosen for ministry within the Church. The congregation gives its assent to this election. Then the candidate is instructed in the nature of the duties he is about to assume, and his willingness to accept those duties is examined. This is followed by a recitation of the litany of the saints. The local church calls upon the entire Church on earth and in heaven to pray for the ordinand as he assumes his new role within the communion of saints. The candidate then kneels before the bishop who lays hands on the head of the ordinand and offers the prayer of consecration.

In the Latin rite, the prayer of consecration for a bishop is as follows:

> *Father, you know all hearts.*
> *You have chosen your servant for the office of bishop.*
> *May he be a shepherd to your holy flock,*
> *and a high priest blameless in your sight,*
> *ministering to you night and day;*
> *may he always gain the blessing of your favor*

Around the time of the Middle Ages, a series of minor orders developed. Porters were those who gathered the worshiping community, lectors were readers of scripture, exorcists assisted the bishop in driving away evil and caring for catechumens, acolytes were servers at Mass, and subdeacons assisted the deacon and priest at Mass. Before the Second Vatican Council, all of these minor orders were conferred on seminarians in the months before ordination. Today, the ministries of lector and acolyte are still conferred on men in the months or years prior to their ordination. Also, today, lay people may be admitted permanently to the ministries of lector and acolyte. And, when necessity warrants it and ministers are lacking, lay persons, even if they are not lectors or acolytes, can still fulfill some of the offices of these ministries, for example, reading of the Word, presiding over liturgical prayers, conferring Baptism, and distributing Holy Communion (see CCC, 903).

Name an ordained church leader you respect. Why do you respect this person? What qualities makes this person a good spiritual leader?

and offer the gifts of your holy Church.
Through the Spirit who gives the grace of high priesthood
grant him the power
to forgive sins as you have commanded,
to assign ministries as you have decreed,
and to loose from every bond by the authority which you gave to your apostles.
May he be pleasing to you by his gentleness and purity of heart,
presenting a fragrant offering to you,
through Jesus Christ, your Son . . . (Roman Pontifical, Ordination of
Bishops, #26).

There are several additional rites which follow the solemn consecration in the Roman Catholic Church. These rites express and complete the mystery that is accomplished in ordination:

> Bishops and priests are anointed with holy chrism as a sign of the special anointing of the Holy Spirit given in ordination. The new bishop is then presented with the book of the Gospels as a sign of his apostolic mission to proclaim the word of God. He is given a mitre and a ring as a sign of his office and his fidelity to the Church, the bride of Christ. Finally he is presented with a crosier (staff) as a sign that he is a shepherd of God's people.
>
> When a priest is ordained, he is given a paten and chalice. These represent the "offering of the holy people" which he is called to present to God.
>
> A deacon is given the book of the Gospels because he has received the mission to proclaim the Gospel.

Historical Development of the Sacrament of Holy Orders

The priesthood of the Old Testament prefigured the priesthood of the New Testament. The entire nation of Israel had a priestly role to the world through one tribe. The tribe of Levi was chosen to act as priests within the Israelite community. The Levites had a particular responsibility for the liturgical life of the community; and it was their job to act on behalf of the community in offering gifts and sacrifices to God. But the sacrifices which the flawed human priests could offer were never perfect and could never completely reunite God and humanity.

Jesus came as the one high priest who could offer the perfect sacrifice. He fulfilled the task of the Levitical priesthood. He then chose twelve apostles to continue his priestly work. The number twelve was significant. It symbolized the twelve tribes of Israel and thus the completeness and the universality of the new nation—the Church—which Jesus was founding. The importance of this symbolism was underscored by the fact that the apostles felt that it was necessary to choose someone to replace Judas before they began their formal priestly work (see Acts 1:15-26).

The apostles saw their priestly task as missionary. They understood their primary role to be that of bringing the message of Jesus to those who had not yet heard it. As new communities of Christians came into being, the apostles also saw it as their duty to guide them and to settle any disputes which arose.

As the number of Christian communities began to gather without an apostle present, an increasing number of false teachers emerged. As mentioned before, many of these used the name of Christ to teach and do things that were far from what Christ intended. Because of this there was a growing recognition of the need for good order and formal structures for leadership.

Jewish Christian communities adopted the organizational model used in Jewish synagogues with elders, prophets, and preachers. The early gentile Christian communities developed their own formal structure with bishops (or overseers) and deacons. The elders and bishops were responsible for overseeing the religious and moral life, for ensuring that those in need were cared for, and for safeguarding doctrine. As the number of local communities or parishes outside major centers began to increase, presbyters (priests) were given pastoral care of these parishes. Deacons were ordained to help the bishops, particularly to help them in caring for those in need.

By the beginning of the second century, Ignatius of Antioch decreed that only a bishop or his appointee was to preside at Eucharist or to baptize. In the early Church, bishops and other Church leaders were chosen by the community as a whole. A person was chosen as bishop because of the apparent presence of the Holy Spirit within him. After his election a bishop received imposition of hands from another bishop. He was ordained to proclaim the word, forgive sins, preside at Eucharist, and supervise the work of presbyters and deacons. Presbyters were ordained by the bishop and other presbyters joined in the laying on of hands at the rite of ordination. Deacons were ordained by the bishop alone, and were ordained specifically to assist the bishop in his ministry.

Following the edict of Constantine and the legalization of Christianity in 313, bishops and presbyters were given civil authority and status. The state gave special privileges to the ordained. The ordained came to be called "clergy" and a gap developed between them and the laity. A view took hold that the clergy were people devoted to "higher things of the spirit" while lay people were obliged to the "lower things of the flesh."

The desire of the people to elect a particular person as bishop was no longer enough to guarantee that he would become a bishop; the approval of the state was also necessary. Still, the Council of Chalcedon (451) stated that priests were to be called by the people of a particular parish and ordained for work within that parish. Any other ordination was considered null and void. Bishops and priests were paid salaries by the state.

Between the sixth and twelfth centuries, the increase of the monastic life influenced priesthood a great deal. Though most monks were not priests, many priests did adopt the religious habit, prayers, study, and strict discipline of monasticism, including celibacy. This movement helped lead to the requirement of celibacy for the ordained in 1215. Prior to this time priests were permitted to be married, though many priests already lived a single, celibate life.

Debate the validity of this statement: In general, priests are holier and more devoted to God than lay people.

Share an example of Christian living you have learned from a priest.

Reaffirming and Reteaching Priesthood

The Reformation and the ensuing Council of Trent had a dramatic effect on the priesthood. Martin Luther and other reformers emphasized the common priesthood of all believers and said that there was no special ministerial power received through the sacrament of Holy Orders. The Council of Trent countered this argument by asserting that Holy Orders was one of the seven sacraments and stating that bishops, priests, and deacons do not depend on a call from the Church for their authority and power. The Council of Trent inspired reform in the church, including the establishment of seminaries for assisting the preparation of candidates to the priesthood.

The Second Vatican Council reminded the Church of the differences between the ministerial or hierarchial priesthood and the common priesthood, and also pointed out their interrelation. Each of them in its own special way is a participatioin in the one priesthood of Christ. Yet, they differ essentially. The common priesthood is exercised by a living out of the baptismal graces. The function of the ministerial priesthood is to help unfold the baptismal graces of all Christians.

What is more, the Council reaffirmed that the role of the priest, bishop, and deacon is not a role of power but a role of service. Priests, bishops, and deacons are ordained not for themselves but for the Church as a whole. They are to facilitate the action of God's grace within the Church so that lay people may receive grace within the sacraments and then carry that grace into the world. Bishops, priests, and deacons are called to do for the Church what the members of the Church are called to do for the world.

Only Men Can Be Priests

How do you think the work of priests will change in the future? How will it remain the same?

In 1995 Pope John Paul II stated that the Catholic practice of ordaining only men to the priesthood was not something that could be changed. He said that the teaching that priests must be male is part of the "deposit of faith" which the Church has received from Christ. As such, it must be accepted in faith.

For many people living in the twenty-first century this is a very difficult thing to accept even as a matter of faith. We live in a world in which we are becoming increasingly aware of the fundamental equality of men and women. In all areas of life people are making concerted efforts to translate this equality into reality. When we are told that there is something which women cannot do simply because they are women we are quick to suspect injustice.

But the Church's teaching is not rooted in injustice. In fact, in recent years the Church has

(Only Men Can Be Priests cont.)

stressed the fundamental equality of men and women. The Church's teaching regarding ordination is rooted in a belief that although men and women are fundamentally equal, they are not the same. Our gender is not incidental. It is an essential part of who we are. For this reason it has an impact on all of our relationships, including our relationship with God and with God's Church.

When Jesus chose the twelve apostles to carry on his work he chose only men. According to Catholic teaching, this cannot be interpreted as a caving in to the societal norms of his day. Jesus regularly interacted with a group of women. He talked with women as friends in a society in which women and men were not normally friends. He taught women and allowed them to sit at his feet to learn as disciples in a society where women were not normally allowed to learn. He sent women to proclaim his resurrection to the others. Nonetheless, he did not count women among the twelve. Furthermore, when the apostles chose their successors they also did not choose women. Even Mary, the mother of Jesus was not chosen to replace Judas among the twelve even though she was regularly with the apostles.

When the Church says that the practice of ordaining men and men only is part of the deposit of faith, she is saying that if the Church ordained women, a fundamental truth which Jesus wanted to preserve would be lost.

In official pronouncements regarding the inability of the Church to ordain women, the Church's leadership has often stressed the significance of the role of motherhood. Like motherhood, ordination can only be received as an unmerited gift. Also, as motherhood is not primarily for the benefit of the mother but for the good of the child, priesthood is primarily for the service of others.

It is also important to remember that although women cannot be ordained as priests, they can hold many other leadership positions within the Church. Too often the Church has been influenced by the patriarchal societies around us and has not recognized that the dignity of women is equal to that of men. Too often the Church has excluded women from

(Only Men Can Be Priests cont.)

certain things, not out of fidelity to Jesus' teachings but out of its own sinfulness. All of us within the Church have a responsibility for working to overcome the gender inequalities which are the result of sin within the Church.

Many things which have traditionally been done by those who are ordained do not actually require ordination. Many of the Church's ministries must be exercised under the direction of the bishop, but they can be exercised by ordained and lay persons, by men and women. Furthermore, all baptized Christians—men and women—are called to live out the graces of Baptism by living a life of faith, hope, and charity, according to the promptings of the Holy Spirit.

Called to Serve

Each person has been created by God for a special purpose and is called to serve God in a unique way. When we respond to our call we will find the joy which Jesus promised us, a joy which will fill us to overflowing if we allow it to. God's call to us is an invitation to live in the way that will allow our unique gifts and talents to flourish and to produce a good greater than we would have imagined possible. Our call is an invitation to become the good soil which yields thirty, sixty, and one hundredfold (see Mk 4:20).

It is important to spend regular time in prayer, listening for God's call in our lives. All of us need to ask ourselves how we can best serve God and his people. Unless we do this, we cannot be faithful to the commitments we made in Baptism and Confirmation. Not only should we spend time in private prayer, we should also pray with others in our Church community, and we should take time to share our faith and discuss our sense of call or our inability to hear a call.

Young men should take special care to discern if they have a vocation as a priest, deacon, or religious. In the same way, young women should examine their hearts carefully to see if the Lord is calling them to a vocation as a sister. If you discover in your heart that God is indeed calling you to one of these vocations, you should find a priest, sister, brother, or trusted teacher to talk over what your heart might be telling you.

God does not call us just for ourselves, but also for others. For this reason we need the help of others to hear God's call. No person can determine his or her call in isolation; all of us need to rely on the support, prayers, and discernment of other people of faith. We also need to remember that those other people of faith are depending on us. If we think that God is calling someone to a particular ministry, we have a responsibility to tell that person.

Remember: If you think that God may be calling you to a particular ministry as a priest, brother, or sister, take time to find out more about that ministry, to pray about it, and to talk with others about it. Do not try to run away from God. For as St. Augustine said, "our hearts are restless until they rest in God." If God is calling you to do something specifically, even something that appears difficult, he will give you the strength and the ability to do it, and he will enable you to find joy in it.

Have you ever told someone that he may have the gifts necessary to be a candidate for priesthood?

Chapter 8
Review Questions

1. Which two sacraments are directed to the salvation of others?

2. What does the ministerial priesthood insure for the Church?

3. Why was the issue of apostolic succession important in the early Church?

4. What does the sacrament of Holy Orders confer?

5. What does it mean to say that the bishop and his priest designate act in the person of Christ?

6. How is the position of bishop and priest really one of complete powerlessness?

7. How does the sacrament of Holy Orders change a person's character?

8. How do bishops and priests exercise their ministries within community?

9. Where is the fullness of the sacrament of Holy Orders found?

10. Explain the three dimensions of the gift of infallibility.

11. What are priests ordained for?

12. What is the primary ministry of deacons?

13. Why are only men eligible for ordination?

14. What is the primary rite of ordination?

15. How did the apostles understand their priestly task?

16. What differing views on the clergy and laity developed after the edict of Constantine?

17. When did celibacy become a universal requirement of priesthood?

18. What should people do to help determine their special calling from God?

Endnotes

1. The Anabaptists were a group of Christians who broke away from the Catholic Church during the Protestant reformation. They believed that baptism was an adult commitment to Christian faith and therefore rebaptized those who had been baptized as infants. It is impossible to intend what the Church intends in a rebaptism because the intention of baptism is to wipe away original sin (something which cannot be done more than once) and to mark a person as an adopted child of God (something which is done once and for all.) It is important to note that the Catholic Church does recognize the validity of all baptisms which are done in the name of the Trinity if the person being baptized has never been baptized before. The Church does not recognize any repeat of baptism no matter who is doing the baptizing.

Matrimony

9

The Mystery of Love

We know from popular songs that "love is the answer."

But, what is love?

Is there any other question which has received as much attention over the centuries? Millions of books, plays, poems, movies, and songs have been written about love. Scientists and psychologists have tried to explain why people love. Wars have been fought for love. Peace has been made for love. Our own scriptures tell us that "God is love."

Still, we ask, "What is love?"

Over 2,500 years ago a Jewish poet described the desires of love in this way:

> *More delightful is your love than wine!*
> *Your name spoken is a spreading perfume—*
>
> *On my bed at night I sought him*
> *whom my heart loves—*
> *I sought him but I did not find him.*

I will rise then and go about the city;
in the streets and crossings I will seek
Him whom my heart loves.
I sought him but I did not find him.
The watchmen came upon me
as they made their rounds of the city:
Have you seen him whom my heart loves?
I had hardly left them
when I found him whom my heart loves.
I took hold of him and would not let him go. . . .

Set me as a seal on your heart,
as a seal on your arm;
For stern as death is love,
relentless as the nether world is devotion;
its flames are a blazing fire.
Deep waters cannot quench love,
nor floods sweep it away.
Were one to offer all he owns to purchase love,
he would be roundly mocked (Sg 1:2-3, 3:1-4, 8:6-7).

✔ **Write your own personal definition of love.**

These words are part of the Song of Songs from the Old Testament. This inspired text has been viewed by both Jews and Christians as a description of the love between God and his people. It has also been understood as a God-given description of the sacredness, beauty, and wonder of married love. In the wonder of ideal human love God welcomes us into the mystery of divine love. When we open ourselves to the mystery of divine love we are able to experience ideal human love. God has chosen to intertwine human and divine love to such an extent that when we know one we will know the other.

The sacrament of Matrimony, or marriage, celebrates the universal human relationship of wedded life between a man and a woman and their relationship with the divine. An understanding of the nature of Christian marriage, its history, and its rites are presented in this chapter.

Marriage imagery is used over and over in the scriptures to help us understand God's loving plan for creation. The Bible begins with the story of the creation of man and woman as partners made in the image of God and it concludes with the wedding feast of the Lamb in the book of Revelation (see 19:5-8). It is in human marriage that we get a glimpse of the tremendous love which Christ has for the Church and it is in human marriage and family life that we have a foretaste of the intimate communion and tremendous joy that will be ours in heaven (see *CCC*, 1642).

Marriage in God's Plan

According to the second story of creation in Genesis 2:4-25, when Adam was created he had a very close relationship with God. After God created Adam, he created all of the beauty of the earth. All was for Adam. God gave Adam the garden of Eden as his home and as a place that he could shape according to his own wishes. God made Adam comfortable, God conversed with Adam and he invited Adam to share his work. But still Adam was lonely.

God said, "It is not good for the man to be alone. I will make a suitable partner for him." And so God created the various animals and brought them one by one to Adam. Adam named the animals, but none of the animals could truly ease his loneliness. Finally, God put Adam into a deep sleep and created a woman from Adam's own flesh. When Adam saw the woman he said, "This one, at last, is bone of my bones and flesh of my flesh."

In Eve, Adam had at last found "his counterpart, his equal, his nearest in all things" (see *CCC*, 1605).

The message of this passage is that *men and women are created for each other*. God established the intimate communion of life and love which is the essence of married life (see *Gaudium et Spes*, 48). God made married life the foundation of human society. From the beginning, one of the primary ways in which God has shared his love with men and women has been by giving them a way of sharing a deep and unifying love with each other. When a husband and wife truly become one they are given a glimpse of the love and unity which is shared in the Trinity, a glimpse of the love that the first letter of John refers to in the words, "God is love" (4:16).

Marriage was given to people as a way for them to participate in the experience of divine love and divine unity. Too often, however, men and women experience more discord and conflict in their relationships than they do pure love and unity. Pure love, the kind of love that results in true unity, is patient and kind; it is never jealous or pompous, rude or self-seeking. It is not quick tempered and it does not brood or sulk. The love which God intended for husbands and wives bears all things, believes all things, hopes all things, endures all things and never fails (see 1 Cor 13:4-8).

The fact that this is not the love that we see all around us has led many to scoff at the notion of perfect love or complete unity, and to say that such a love is not in human nature. According to our faith, however, the discord between men and women is not the result of basic human nature or of some fundamental difference in the way men and women think.

Men and women have been created as one, to be one. The disharmony between the sexes and within marriages is not the result of our natures but the result of our sin. The first consequence of the original sin was the rupture of the communion between man and woman. After they ate the forbidden fruit, Adam and Eve no longer saw their similarities, but rather their differences. They hid because suddenly the differences that were revealed in their nakedness were not a source of unity but a means of separation. No longer did they see themselves as flesh and bone of one another, instead they saw themselves as competitors.

Even though sin damaged the complete union between man and woman, God's plan for that union still remained. After the fall, the complete union of a man and a woman was not an automatic consequence of their coming together physically. Men and women needed and continue to need God's help to overcome the effects of sin in their lives so that they may find that unity for which they were created.

God has offered help to men and women through the institution of marriage. Marriage helps people to overcome their self-absorption and their tendency to put most of their energy into pursuing their own pleasure. Marriage by its very nature encourages spouses to give of themselves and to help each other.

Marriage involves giving yourself completely to another person and not letting any other relationship come between you and the loved one. Practically, what kind of actions does this entail?

The Nature of Christian Marriage

Jesus consistently taught that God intended marriage as a permanent union in which two people truly become one (see, for example, Mt 19:1-12). Although Mosaic law—which was understood as divine law—allowed for divorce, Jesus said that was only because of the people's hardness of heart. Jesus himself came to remove our stony hearts and give us hearts of flesh (see Ez 36:26). Jesus made it possible for men and women to achieve a permanent union. He made it possible for them to live as one, the way God intended from the beginning.

The fact that Jesus performed his first miracle at the wedding of Cana is understood by the Church as Jesus' confirmation of the goodness of marriage. It is also understood as a proclamation that from that time on Christ himself would be present in the marriages of his followers.

As with the other sacraments, Christ instituted the sacrament of Matrimony. Marriage was already a gift from God and a structure which could help people in their struggle against sin; Jesus made it an actual source of God's grace (see *CCC*, 1609, 1613). When a man and a woman pledge themselves to each other before the Father and through the Son, the Holy Spirit seals their pledge and gives them the strength they need to keep it. Jesus restored marriage to its original state as a union confirmed by God. It holds then that what God has joined, no person has a right to separate.

From the Old Testament, fidelity in marriage was already seen as an image of God's fidelity to his people. The prophet Hosea was told by God to remain faithful to a wife who was continually unfaithful (see Hos 1–3). His faithfulness was to be a prophetic sign of God's own faithfulness. By raising marriage to a sacrament Jesus made every marriage a sign of God's faithfulness. The loving and faithful relationship between a husband and wife is now the visible sign of the loving and faithful relationship between

Interview at least one married couple. Ask them to name visible ways that God's grace has been present in their married life.
What do you think it means to "take up one's cross" in the context of marriage?

Christ and his Church. The love which sustains the Church and makes it one is the love which allows a man and a woman to truly become one—one body, one heart, one mind, and one soul.

The Two Shall Become One

When God calls two people to become one, he is not calling upon them to give up their individual identities. A man and a woman do not become one flesh in the same way that two streams become one river. The model for the union of two people in marriage is found in the Trinity. The Father, the Son, and the Holy Spirit are three distinct persons, yet they are one God. They relate to each other as distinct persons. When the Father loves the Son he is loving another person; he is not just loving himself. When the Son is obedient to the Father, he is doing the will of another. Yet even though they are separate, they are one. There is no competition among them and there is no division of will—one never wants something that the others would oppose. Furthermore, whatever one person of the Trinity does is owned by the other two persons as well.

The unity of the Trinity is a total lack of selfishness and a total loving commitment to the other. When God calls two people to become one, he is calling them to give up their selfishness and seek what is truly best for the other and best for the family. When each person places the other at the center of his or her heart, when each person makes the well-being of the other his or her goal, the two will indeed be one.

The sacrament of Matrimony gives a husband and wife the grace that they need to work toward and ultimately achieve this unity. The sacrament gives husbands and wives the grace to love each other in the way Christ loved his Church. As with every other sacrament, however, the degree to which this grace bears fruit and

(*The Two Shall Become One cont.*)

accomplishes its purpose depends upon the dispositions of the ones who receive it. The sacrament of Matrimony makes true unity possible. The existence of sin in the world makes true unity difficult.

While it may be that no couple will ever experience perfect unity all the time in their marriage, those who open themselves to the grace of the sacrament will experience moments of perfect unity. Furthermore, even in their moments of disunity the sacrament will give them the strength to forgive one another and work through their difficulties, frequently deepening their unity in the process. The grace of the sacrament perfects the human love of the husband and wife, strengthens their unity, and allows them to grow in holiness on the way to eternal life.

St. Paul described marriage as a mystery (mystery is a word that translates to Latin as "sacrament"). He writes that the love of a husband and wife in marriage mirrors the love Christ has for his Church:

So [also] husbands should love their wives as their own bodies. He who loves his wife loves himself. For no one hates his own flesh but rather nourishes and cherishes it, even as Christ does the church, because we are members of his body (Eph 5:28-30).

The second creation story says "It is not good for [a person] to be alone" (Gn 2:18). Explain how you have found this statement to be true.

The Marriage Covenant

The true nature of marriage is in the mutual self-giving of the husband and wife. This self-giving takes the form of a covenant as opposed to a contract. A contract involves the exchange of services. It establishes rights and responsibilities within a known context. If circumstances change significantly, a contract can cease to be binding. A contract is an agreement to do certain things for each other. A covenant, on the other hand, establishes a relationship which will be maintained even in the face of changing circumstances. A covenant is a commitment to work with each other to do whatever needs to be done. While contracts do not change over time, covenants can and should grow stronger and deeper over time.

When a man and a woman establish a covenant with each other in marriage, they establish a relationship of self-giving. Each one makes a commitment to give himself or herself to the other without reservation. This self-giving is not something that happens once and for all on the day of the wedding. The self-giving of marriage must be repeated day after day in big and small ways. With each act of self-giving the marriage covenant grows stronger. Since marriage involves the total self-giving of each spouse, fidelity and permanence are both necessary parts of the marriage covenant.

The intimate union of a husband and wife in marriage needs to be exclusive if it is going to continually grow stronger and deeper. Infidelity shows a desire to withhold something from one's spouse. It weakens the essence of marriage. Likewise an intention or openness to ending the union at some future time shows an incomplete self-giving and weakens the essence of marriage.

However the Church recognizes that there are some situations in which it becomes practically impossible for a husband and wife to live together, for a variety of reasons. In these cases, the Church permits the *physical* separation of the couple though the spouses remain husband and wife and are not free to begin a new relationship. Hopefully, reconciliation can take place. In any case, the Church is called to help these persons live their situation in a Christian manner in fidelity to their indissoluble marriage bond. Catholics who are divorced civilly but continue to live chastely out of respect for their marriage vows can participate fully in the sacraments and in the life of the Church.

The sacrament of Matrimony makes each marriage a living sign of God's fidelity. The commitment of the spouses to each other becomes a part of God's commitment to his people. Since God's commitment is permanent and unfailing, all commitments which are caught up in his must also be permanent and unfailing.

Finish this sentence with several similes: "A marriage based in covenant relationship is like...."

The Purpose of Marriage

Marriage has been established by God for two reasons: for the good of the husband and wife, and for the procreation and education of children. Marriage offers a way for men and women to support each other and to help each other grow in love. The deeper a person's understanding of and experience in love, the closer that person will be to God.

Marriage also creates a communion of love into which children can be born. The documents of the Second Vatican Council teach that

> By its very nature the institution of marriage and married love is ordered to the procreation and education of the offspring and it is in them that it finds its crowning glory (Gaudium et Spes, 48 § 1; 50).

God creates each person out of love. God wants each person to experience that love from the moment of his or her birth. This is most likely to occur if the child is born into a permanent relationship of love. When God created the first man and woman, he told them to "be fruitful and multiply" (Gn 1:28). God established marriage because it was not good for a person to be alone. God also established marriage because the loving union of a husband and wife creates the environment into which God wishes to send his children. Beginning with Adam and Eve, God called husbands and wives to join him in his creative work by creating an environment of love and by welcoming children into that environment.

Just as marriage has two purposes, sexual intercourse, which is the act that most clearly expresses the marriage covenant, also has two purposes. Indeed, it has the same two purposes: the unity of the spouses (mutual love and support) and procreation. Sexual intercourse involves the self-giving of the entire person. All the aspects of the husband's and the wife's person enter into their sexual relationship. Their sexual relationship involves a giving of their physical selves, including their instinctual attraction to the opposite sex. It also involves a sharing of their emotions and feelings, a commitment of their spirit and a deliberate choice of their will.

The Church teaches that children are to be viewed as a great blessing of marriage. A blessing is a "gift of divine favor." How does this view of having children contradict with popular views of society at large?

Sexual intercourse aims at a deeply personal unity, a unity that, beyond union in one flesh, leads to forming one heart and soul. Sexual intercourse can only be what it is meant to be if it occurs within a marriage. New life is the natural outcome of sexual intercourse. That is why the Church has always taught that every act of sexual intercourse in marriage should remain open to the procreation of human life.

Part of a married couple's responsibility to welcome children into their lives involves the regulation of procreation, or the spacing of births between children. For just and moral reasons, a couple may regulate the spacing and birth of their children. These reasons include the physical and psychological health of a spouse, family finances, or the current number of children. However, selfishness or greed—for example, not wanting a child in order to maintain a certain financial level—would be a sinful motive for practicing birth control.

The Church supports natural means of birth regulation based on the observation of a women's fertility cycle. Part of this natural means also includes periodic abstinence from sexual relations. Most dioceses sponsor classes that help train couples in natural methods of family planning. Two popular and effective methods are the sympto-thermal method and the ovulation method. Oppositely, every artificial means of contraception is against Church law and contrary to God's will. Artificial birth control refers to pills or devices (like condoms or diaphragms) that interfere with the conception of a child. The Church also teaches that sterilization—rendering unfruitful the reproductive organs—is immoral unless the organs are diseased and the health of the person is at risk.

Children are "the supreme gift of marriage" (*Gaudium et Spes*, 50). For that reason, "each and every marriage act must remain open 'per se' to the transmission of life" (*Humanae Vitae*, 11). Children offer married couples a profound way of cooperating with and participating in God's creative love. The life-giving nature of sexual love is seen not only in the physical life which comes into being when a child is conceived, but also in the moral and spiritual life which parents pass on to their children through education. Parents are the first ones to teach their children how to live in the fullness of life that they received in baptism. As parents share life, love, and faith with their children the family takes its place at the heart of community life and at the heart of Church life.

The Domestic Church

The family is called the *domestic church*, meaning that the family is the "church of the home" (*CCC*, 2204). The family is the "original cell of society" (*CCC*, 2207) The family is where the church in its smallest form cultivates and shares the good news of Jesus.

Relationships within the family create the foundation for all other relationships. The unity of heart that is learned in the family prepares us to embrace the unity of heart that is essential to the Church. In a world that is often hostile to faith, believing families are important centers of living faith. The majority of people who come to the Church come because they have experienced the love and faith of a Christian family, be that the love and faith of their biological family or of another family that has welcomed them.

All married couples, whether they have children or not, are called to establish the kind of home—one that offers love, acceptance, and support—that welcomes those who would otherwise be without a family. All families are called to become domestic sanctuaries of the Church (*Apostolicam Actuositatem*, 11). In other words, the family is to be a place where the grace of God is clearly visible. Everything that family members receive in the sacramental life of the Church they are called to share with one another. Within the family parents and children exercise the priesthood of the baptized in a very special way. Together they establish a holy place in which the covenant of love among God's people and with God becomes visible and tangible.

More concretely, children have several obligations to their parents. First, children owe their parents gratitude for the gift of life. They do this by being respectful and obedient to their parents as long as they live in their parents' home. Even when they are grown up, children owe their parents respect. They should help their parents with their physical and spiritual needs in times of illness and loneliness especially associated with old age. Children are also obliged to live in harmony with their brothers and sisters, and to show special gratitude to others—besides parents—from whom they have received the gift of faith: grandparents, godparents, and catechists.

Parents are, of course, obliged to their children as well. Specifically, parents must "regard their children as *children of God* and respect them as *human persons*" (*CCC*, 2222). Parents are responsible for the education of their children. They do this by creating a home where tenderness, forgiveness, respect, fidelity, and disinterested service are prevalent. The home is the natural place for parents to educate their children in the virtues, that is, good habits. This is primarily done by

The origins of the family as domestic Church can be found in Jesus' words: "For where two or three are gathered in my name, there am I in the midst of them" (Mt 18:20). Recall and name some of the ways you first came to know Jesus in your own family.

their good example, teaching them to follow the Lord and encouraging them to listen to how the Lord may be calling them to a vocation to the priesthood or religious life. In fact education in the faith should begin in the child's earliest years. Parents have the duty to teach their children to pray and to discover their vocation as children of God. The *Catechism* calls the home "the first school of Christian life" (1657). It is in the home that all family members learn about the joy of work, love, forgiveness, divine worship in prayer, and the offering of one's life.

Beyond supporting one another and establishing a community of love, families also have a mission and responsibility with respect to the larger world. The sacrament of Matrimony sends husbands and wives and any children they have into the world to bear witness to the sacredness of marriage and the centrality of family life. Their lives should be a sign of the permanence of marriage and of the generous and life-giving nature of married love. They are to help others understand the type of relationship that God intended for men and women. Furthermore they should work within society to see that the dignity and the "legitimate autonomy" of families are always respected. It is part of our Christian responsibility to work for legislation, social policies, and employment practices that give consideration to the needs of families.

Historical Development of the Sacrament of Matrimony

Christ did not establish the institution of marriage. But Catholics believe that Jesus did bless the relationship between husband and wife and invest it with special meaning. Jesus' presence at the wedding feast at Cana shows his respect for the goodness, necessity, and naturalness of marriage (see Jn 2:1-12). In his preaching, Jesus spoke of marriage, saying that marriage belongs in this world only and that there are no marriages "at the resurrection" (Mt 22:30); in fact, some may choose not to marry for the sake of the kingdom of heaven (Mt 19:12).

Christ also restored the model of marriage that was present at the beginning of creation. He said that the permission given by Moses for divorce was a concession to the hardness of hearts of the people. He added, "Therefore, what God has joined together, no human being must separate" (Mt 19:6).

The letters of St. Paul also contain some important teachings about marriage. Paul wrote that the rights of both husbands and wives must be upheld in marriage: "The husband fulfils his duty toward his wife, and likewise the wife toward her husband" (1 Cor 7:3). Other examples of New Testament attitudes toward marriage are more ambiguous. Paul tells the people of Corinth that, if they can contain their lust, it is better not to marry (see 1 Cor 7:8 ff.) Yet, Paul concluded that marriage is a great mystery that mirrors the Lord's relationship to the Church:

Jesus' teachings on the kingdom of God influence how we understand marriage. Jesus' positive treatment of women helped speed the understanding that women were not to be treated as property in marriage. Read and report on Jesus' attitude towards women. Use passages like the following: Matthew 9:18-26, 15:21-28, 26:6-13, and 28:1-10.

This is a great mystery, but I speak in reference to Christ and his church. In any case, each one of you should love his wife as himself, and the wife should respect her husband (Eph 5:32-33).

By the fifth century, Church fathers like St. Augustine expanded on Paul's writings, teaching that marriage is a sacrament of the relationship between Christ and his Church. Augustine found sexual relations during marriage tolerable, but he did not see sex as the primary purpose of marriage. He held that sexual intercourse was only morally justifiable with the couple's intention to have children. He also believed that original sin had so affected human sexuality that intercourse always carried some moral evil. For Augustine, the primary purpose of marriage was to increase the couple's holiness.

During the twelfth century, theologians and canon lawyers named marriage as one of the seven sacraments. Both the Council of Florence (1439) and the Council of Trent (1563) taught this doctrine. Also at Trent, the Church reaffirmed Christ's teaching that marriage is a sacrament lasting until the death of a spouse.

Changing Wedding Customs

In the first century marriage rites presumably followed Jewish and pagan customs with the elimination of anything that was explicitly objectionable to Christians. The majority of marriages took place in the home and were private celebrations that did not require the presence of Church leaders. A marriage contract was publicly agreed upon by both families. The groom and the veiled bride were brought together and blessed by a family member, often the bride's father. A feast followed.

Late in the first century Ignatius, the bishop of Antioch, said that it was better if Christians married with the approval of the local bishop so that "their marriage may be according to the Lord, and not after their own lust" (*Letter to Polycarp*). He did not, however, suggest any particular form for a Christian marriage and neither he nor the Church said that the bishop's approval was required for a marriage. In 866 Pope Nicholas said that marriage by mutual consent was valid without the presence of any clergy and without any type of ceremony.

It was not until the eleventh century that bishops started calling for the blessing of secular weddings, and not until the twelfth century that there was an established (although not required) liturgical wedding ceremony. It was only at the Council of Trent in the sixteenth century that the Church declared that a marriage was only valid if it was celebrated before a priest and two witnesses. This significant development was primarily aimed at eliminating the problem of clandestine marriages, which disrupted society because they made legal rights and responsibilities difficult to assess particularly in relation to the inheritance of property.

Name some of the benefits of proclaiming wedding vows publicly. How do some of the benefits you gave contradict the argument for couples living together before marriage?

Describe the married life of a couple you consider to have a good marriage. What makes it so? If you were married, what part of their life together would you want to emulate?

Although a religious ceremony was not required for a Christian marriage before Trent, certain specifically Christian customs started to develop for weddings much earlier. After the fourth century, Christian weddings became increasingly common. The marriage blessing began to take on a definite liturgical structure and there was an increasing reluctance on the part of Christians to marry during Advent or Lent. In some places a celebration of the Eucharist followed the blessing of the couple, and on occasion the Eucharist actually replaced the traditional wedding feast.

The primary image of marriage through most of the first two millenniums was that of a contract. In the Middle Ages the front steps of the church became the place where legal contracts were ratified before God and before the Church; therefore, marriages gradually moved from the home to the outside steps of the church. The push to have marriages take place *inside* the Church grew stronger as the need grew for written documentation to prove the man and woman's legitimate births and the rights of inheritance. Priests were the only people in most villages who could read and write; therefore it became necessary to have a priest present at the wedding. It was only around the sixteenth century that all marriages moved into the church and that the celebration of a nuptial mass became the norm.

During the Middle Ages there was a great deal of debate over the essential act that legitimatized a marriage. According to Roman custom, the essential element for a marriage was the mutual consent of the couple. However, the Germanic custom saw families arrange the marriages of men and women of the right age. Under this custom, the marriage was ratified when the couple consummated the marriage, that is, as soon as they had sexual intercourse. Ultimately, a series of popes taught that the immediate cause and validity of marriage was a couple's consent, nothing else.

Wedding vows had to be pronounced both freely and in public. Thus they became the first liturgical pieces in the vernacular, the common language of the people. Wedding vows themselves have changed very little over the centuries.

One of the major changes in the wedding ceremony since the Second Vatican Council has been the stress on the equality of the marriage partners. The pre-Vatican II rite included a prayer for the bride that she be "faithful to one embrace . . . honorable in her chastity." There was no similar prayer for the groom. Today's rite contains no such inequalities.

As a sacrament, marriage must be something which God has given to us to both reveal God and to make God's presence a tangible reality. Marriage does not just limit something negative; it offers something positive. The Second Vatican Council said, "Authentic married love is caught up into divine love." Through mutual self-giving, the spouses sanctify one another and cooperate with the life-giving love of God (*Gaudium et Spes*, 48-50). Marriage is "ordered toward the good of the spouses and the procreation and education of offspring" (*CCC*, 1601).

Catholic Marriage Today

A good challenge question to stump a Catholic friend might be "Who is the minister of the sacrament of Matrimony?" In the Latin rite the ministers of the sacrament of Matrimony are the spouses themselves. The essential element of marriage remains the exchange of consent by the bride and groom. The priest or deacon who presides at the wedding receives the consent of the couple in the name of the Church and offers the blessing of the Church on the marriage.

The rite of marriage itself begins with the priest or deacon asking the couple to express their desire to marry and their understanding and acceptance of the permanence of marriage and of the two ends of marriage. The couple then makes a lifelong, unconditional covenant with each other through the exchange of vows. If the couple is exchanging rings, the priest or deacon blesses the wedding rings and the couple exchanges them as a sign of their love and fidelity. The wedding liturgy concludes with a blessing of the couple.

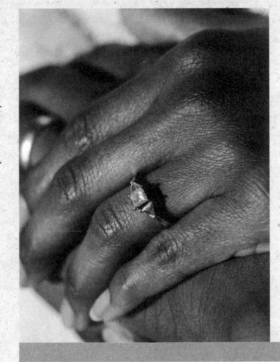

A sacramental marriage is important because as a liturgical act it establishes rights and duties within the Church. All who are baptized are members of the body of Christ, which is the Church. No member of the body can do anything without affecting and being affected by the rest of the body. When a member of the body marries, the body is changed. A Church marriage acknowledges the fact that the marriage will affect the Church community and that the Church community will have a role in the marriage.

When two Catholics marry, the rite of marriage itself normally takes place during a Mass after the homily. When a Catholic marries an unbaptized person the rite of marriage takes place outside of Mass and is preceded by the liturgy of the Word. When a Catholic marries a baptized non-Catholic, the rite of marriage may take place within or outside of the Mass, although since the non-Catholic cannot receive the Eucharist many feel that it is preferable to have only a liturgy of the Word.

The Rite of Marriage

The rite of marriage begins with the priest (or deacon) asking the bride and bridegroom to state their intentions. He questions them about their freedom of choice, their faithfulness to each other, and their willingness to accept and raise children. He asks three questions like the following, with each person answering separately.

N. and N., have you come here freely and without reservation to give yourselves to each other in marriage?

Will you love and honor each other as man and wife for the rest of your lives?

Will you accept children lovingly from God, and bring them up according to the law of Christ and his Church?

The priest then asks the couple to declare their consent before God and the Church. They join hands and take turns saying their vows. One of the two forms they may select is:

I, N., take you, N., to be my wife/husband. I promise to be true to you in good times and in bad, in sickness and in health. I will love you and honor you all the days of my life.

Receiving their consent, the priest says:

You have declared your consent before the Church. May the Lord in his goodness strengthen your consent and fill you both with his blessings. What God has joined, men must not divide.

The blessing and exchange of rings follows. Then the minister offers a blessing on each of them and their life together.

✔

Explain what each of these marriage vows means to you:
- I promise to be true to you . . .
- I will love you . . .
- I will honor you . . .

Choosing Who to Marry

Catholics are encouraged to marry other Catholics. When spouses do not share the same faith or the same religious practices, tensions can arise, especially when it comes to educating children. When a Catholic marries a baptized non-Catholic, there is a danger that the couple will experience the pain of Christian separation even in the heart of their own home. When a Catholic marries an unbaptized person the disparities of faith are often even greater and the resulting tensions can be more difficult to overcome. Couples with very different perspectives on faith may be tempted toward religious indifference.

If a Catholic wishes to marry a baptized non-Catholic, he or she needs the express permission of the bishop in order for the Church to recognize the marriage. If a Catholic wishes to marry an unbaptized person he or she needs a special dispensation in order for the marriage to be valid.

In order to receive either permission or a dispensation both members of the couple need to understand and accept the essential ends and properties of marriage. Both have to understand and accept the permanent and exclusive nature of the marriage covenant, and the importance of mutual love and support. They must be open to having children. Furthermore, the Catholic partner has to promise that he or she intends to remain a Catholic and to do what is reasonably in his or her power to pass on the Catholic faith to any children that the couple might have. The non-Catholic partner must be made aware of the Catholic partner's promises. Nevertheless, the non-Catholic remains free to do all that is reasonably in his or her power to share his or her own faith with the child. When the priest or deacon who will officiate at the marriage has questioned the couple about these things and received their consent, he applies to the bishop for the particular dispensation.

How important is it to you to marry a person of your own religious faith?

Divorce, Remarriage, and Annulment

Jesus spoke clearly on the permanence of marriage: "What God has joined together, no human being must separate;" and, "Whoever divorces his wife (unless the marriage is unlawful) and marries another commits adultery" (Mt 19:6, 9). The Church has consistently taught that divorce and remarriage is unacceptable.

Divorce, of itself, is a "grave offense against the natural law" (*CCC*, 2384). It is a serious offense against the sacramental bond of marriage. Sometimes it involves the desertion of a spouse and children, which is a particularly callous disregard for God's law. In many cases, one of the spouses is an innocent victim of a civil divorce. There is a great difference between a spouse who has consistently tried to be faithful to the promises of the sacrament of marriage, and one who has been unfaithful, abandoned the other, or through sin has destroyed a marriage.

One cause of divorce is *adultery*, or marital infidelity. When two people, at least one of whom is married to another partner, have sexual relations of any kind, they commit adultery. Christ called even the mere desire for sex outside of marriage adultery: "But I say to you, everyone who looks at a woman with lust has

How do you think the Church should reach out and support spouses and other family members who have been affected by divorce?

already committed adultery with her in his heart" (Mt 5:28). Adultery is a sin against the sixth commandment.

Due to adultery of one spouse or for other reasons in which a couple may not be able to live in harmony, the Church allows them to choose to live apart, but they are still married before God. The spouses do not cease to be husband and wife, and they are not free to begin a new union with someone else. Even if a person receives a civil divorce, he or she remains fully in communion with the Church and is able to receive the sacraments. The best solution in this situation is the reconciliation of the spouses, if possible. The Christian community is responsible to help persons in this situation remain faithful to their marriage bond which is unbreakable.

The Church does not permit divorce and remarriage because Jesus forbade it. Although the state has authority to dissolve certain legal aspects of a marriage (called a civil divorce), it has no authority to dissolve a sacramental marriage. The Church teaches that a second marriage is not valid if the first marriage was valid. This is because a second marriage in such a case is seen as a direct violation of the plan and law of God as taught by Christ. When divorced people are remarried civilly, they cannot receive the Eucharist as long as the situation remains the same.

Reconciliation through the sacrament of Penance is granted to those who repent, and who are committed to living chastely. The Church responds pastorally to divorced people who have remarried civilly in many ways so that they can keep their faith and bring their children up in the faith. Pope John Paul II taught in *Familiaris consortio* that these baptized members of the community should continue to listen to God's Word, attend Mass, pray, do works of charity, raise their children in the Catholic faith, practice penance, and seek out God's grace each day.

In some instances the Church recognizes that even though a couple was legally married, they were never in fact joined by God. In such cases the Church may grant an *annulment* so that the man and woman may marry again. The primary grounds for an annulment is found in an attitude which goes against the most basic Catholic understanding of marriage. If one of the spouses rejected one of the purposes of marriage or one of the primary characteristics of the covenant relationship, that would be an indication that a true covenant was never established and sealed by God.

For example, an annulment may be granted if one partner did not want children, if one partner never viewed marriage as permanent, if one partner did not think that fidelity was important, or if one partner had no intention of loving and supporting the other.

Annulments may also be granted if the original consent given by the couple was seriously flawed in some way. An annulment may be given if consent was the result of force or fear, if one or both people were incapable of understanding the true nature of consent, if one or both people were unable to fulfill the obligations of marriage, or if one or both people believed that they were giving their consent to someone other than the person to whom they were actually giving it. Finally, annulments may be granted when the two people contracted a marriage that was not legal according to the laws of the Church.

It is important to remember that an annulment does not affect the legitimacy of any children. What is more, an annulment does not imply that there was no good in the relationship. An annulment is simply a recognition by the Church that this particular union was never a sacramental marriage.

Other Offenses Against Marriage

The *Catechism of the Catholic Church* names three other offenses against the dignity of marriage. They are:

- *Polygamy* is the offense of a man who has more than one wife.

- *Incest* involves a person who has intimate relations with a relative or in-law within a degree of kinship that prohibits marriage between them. Connected to incest is any sexual abuse by an adult to children or adolescents in their care.

- *Free union* refers to couples who live together without exchanging marriage vows. A free union is contrary to moral law, as sexual intercourse must take place exclusively within marriage. Outside of marriage it is always a serious sin keeping the person(s) from sacramental communion. Related to free union is the so-called "trial marriage" where the couple intends to get married later. This behavior, too, is sinful and not permitted by the Church for the same reasons as described above.

Chapter 9
Review Questions

1. According to our faith tradition, when did God establish the essence of married life?

2. What is the cause of the disharmonies that often exist between men and women in marriage?

3. How does marriage help men and women overcome the effects of sin?

4. How did Jesus elevate marriage to a sacrament?

5. How is the model for the union of two people in marriage found in the Trinity?

6. What is the true nature of marriage? How is this nature lived out?

7. Name the two reasons God established marriage.

8. What are the two purposes of sexual intercourse in marriage?

9. What does the Church teach about children in a marriage?

10. What is meant by the term "domestic church"?

11. Besides supporting one another and raising children, what are some other responsibilities of a married couple?

12. Summarize the Church's attitude toward marriage, and sex within marriage, as represented by St. Augustine.

13. Why did the marriage rite eventually move from the home to churches, from not having a church official present to having a bishop or priest witness the wedding?

14. What is the essential element of the sacrament of Matrimony?

15. Who is the minister of the sacrament of Matrimony?

16. Why are Catholics encouraged to marry other Catholics?

17. Is a divorced Catholic able to receive the sacraments? When might this not be so?

18. What are some of the primary grounds of an annulment?

19. Define these offenses against the dignity of marriage: *polygamy, incest,* and *free union.*

Appendix: Another Look

The material in the appendix is designed to whet and refresh your memory of the material covered. It is not a comprehensive review. For detailed material relevant to the sacraments, please review Chapters 1 to 9.

Sacraments Draw Us Into the Mystery of God

According to Jewish legend a Caesar once went to Rabbi Joshua and said, "I want to see your God."

"You cannot." Rabbi Joshua told him.

"I am Caesar, and I insist that you show me your God."

"Very well," Rabbi Joshua said, "Meet me at noon on the day of the summer solstice."

The Caesar met the rabbi at the agreed-upon place on the day of the solstice. "Now show me your God," he said.

"First," Rabbi Joshua replied, "you must stand here and look directly at the sun."

"But I cannot!" Caesar exclaimed.

Rabbi Joshua responded, "If you cannot look directly at the sun which is only one of the thousands of minions who serve the Holy One, how much less could you look on the Presence itself!"

We cannot look upon God. We cannot touch him and we cannot fathom him. God is infinitely beyond us. His thoughts and his ways are as high above ours as the heavens are above the earth. God is unsearchable mystery. And yet, God wants us to know him, love him, and serve him. For this reason God comes to us in ways that we can see, feel, and understand. God comes to us in sacraments.

Christ Is the Primordial Sacrament

The most basic definition of a sacrament is a *visible and efficacious sign of invisible grace.* Sacraments allow us to perceive God's grace. Sacraments also allow us to experience that grace; through the sacraments we touch God. Jesus is the primordial sacrament. The second person of the Trinity became man in order that we might know the unknowable, touch the intangible, and see the invisible. By the power of the Holy Spirit, Jesus draws us into the mystery of God the Father. He makes the Father accessible to humanity. He makes divine grace part of human history.

The Church Is the Primary Sacrament of Christ

Following Jesus' ascension, the Church became the tangible and effective way in which Christ remained present in history. Jesus established the Church as his body on earth, so that through the Church all people might come to know God. All of us who are members of the Church are part of Christ's body. We are the hands of Christ reaching out to comfort and heal. We are the eyes of Christ looking upon people with compassion and forgiveness. We are the feet of Christ carrying the message of hope and acceptance to those who are outcasts.

The Sacraments of the Church Make It Possible for Us to Live as the Body of Christ

But how can we who are sinners be the body of Christ? How can we bring Christ's love, or healing or forgiveness to others when we so often ignore it ourselves? Jesus gave us the sacraments of the Church in order that we might truly act as the body of Christ on earth. Jesus bound the seven actions of Baptism, Confirmation, Eucharist, Penance, Anointing of the Sick, Holy Orders, and Matrimony to himself in such a way that whenever the Church performs these actions, it is Jesus himself performing them.

Each time the Church baptizes, Jesus gives new life. Each time the Church confirms, Jesus sends the Holy Spirit to dwell in the one who is confirmed. Each time the Church celebrates the Eucharist, Jesus nourishes his people. Because the sacraments are actions of Christ, they confer grace. That is, they invite us into the life of God. The sacraments guarantee that the Church will always do what Christ wants her to do, even if at times the members of the Church also do things that Christ does not want them to do.

Through the celebration of the sacraments the people of the Church are regularly drawn into their identity as the body of Christ. The sacraments sanctify men and women, build up the body of Christ, and give worship to Christ. The fruits of the sacraments—the degree to which they change those who receive them and make people more Christ-like—are dependent upon the disposition of the one receiving them. Although grace is always given in the sacraments, that grace can only bear fruit in our lives if it is accepted and acted upon. All who encountered Jesus encountered God; but those who refused to acknowledge that Jesus was God could not accept what Jesus offered. The same may be said for each of the sacraments: all who participate in the sacraments encounter God, but if they do not recognize God and accept the gift that he is offering their lives will remain unchanged.

The Sacraments Make All of Salvation History Part of an Eternal Today

The sacraments alter our relationship to time. They take us beyond time so that in the celebration of the sacraments there is no distinction between the past, the present, and the future. The sacraments allow us to participate in the Paschal mystery. They make Christ's life, death, resurrection, and ascension part of our own personal history. All of the sacraments of the Church are directed toward the liturgy which is *the* celebration of the Paschal mystery. The sacraments of Baptism, Confirmation, Penance, Anointing of the Sick, Holy Orders, and Matrimony all enable us to participate fully in the Sunday celebration of the Eucharist and to live out the Eucharist in our daily lives.

The Liturgy Makes the Paschal Mystery Part of Our Own Experience

The liturgy is the source and summit of the entire Christian life. In the liturgy the Holy Spirit prepares us to encounter God. The Spirit reveals Christ and makes him present to all who are gathered. Finally, the Spirit unites the Church to the life and mission of Christ. We call the liturgy the summit of the Christian life because as we share in Christ's mission we participate in the world as God wants it to be.

In the liturgy God's kingdom has come and God's will is done. In our worship we are people who ask for forgiveness, accept forgiveness, and offer forgiveness to others. We are people who listen and say "yes" to God's Word. We are peacemakers. We are united with one another and we are people who share all that we have with each other. We are people who offer our lives to praise and honor God. Our worship is an expression of who we are becoming through the grace of God. We call the liturgy the source of Christian life because in the liturgy we receive the grace that we need in order to truly live as the body of Christ in the world.

The Liturgy Is the World "Done Right"

The word "liturgy" means "a public work." The liturgy is our public work. We participate in the liturgy for the good of the community. In our liturgical celebrations we participate in the world as God intended it to be. When we leave the liturgy we leave with a better understanding of what God wants the world to be. We leave filled with the grace we need to help recreate the world in light of our new understanding. When we take an active part in the liturgy, we give glory to God, we receive what we need for ourselves, and we receive what we need to be able to help others.

The Liturgy Is a Blessing

All of God's work throughout history is a blessing—in other words, a gift of life. In the liturgy we are given a share of this blessing. We become participants in God's saving and life-giving actions. Through the liturgy we also return blessings to God. We surrender our lives to him and commit ourselves to his work. The more completely we return blessing to God, the more deeply we will experience God's blessings in our lives.

The blessing of the liturgy belongs to the whole Church, both the Church on earth and the Church in heaven. Through our earthly sacramental liturgy we participate in the eternal liturgy of heaven. We experience the feast of life and the communion of all people with each other and with God who is in heaven.

Although the liturgy is always a foretaste of heaven, we can only experience it as such if we participate actively. It is not just the priest and those with special ministries who have a ministry to fulfill during the Mass. The entire assembly—the people in the pews—have an active role to play during the liturgical celebration. The prayers and gestures of the people are the signs of the relationships of love and unity which the Eucharist establishes and maintains. Unless we actively participate in the liturgy we will not be disposed to participate in the relationships which the liturgy establishes, and we will be unlikely to benefit from the grace which the liturgy imparts.

Our Worship Shapes Our Faith

The prayers and gestures of the assembly are not just there to hold our attention. They have been carefully chosen because they help form us as the people we are called to be. All of the rites of the Church provide a structure for worship that is in keeping with the faith that Jesus handed on to his apostles. The particular structure of Catholic worship is not merely a matter of taste or style; the way that we worship shapes what we believe. This is why the basic shape of our worship and the basic symbols of our worship life have changed very little over two thousand years.

The Church has ensured that our worship teaches us the faith which Jesus taught to his followers. In the sacramental life of the Church, we use specific signs and symbols taken from daily life which have been handed down to us from Jesus and the apostles. These signs and symbols have many layers of meaning; if they were replaced some of that meaning might be lost and new meanings which were not part of the faith given to us by Jesus might be added. Although the Church allows for some cultural adaptation in the liturgy, she insists that nothing be done which could obscure or confuse the essential message of the sacraments or the divine truth which has been handed down through the apostles and their successors.

Jesus' own life as presented in scripture gives us the form for our worship. The actions of the liturgy signify what the word of God expresses. The prayers of the liturgy are our response to the word of God. For this reason the liturgy of the Word is an integral part of the celebration of the sacraments. The liturgy of the Word also gives shape to the liturgical year. Over the course of the year all of the major points of salvation history are remembered and made present to us as the liturgy of the Word carries us through the scriptures.

The Liturgical Year Allows All of Salvation History to Unfold in Our Lives

In the liturgical year God uses the rhythms of our daily, weekly, and yearly calendar to plunge us more deeply into the mystery of salvation. As we move through the year the major events of salvation history become part of our own personal history. Thus Easter and Christmas are not just ancient historical events, but part of our own lived experience.

Easter is the main pillar of the liturgical year. During the Easter Triduum we enter into the events of Jesus' passion, death, and resurrection. In the fifty days of the Easter season—from Easter Sunday to Pentecost—we immerse ourselves once again in the mystery and wonder of the new life which God has given us. In the forty days which precede Easter (the season of Lent), we cleanse our lives of all those things which blind us to the wonder of God or prevent us from receiving God's grace.

The second pillar of the liturgical year is Christmas. Christmas is also a celebration of the Paschal mystery—a celebration of all that Jesus has accomplished for us—but it is a celebration which focuses on the wonder of the incarnation and the promise of the second coming.

Just as Easter is the main pillar of the Christian year, Sunday is the main pillar of the Christian week. Each Sunday is a "little Easter." Each Sunday makes the saving events of Christ's passion, death, and resurrection present to us. Although Christians are called to pray daily, Sunday is the preeminent day for gathering to pray as a community. Sunday is both the first day of the week and the eighth day of the week. It is the day which knows no evening, the day of the new creation. Christians gather on Sunday to participate in the new creation which was assured by Jesus' resurrection but which will not be complete until his second coming. Through the Sunday celebration we are invited into the mystery of the kingdom of heaven which is already in our midst and not yet fully visible.

Baptism

Sin Separated Us From God and Resulted in Suffering and Death in the World

The world God planned for us was a world free from suffering and death. Our world is not that world. Our world is fallen, marred by Adam and Eve's decision to walk away from a partnership with God and to try and make it on their own. Sin, suffering, and death were not punishments for this decision, they were merely its inevitable results. Life and joy are gifts from God. But they are not gifts that we can separate from the Giver. Life and joy are gifts of God's love and they can only be experienced in his presence.

All children are born into the world which their parents inhabit. Since the time of Adam and Eve, children have been born into a world which has distanced itself from God. They have been born into a world where they are seen as belonging not to God, but to themselves. They have been born into a world in which they are expected to "make it" on their own. This is the meaning of original sin. Original sin—the sin by which the first human beings disobeyed God's commands, choosing to follow their own will rather than God's will—is an essential truth of our faith. However, it is only through the long journey of revelation which culminates in the death and resurrection of Jesus Christ that original sin can be fully understood.

Jesus Overcame the Power of Sin and Death

Human beings were unable to break through the isolation of sin, suffering, and death in order to be reunited with God. Only God could reunite us to himself. Jesus came into the world in order to destroy suffering and death and create a pathway to God. Through his own suffering, death, and resurrection, Jesus reunites God with those who suffer and die. Through the sacrament of Baptism, Jesus makes it possible for us to follow him through suffering and death to be united with God. Through Baptism Jesus invites us to follow him into a new world—the kingdom of God—in which there is no separation between God and his people.

Jesus is the savior of the human race. All people would have been separated from God if Jesus had not healed the rift between God and humanity. Jesus broke the power of suffering and death by freely accepting them and remaining faithful to God. We are able to break the power of suffering and death in our lives by uniting ourselves with Christ's actions. We do this through the sacrament of Baptism. In Baptism we die with Christ. The life that we live after Baptism is one that is free from the power of sin and death, a life that is a foretaste of the life of heaven.

Following our Baptism we can say with St. Paul:

> I am certain that neither death nor life, nor angels nor principalities, nor present things nor future things, nor powers, nor height nor depth nor any other creature will be able to separate us from the love of God in Christ Jesus, our Lord (Rom 8:38-39).

Baptism Is the Seal of Eternal Life

God has given us Baptism as a means of entry into heaven. When we are baptized we are sealed with the sign of eternal life. All who are baptized who do not destroy the fruits of Baptism by preferring sin to God will be welcomed into the kingdom of heaven. God has promised that salvation is one of the gifts of Baptism. We believe that this same gift of salvation is given to all of those who specifically desired Baptism but died without receiving it. Catechumens and any who died for the faith—even though they were not baptized—are given the salvation that comes with Baptism. We do not know of any other specific way to gain entry into heaven, but that does not mean that no other way exists. God is not bound by the sacraments. He can act outside of them.

Baptism Gives Us an Indelible Spiritual Character

Baptism gives us a new identity. When we are reborn through the waters of Baptism we are not reborn as isolated children of Adam and Eve, but as sons and daughters of God and as members of the body of Christ. Our fundamental identity is changed. Furthermore, all of our relationships are changed. As children of God we can never again be completely separated from God. As members of the body of Christ we are one with everyone else who has been baptized. Baptism restores all of the relationships that were broken in the fall of humanity. Because Baptism gives us a new and indelible identity (or character) it can never be repeated.

Baptism Is the Gateway Into Life in the Spirit

Baptism is the embrace of God who first loved us. In Baptism God reaches out to us and offers us his Spirit even though we do not and cannot deserve it. The gratuitous nature of Baptism is clearly seen in the ancient Catholic practice of baptizing infants. Once we have received the Spirit, it is up to us to allow him to shape our lives. It is up to us to live as the children of God and not as the children of Adam and Eve. In Baptism the light of God enters us. We have the rest of our lives to learn to let that light shine out of us and brighten the world. For all who are baptized, whether children or adults, faith must continue to grow after Baptism. Baptism places us on the threshold of new life. It is up to us to live that life to the full.

The Essential Rite of Baptism

The normal minister of Baptism is a bishop, priest, or deacon. In an emergency, however, anyone can baptize. The essential rite of Baptism consists in immersing the candidate in water or pouring water on his or her head while saying: "I baptize you in the name of the Father, and of the Son, and of the Holy Spirit."

Through the sacrament of Baptism we are invited into the mystery of life as God intended it to be.

Confirmation

Confirmation Completes Baptism

All-powerful God, Father of our Lord Jesus Christ,
by water and the Holy Spirit
you freed your sons and daughters from sin
and gave them new life.
Send your Holy Spirit upon them
to be their Helper and Guide.
Give them the spirit of wisdom and understanding,
the spirit of right judgment and courage,
the spirit of knowledge and reverence.
Fill them with the spirit of wonder and awe in your presence.
We ask this through Christ our Lord.

This is the prayer that the bishop (or priest) says before he confirms someone; and this is the prayer that is answered in Confirmation. Through the sacrament of Confirmation a person receives strength to live as a member of the body of Christ in the world.

In the sacrament of Confirmation, the bishop lays his hand on the forehead of the candidate and anoints him or her with chrism saying the words, "Be sealed with the gift of the Holy Spirit." This action completes the sacrament of Baptism. In Baptism, the newly baptized receive forgiveness of sins, adoption as children of God, and the character of Christ. In this way they are *made members of the Church and become sharers in the priesthood of [Christ]....*

...Through the sacrament of Confirmation those who have been born anew in Baptism receive the inexpressible Gift, the Holy Spirit himself, by whom "they are endowed...with special strength...."

...Finally, Confirmation is so closely linked with the holy Eucharist that the faithful, after being signed by Baptism and Confirmation, are incorporated fully into the Body of Christ by participation in the Eucharist (Apostolic Constitution on the Sacrament of Confirmation).

In the early Church, Baptism, Confirmation, and first Eucharist were all celebrated at the same time. In the Eastern Church this is still the practice. Confirmation is administered immediately after Baptism for both infants and adults and is followed by participation in the Eucharist. In the Latin Church there was a desire to maintain the bishop as the minister of Confirmation and thus symbolize the unity of the new Christian with the universal Church. When the majority of Baptisms were performed by priests, Confirmation was withheld until a time when the bishop could be present. Eventually Confirmation was moved to some time after a person reached the age of reason.

Even when Baptism and Confirmation are celebrated separately, the Church aims to make their unity with each other and with the Eucharist clear. When infants are baptized but not confirmed, they are anointed with oil as a sign of the anointing by the bishop which is still to come. Then, in order to show the connection of Baptism with the Eucharist they are brought to the altar for the praying of the Our Father. When Confirmation is separate from Baptism, the liturgy of Confirmation begins with a renewal of baptismal promises.

Confirmation Changes Our Identity

Following his resurrection Jesus breathed the Holy Spirit upon his apostles and gave them the power to forgive sins. At Pentecost he sent the Spirit in an even more striking manner. The apostles who had been hiding in fear were suddenly filled with a new strength and courage. They began to proclaim all of the marvelous things that God had done culminating in the resurrection of Jesus and the coming of the Spirit. From the day of Pentecost on the apostles baptized people and then laid hands upon them so that they would receive the Holy Spirit. The laying on of hands is recognized by the Church as the origins of the sacrament of Confirmation. It was the gift of the Spirit which made a person a Christian—that is, an "anointed one."

When we receive the gift of the Holy Spirit our identity and our relationships are changed forever. Like Baptism, Confirmation imprints an "indelible spiritual mark" on the person who is confirmed. Once the Holy Spirit has been given to a person he cannot be taken away and he will not go away. A person may choose not to listen to the Spirit dwelling within him or her, but that will not change the fact that the Spirit is there. For this reason Confirmation cannot be repeated.

Who May Be Confirmed?

Confirmation is a sacrament for all those who have been baptized and have reached the age of reason (age seven). It can and should be given earlier if a child is in danger of death. When a person is confirmed he or she becomes like an apostle, that is "one who is sent" into the world to share the faith of the Church with others. There needs to be a period of preparation preceding Confirmation so that the person being confirmed will be better prepared to take on this apostolic responsibility. Furthermore, those who are to be confirmed should be in a state of grace. If they have committed a serious sin, they should receive the sacrament of Penance before their Confirmation. If they have not, the sacrament of Penance will enable them to be better prepared to receive the gift of the Holy Spirit.

The celebration of Confirmation normally takes place during the celebration of the Eucharist. Before the homily, those who are to be confirmed are presented to the bishop. After the homily, the candidates are asked to renew their baptismal promises. The bishop then extends his hands over the heads of those who are to be confirmed and prays for all of them. Finally, he confirms each candidate individually. He makes the sign of the cross with chrism on the one to be confirmed addressing him or her by name and saying, "be sealed with the Gift of the Holy Spirit."

Confirmation Binds Us More Closely to the Church

Confirmation binds us more closely to the Church and commits us to prayer and action, which are the work of the Church. In Confirmation the law of God is written on our hearts. Our very identity is linked to God. Once we are confirmed our own nature will constantly pull us back to God. When sin tempts us to wander away from God, an inner restlessness will call us back. The wonder and mystery of Confirmation is that God has chosen us, imperfect though we are, to be his home, so that we will always be able to find and approach him.

Eucharist

The Eucharist Is at the Center of Christian Life

The Eucharist is the center and culmination of Christian life and community. All that we are and all that we strive to be as Christians can be found in the Eucharist. The Eucharist is our heart and soul. When a person receives communion he or she is entering the innermost life of the community. This is why the Church calls the Eucharist the sacrament which completes Christian initiation.

A Catholic only receives one Baptism and one Confirmation but is able to participate at Eucharist and receive holy communion many times. Nevertheless, Eucharist reenacts the same event as Baptism and Confirmation. In the Eucharist we experience Christ's death and resurrection. We also experience the gift of God's life within us. Through the Eucharist we recommit ourselves to our Baptism at every stage and every moment of our lives.

The Eucharist Draws Us Into the Great Events of Salvation History

On the night before he died Jesus anticipated his own passion and death and interpreted them in the terms of the Jewish Passover and its sacrifice. At the same time he gave the Eucharist to his followers as a means of remembering his passion and death. Jesus made the Eucharist the new Passover, the new eternal today. When we celebrate the Eucharist we proclaim the great events of salvation from creation to the Exodus, to the death and resurrection of Jesus and the coming of the Holy Spirit, to the second coming of Christ and the establishment of a new heaven and a new earth. As we proclaim these events, we are caught up in them.

The Eucharist is the means by which God imprints the events of salvation history upon our memories so that we will constantly remember our covenant with God. When Jesus took the cup at the Last Supper, he said, "This cup is the new covenant in my blood, which will be shed for you." Jesus' body and blood are the new covenant which the prophets foretold. When God enters us through the Eucharist, he writes the covenant upon our hearts.

Jesus Is Present in the Eucharist

In the Eucharist God makes his dwelling with us. Jesus is present in many ways in the celebration of the Eucharist. He is present in the community which is gathered in his name. He is present in the scripture which is his word. He is present in the person of the priest. But he is present in a unique way in the bread and wine which become his body and blood.

The Eucharist Is the Holy and Acceptable Sacrifice

The Eucharist has been understood as a sacrifice since the earliest days of Christianity. Jesus is a high priest who offers sacrifice on behalf of the people. But unlike the sacrifices offered by every other priest, Jesus' sacrifice is perfect. His sacrifice is his own body and blood, the body and blood of the Son of God. Jesus is a high priest according to the order of the Old Testament priest Melchizedek. The sacrifice which Melchizedek offered was a sacrifice of bread and wine. Jesus also uses bread and wine. He continues to offer the sacrifice of himself in the bread and wine of the Eucharist. The Eucharist is not a new sacrifice. The Eucharist is the presence in our midst of the one eternal sacrifice which Jesus made on the cross.

In a Jewish context, a sacrifice was a gift to God offered as a sign of a person's desire to give of himself. Jesus' sacrifice is a perfect sacrifice because he offered himself completely. Out of love for God and for God's people he held nothing back. When Jesus gave us the Eucharist, he gave us a way to change our imperfect offering into his perfect offering. When we offer the sacrifice of the Eucharist, we offer the one sacrifice which can and does restore our relationship with God. Our sins do not keep adding up to create an unbridgeable gulf.

Our efforts to love and care for one another are always imperfect. In the Eucharist, however, we unite these imperfect efforts to the work of Christ. They are thereby given new meaning and value. Even our smallest efforts to love have power when they are united to the love of Christ and the love of the members of his body throughout history. The fact that we can unite our love to Christ's love keeps us from despairing. Without the Eucharist we might well say that our love is so inadequate that we should just give up. With the support of the Eucharist, we keep on doing what we can. The Eucharist constantly helps the Church to become more loving.

The Eucharist Is a Sacred Meal

Jesus instituted the Eucharist in the context of a Jewish ritual meal. Because of its context within a meal, the Eucharist is not just a sacrament of self-giving love and sacrifice, it is also a sacrament of fellowship, of mutual give and take. When we examine all of the dynamics of people eating together we gain a better understanding of the meaning of the Eucharist.

Meals unite people. In many cultures sharing a meal is a pledge of friendship and support. The Eucharist is just such a meal. It is the sign and source of our unity as a Christian community, a unity which encompasses both the Church on earth and the Church in heaven. The Eucharist is the foretaste of the great feast of joyful unity which we will share in heaven.

The Eucharist Sends Us Into the World to Be the Body of Christ for the World

The word "Mass" comes from the Latin word for dismissal. In a sense, the aim of the Eucharist is to dismiss us, to send us out into the world to be Christ for the world, especially to those who are most in need of Christ's presence. The Eucharist does for our spiritual selves what ordinary food does for our bodies; it nourishes us and strengthens us so that we can live and so that we can do the other things we want and need to do.

In the Eucharist we receive Christ's body and we become Christ's body. The Eucharist sends us out into the world to act as that body, separated from sin and able to love and serve generously. The Eucharist gives us the strength to find love and hope even in the most difficult situations. When we have been nourished by the Eucharist, we have been nourished by Christ himself. The One who has already conquered death and despair is within us. Death and despair no longer have the power to defeat us.

Penance

God Never Abandons Us to Sin

God has not chosen to remove all pain and sorrow from our world. He has not chosen to eliminate sin and its consequences. But he has refused to allow pain, sorrow, or sin to destroy what he has made. In the midst of evil God continually creates a path of love and he invites us to walk that path. Through the gift of the sacrament of Penance God makes it possible for us to recognize and turn away from sin, and to draw closer to him in the process.

The sacraments of initiation—Baptism, Confirmation, and the Eucharist—are the primary way in which we turn away from sin and embrace the life of love and joy which Jesus offers. In the sacrament of Baptism we turn away from the darkness of sin and receive the light of Christ, the light of life. The sacraments of Confirmation and the Eucharist make it possible for that light of life to burn stronger and brighter. But the flame of life which we receive in the sacraments of initiation is carried in "earthen vessels." Those vessels can fall and crack or break and the light of life which we have received can be weakened or even lost. We can find ourselves wandering once again in the darkness of sin and despair. When we fall back into darkness God calls us to the light once more. He does this through the sacrament of Penance.

The Sacrament Helps Us to Reorient Our Lives to God

The word reconcile means "to flow together again." The purpose of the sacrament of Penance is to help us turn our lives around so that they flow again with God. The focus of the sacrament is not on changing a few sinful beliefs or behaviors. The sacrament affects the fundamental orientation of our entire lives. The purpose of the sacrament is to help us be more faithful.

Baptism is the sacrament of faith. It is the sacrament which establishes our intimate relationship with God, a relationship which shapes every aspect of our lives. The sacrament of Penance is the sacrament of renewed faith. It is the sacrament which restores and strengthens our relationship with God after it has been damaged by sin. Baptism reveals the mystery of God's love for us. The sacrament of Penance shows us that God's love is without limits. Both Baptism and Penance are completed in the sacrament of the Eucharist which embodies and strengthens that union.

The Sacrament Restores Our Relationship With God and With the Church

After he had risen from the dead, Jesus appeared to his apostles and instructed them to continue his mission of reaching out to sinners and calling them back to God and back to the community. He said to them, "Receive the holy Spirit. Whose sins you forgive are forgiven them, and whose sins you retain are retained" (Jn 20:22). The Church understands that with these words Jesus instituted the sacrament of Penance. He made the apostles and their successors the instruments of God's forgiveness.

Even though forgiveness is expressed through the Church, God alone can forgive sins. The Church is the body of Christ. Christ is the head. If Christ chooses something, the Church must do it. If Christ reestablishes a relationship with a sinner, then the Church must reestablish that relationship. The Church is the sign of what God has done, and the instrument through which God acts. In the sacrament of Penance the Church is the sign and instrument of restored unity and wholeness. Each time a priest offers sinners God's forgiveness, he also welcomes them back into the life of the Church. Thus both the repentant sinner and the Church find new wholeness in the sacrament.

The Essential Elements of the Sacrament

The sacrament of Penance consists of two equally essential elements: the acts of the person who undergoes conversion and the intervention of the Church. The person who undergoes conversion has three tasks as part of the sacrament: contrition, confession, and satisfaction. The minister of the sacrament (the priest) also has three tasks: to forgive sins in the name of Jesus, to determine the manner of satisfaction, and to assist the sinner through his own prayer and acts of penance. In this last task the priest should be joined by the whole Church.

God calls us to conversion. Christ, the light of the world, reveals our sinfulness and shows us both what we are and what we could be. The process of conversion begins when we recognize our failings and long to do better. Conversion begins when we turn our focus to God and make union with him our goal. But conversion requires more than just a focus on a distant God. It requires movement towards God. This movement begins with contrition. Contrition is heartfelt sorrow and aversion for the sin committed. It must be accompanied by the intention not to sin again. When we love God above all else we experience what is known as perfect contrition. We willingly let go of all of those things which pull us away from God.

True contrition results in confession. Confession is the external expression of our sorrow and of our willingness to accept responsibility for damaging or breaking the covenant. Because we do not live purely interior lives, our conversion and contrition cannot remain purely interior. They must have an outward form. Confession is also an expression of faith in God. When we confess our sins to God we are in fact proclaiming our belief in God's love and God's mercy. When we confess our sins within the Christian community we are also expressing our belief in the goodness of the community. When we confess our sins to a priest, we are admitting the harm that we have caused to the other members of the body and we are asking the priest to forgive us in the name of Christ. All Catholics are expected to confess their serious sins at least once a year.

A person who has experienced contrition and confessed his or her sins must then work to build a new life with God and with God's people. It is the effort to correct the mistakes of one's old life and to build a new life which completes the process of conversion. In order to begin building a new life with God and with God's people, the repentant sinner must do everything possible to repair the damage which he or she has caused.

Correcting our sins (giving satisfaction) means meeting the basic demands of justice: returning anything that has been taken, offering compensation for injuries, working to rebuild reputations which have been destroyed. It also means making an effort to strengthen those things which have been weakened by sin. Our conversion is not complete until we do what we can to rebuild our relationships with God and with other people and to reinforce our own commitment to love.

The sacrament of Penance is begun in the acts of the penitent, in contrition, in confession and in the effort to correct the harm one has caused. The sacrament of Penance is completed in the act of the priest who grants absolution. When the priest sees that a person's conversion is genuine, he imposes hands on that person and pronounces God's forgiveness.

The Effects of the Sacrament

When a person is forgiven, all the obstacles to a complete union with God and with God's people are removed. God's love once again flows through the repentant sinner. The person's own efforts to love will be effective because they are united to Christ's love. Through the sacrament of Penance we make peace with God, with our neighbor, with ourselves, and with all of creation. Those who approach the sacrament of Penance with a contrite heart and an openness to God usually experience peace, serenity of conscience, and a deep sense of God's love.

The sacrament of Penance reveals the mystery of God's unending love for us. No matter what we do, God never ceases to love us and reach out to us. No matter how many times we turn away from God, God will always make it possible for us to turn back.

Anointing of the Sick

Jesus Accompanies Us Through Suffering

Jesus did not come to explain suffering or to completely eliminate it. He came to be with people as they suffered and to teach them how to respond to suffering. Through his response to those who were suffering and through his own example in suffering, Jesus teaches us that suffering should not lead us into despair or revolt against God. The fact that we are suffering does not mean that God is not there or that God does not care.

Jesus showed a preferential love for people who were suffering. He spent a great deal of time with them and shared his love for them in a unique way. Because of their suffering they were invited to participate in the kingdom in ways that those who were healthy could not. Because they understood brokenness and isolation, because they were acutely aware of their own mortality, they were able to experience the wonder of wholeness, inclusion, and new life. They understood the significance of healing as a sign of the coming kingdom in a way that the healthy could not. Jesus called us to show a similar preferential love for those who are sick and suffering. He said that as often as we visit and care for those who are sick, we visit and care for him.

Jesus healed many people, but he did not heal everyone. The healing that he did was a sign of the coming kingdom of God. Only when the kingdom comes in its fullness at the end of time will everyone be healed. Then suffering and illness will end and every tear will be wiped away. Until then, illness, suffering, and death will continue to be part of our lives.

Jesus Made Suffering Redemptive

Even though Jesus did not put an end to all suffering, he did build on the meaning of suffering cultivated since Old Testament times. Jesus' own suffering had value. It was redemptive. Jesus suffered because of his love for God and for God's people. Jesus' suffering was the price he paid to give his gift of love. Because Jesus was willing to give his very self as an act of love, he undid the damage caused by Adam and Eve's selfishness. Jesus' suffering redeemed humanity from isolation and reconnected us with God.

The Sacrament Allows Us to Unite Our Suffering With the Suffering of Christ

Through the sacrament of Anointing of the Sick, Jesus makes it possible for us to unite our suffering to his own. When we love through our suffering, we are united with Christ and our suffering becomes part of Christ's suffering. It becomes a gift of love which will help to change the world. Suffering gives us an extraordinary power to make a difference. From the moment of our Baptism our goal is to be like Christ. When we suffer through no choice of our own, we become like Christ in a very special and profound way. If we love through our suffering even as Jesus did, we will truly be his body, making his love visible and accessible to those around us who see suffering as a negation of God.

The sacrament of the Anointing of the Sick unites the one who is sick or infirm with the passion of Christ. When a person is anointed he or she is in a sense "consecrated" to participate in the saving work of Jesus and to help make Christ's redemptive suffering present to the world. Anointing completes a person's conformity to the death and resurrection of Christ which began in Baptism. In the sacrament of Anointing any sins which still separate a person from Christ are forgiven.

Through the sacrament of Anointing those who are ill or old receive a special grace of the Holy Spirit. This grace strengthens them and gives them the peace and the courage to overcome the difficulties that go with serious illness and old age. This particular gift of the Holy Spirit heals the soul and, if God so wills, also heals the body. It strengthens those who receive it against temptation and anxiety and makes it possible for them to bear suffering bravely and even fight against it.

The Shape of the Sacrament

The sacrament of the Anointing of the Sick is for all who are seriously ill. When a person is in danger of death because of illness or old age or when illness, age, or chronic suffering make thoughts of death a present reality in a person's life, the priest or bishop is called upon to anoint the forehead and hands of the sick person and pray the prayer of the sacrament, asking God for the special grace of anointing.

If the person faces immediate death, *viaticum* is offered as the final sacrament of the Christian journey. Viaticum—"food for the journey"—is the Eucharist received at the close of earthly life. As the sacrament of Christ's Passover, the Eucharist is the fitting sacrament with which to mark the end of this life and the passing over into the next. Just as Baptism, Confirmation, and Eucharist together mark our entrance into the life of faith, so Penance, the Anointing of the Sick, and Eucharist received as viaticum are the sacraments that complete our pilgrimage on earth and prepare us for heaven.

In All Things God Works for Good

Through the sacrament of the Anointing of the Sick, God's healing power is given to the world. Sometimes that power comes in the form of physical healing. Sometimes it comes in the form of a healing of the soul. Always it comes with the opportunity to give the gift of transforming love to the world. At the heart of the sacrament of the Anointing of the Sick is God's power to use all things, even suffering, for good. The sacrament helps us to experience the mystery of love and joy which cannot be quenched even by pain and sorrow.

Holy Orders

We Are a Priestly People

A priest is someone who mediates between God and humanity. A priest makes God accessible to people and consecrates the sacrificial offerings of the people to God. This priestly work is so important to God that the Son of God became man in order to take it on himself. By becoming human Jesus brought God to people. By offering himself to God with absolute faith and love, Jesus consecrated not just the offerings of the people but the people themselves. Jesus became *the* high priest. Jesus is the only true mediator between God and humanity.

At the Last Supper Jesus tied a towel around his waist and washed the feet of his disciples. Although he was their Lord and master he performed the work of a slave, and a low ranking slave at that. Jesus' actions at the Last Supper gave his disciples the context in which to interpret his death on the cross. Both were acts of self-giving love; the focus of both was the needs of others. Jesus taught his followers that the sacrifice of loving service is the most precious sacrifice that can be offered. The gift of self, given out of love is the only gift that can overcome the divisions of sin. The sacrifice of Jesus' loving service is the only sacrifice which is truly acceptable to God—it is the sacrifice which a priestly people must offer.

Having shown us both the nature and importance of the priestly work, Jesus gave us a share in it. He said to his apostles and he continues to say to us, "as I have done for you, you should also do" (Jn 13:15). Jesus showed us God's love, we are to show that love to others. He gave himself for us, we are to give ourselves for others. He united us with God, we are to unite others with God. All of us are called to permeate the world with Christ's love. All of us are called to act as priests and consecrate the world to God. Those who receive the sacrament of Holy Orders—especially bishops and their designated priests—are called to this ministry in a special way as successors of the apostles.

The Ministerial Priesthood Is at the Service of the Common Priesthood

The ministerial priesthood is at the service of the common priesthood of all the faithful. The priesthood of all the faithful is lived out in the unfolding of baptismal grace. The ministerial priesthood fosters the unfolding of this grace through the celebration of the sacraments, the proclaiming of the word, and the governing of the Church.

Through the sacrament of Holy Orders and the ministerial priesthood which arises from it, Christ continues to lead and build up his Church. The ministerial priesthood guarantees that the Church will celebrate the sacraments; and as long as the Church celebrates the sacraments she does what Christ does. Each time the Church celebrates a sacrament she recalls all those present to the priestly work which they should be doing in the world. She reminds them of what Jesus has done for them and what they must do for others.

The Three Degrees of the Sacrament of Orders

There are three degrees of ecclesial ministry, the ministry of bishops, priests, and deacons. Bishops receive the fullness of the sacrament of orders. They are the successors of the apostles. In the celebration of all of the sacraments bishops are given the grace to act in the person of Christ who is the head of his body the Church. Priests are ordained as co-workers of the bishop. They too are configured to Christ so that they may act in his person during the celebration of the Eucharist, Baptism, and the Anointing of the Sick. They may bless marriages in the name of Christ and may share in the bishop's ministry of forgiveness. Deacons are ordained for service and are configured to Christ the servant. Deacons are ordained to help and serve the priests and bishops in their work. While priests and bishops are configured to Christ in order that they might act as the head of Christ's body, deacons are configured to Christ in order that they might serve as he served.

The Rite of Ordination

The essential rite of the sacrament of Holy Orders consists in the laying on of hands by the bishop accompanied by a specific prayer of consecration asking for the grace needed for the particular ministry to which the person is being ordained. The sacrament of Holy Orders confers an indelible spiritual character. Like Baptism and Confirmation it changes the fundamental identity of a person and allows him to act in the person of Christ in a unique way. The sacrament of Holy Orders cannot be repeated, nor can the character which it confers ever be taken away even if the one who was ordained ceases to serve as a minister of the Church.

The Sacrament of Holy Orders Reveals the Mystery of the Kingdom

The sacrament of Holy Orders reveals the mysterious relationship between authority and humility and between power and service. In the normal course of human events, those who have power are served, they are never expected to serve. In the sacrament of Holy Orders those who are ordained receive sacred power but it is a power to rule from the role of a servant. The sacrament of Holy Orders gives us a glimpse of just how different God's ways are from our own. The sacrament of Holy Orders reveals the mystery of a God who came to serve humanity and who continues to serve humanity. The sacrament of Holy Orders helps us to see that in God's kingdom, if we wish to lead we must serve. If we wish to be first, we must be last.

Matrimony

God Created Men and Women to Be One

God established the intimate communion of life and love which is the essence of married life. From the beginning one of the primary ways in which God has shared his love with men and women has been by giving them a way of sharing a deep and unifying love with each other. Men and women have been created as one, to be one. The disharmony which we see so often between the sexes and within marriages is not the result of our natures but the result of our sin. The consequence of the first sin was the rupture of the original communion between man and woman.

The sacrament of Matrimony gives men and women the grace which they need to overcome the division of the sexes (which is the result of sin) so that they may be one as God intended them to be. When a husband and wife embrace the grace of the sacrament and truly become one, they are given a glimpse of the love and unity which is shared in the Trinity. They are given a glimpse of the God who is love.

Jesus Raised Marriage to a Sacrament

The Church understands Jesus' presence and actions at the wedding of Cana to be a sign of the goodness of marriage and a sign of Jesus' intention to make marriage an effective sign of his presence. From the beginning of time marriage has been a gift from God; Jesus raised it to a sacrament, an instrument of grace. Through marriage a man and a woman receive the grace which they need to live in permanent and faithful love for one another.

Since the time of Adam and Eve marriage has been a divine joining of two people. It has been intended as something permanent. But human sinfulness and hardness of heart often made permanence extremely difficult or even impossible. When Jesus raises marriage to a sacrament, he restores the original order of creation and makes it possible for men and women to become one without fear or reservation.

The Marriage Covenant Is a Sign of Jesus' Covenant With the Church

The essence of marriage is in the mutual self-giving of the husband and wife. This self-giving takes the form of a covenant. A covenant is a commitment to work with each other to do whatever needs to be done, and to give themselves to each other no matter what the circumstances. Since the covenant of marriage involves the total self-giving of each spouse, fidelity and permanence are both necessary parts of the marriage covenant.

Jesus made every marriage a sign of God's faithfulness. The loving and faithful relationship between a husband and wife is now the visible sign of the loving and faithful relationship between Christ and his Church. The love which sustains the Church and makes it one is the love which allows a man and a woman to truly become one—one body, one heart, one mind, and one soul. The commitment of the spouses to each other becomes a part of God's commitment to his people.

The Purpose of Marriage

Marriage has been established by God for two reasons: for the good of the husband and wife and for the procreation and education of children. Marriage offers a way for men and women to support each other and to help each other grow in love. The deeper a person's understanding of and experience of love, the closer that person will be to God. Marriage also creates a communion of love into which children can be born. Just as marriage has two purposes, sexual intercourse—the act that most clearly expresses the marriage covenant—also has two purposes. Indeed, it has the same two purposes—mutual love and support, and procreation. Marriage by its very nature should be open to new life and to the gift of children. Every act of sexual intercourse in marriage should be open to the possibility of new life. No artificial means (birth control) should be used to prohibit the chance for new life.

A husband and wife, together with any children God may give them, form a "domestic church." All married couples, whether they have children or not, are called to establish the kind of home that welcomes those who would otherwise be without a family and that offers love, acceptance, and support to all who enter its doors. All families are called to make their home a place where the grace of God is clearly visible. The family is the first place where the gospel is shared and vocations are encouraged. Everything that family members receive in the sacramental life of the Church they are called to share with one another and with all whom they meet.

The Rite of Marriage

In the Roman Catholic Church the ministers of the sacrament of marriage are the spouses themselves. The essential element of the sacrament is their exchange of consent. The priest or deacon who assists at the wedding receives the consent of the couple in the name of the Church and offers the blessing of the Church on the marriage.

The Permanence of Marriage

The Church does not permit divorce and remarriage because Jesus forbade it. The covenant made between two validly married Catholics can only be dissolved by the death of one of the partners. The example of a permanent marriage is a prime way to bring Christ to the world. This is concretely true for children. Children need the assuring love of a solid marriage to develop a healthy attitude toward life and God.

Marriage Gives Us a Glimpse of the Love That Is the Trinity

When married couples surrender to the grace of the sacrament, the light and love of Christ will shine through their love for each other and through them the world will be changed. When they allow the grace of the sacrament to shape their lives, the God who is love is made visible. Marriage draws us into the mystery of God's own love, a love which produces perfect unity.

The Sacraments Are the Answer to Our Deepest Longings

Author's note: When I was in college and going through a difficult period I wrote my father asking for answers to some of the classic questions about life, love, purpose, and success. The letter that Dad sent me in response is one of my greatest treasures. In it he wrote:

> Outside the window there is a robin hopping around in the rain catching worms for dinner. He is upset because it seems that whenever he finds a nice dinner it's raining out and he doesn't like to eat in the rain. He keeps asking why, just once, can't he sit and eat a fat worm in the warm sunshine. The problem is, he has a robin-size brain, and the fact that rain makes the worms come out is a simple but human-size answer. The questions you ask have answers just as simple, but they won't fit in a human-size brain. The important thing is: it's not raining on the robin to spoil his dinner or character, nor to build his tolerance. The robin can't know that without the rain he would starve. And God doesn't like to let robins starve.

Life, love, joy, purpose, and success. These are the great mysteries of human existence. They are the things that were lost in the fall of creation and the things we all pursue today. They are the things no one can guarantee; no one, that is, but God. God is the only answer to the death, hate, suffering, emptiness, and failure which sometimes threaten to weigh us down. But God is so infinitely beyond us, how can we possibly hope to reach him?

The answer is found in the sacraments. In many ways the sacraments are a "book of answers" which God has given to us in response to our deepest questions. The more completely we participate in the sacraments the less we will be plagued by unanswerable "whys." This is not because sacraments fill our minds with logical explanations or because they make us stop questioning, but because sacraments give us *a way of understanding* that will put many of our questions to rest. We cannot know love except by living in a loving relationship. Likewise we cannot know the mystery of God except by living that mystery in the ways that God has made available to us.

Through the sacraments God gives us the life, love, joy, purpose, and success that we long for. Through the sacraments God restores what we lost. The sacraments draw us into the mystery of God. They allow us to stand in the presence of the only one who can give us what we seek. They are always actions of God and they always bring us into God's presence so that we may receive the gifts we long for. In the sacraments we are given a foretaste of heaven. In the sacraments we glimpse a world in which every tear has been washed away and we are able to live life to the full. When we are filled with the grace of the sacraments our lives have purpose. We are filled with love and joy and we know that we are a success.

Photo Credits

Crosiers ....page 15, 18, 26, 52, 55, 64, 66, 72, 73, 79, 81, 82, 87, 91, 96, 97, 101, 111, 113, 114, 115, 116, 118, 121, 128, 129, 147, 168, 183, 184, 188, 190, 191, 192, 194, 195, 209, 211

Bill Wittman............page 21, 37, 39, 41, 42, 49, 51, 61, 99, 137, 145, 153,

Photodisc..................page 43, 50, 77, 95, 103, 109, 119, 123, 141, 149, 166, 177, 207, 210, 212, 215, 216, 222, 229

AP Photo.................page 33, 140

Picturequest.............page 25, 47, 102, 125, 163, 170, 171, 173, 221

Corbis Images..........page 98, 112, 154, 165, 167, 201

Eyewire ....page 9, 13, 30, 35, 45, 100,

Lighthouse
Imaging......................page 88